THE INSECURITY OF NATIONS

The Insecurity of Nations

*International Relations in the
Twentieth Century*

by

CHARLES YOST

PUBLISHED FOR THE
COUNCIL ON FOREIGN RELATIONS

FREDERICK A. PRAEGER, *Publishers*
New York • Washington • London

FREDERICK A. PRAEGER, PUBLISHERS
111 Fourth Avenue, New York, N.Y. 10003, U.S.A.
5, Cromwell Place, London S.W.7, England

Published in the United States of America in 1968
by Frederick A. Praeger, Inc., Publishers

Second printing, 1969

Library of Congress Catalog Card Number: 68–11324

Printed in the United States of America

For

ADLAI STEVENSON

and

ARTHUR GOLDBERG

In Admiration and Affection

Preface

I belong to the generation that grew up just after the First World War. We learned from history then being rewritten that the war had been stupid and unnecessary and from novels, plays and poetry by those who fought in it that those who died did so for the most part ignobly and in vain. The world, outrageous as it seemed, was not better but worse for their heroism and sacrifice.

Yet in the fifty years since 1918 a further great World War and a series of lesser ones have been and are being fought in the same old way, usually in the name of national security, too often with the same disregard for human lives and human values.

Nations are still as insecure as ever—indeed, because of the nature of weapons, more insecure than ever. Governments are learning how to make their people rich but show little capacity for making them safe or sane. The obsolete means that statesmen and soldiers persist in using to promote security do more on the whole to promote insecurity. Recent events in the Far East and the Near East, the reckless "balance of terror" between the United States and the Soviet Union, are new evidence of this ironic fact.

The point is not that the world is worse than it used to be—on the whole it is much better for more people—but that, with all the miracles worked in the past half century, so little has been done about the insecurity of nations. That is to say, so little that corrects or controls it.

This book is dedicated to two statesmen who did know how to make peace, even though they were often not heeded: Adlai

Stevenson and Arthur Goldberg. The United States and the
United Nations owe them a great debt. So do I.

I am also most grateful to those wise and charitable men who,
at the request of the Council on Foreign Relations, went over
the first draft of this book and advised the author. He profited
greatly from their advice. They included that youngest and
gayest of elder statesmen, Henry M. Wriston, as well as John S.
Badeau, A. Doak Barnett, Jacques Barzun, Adolf A. Berle, John
C. Campbell, William Diebold, Jr., George S. Franklin, Jr., Richard N. Gardner, Edmund A. Gullion, Caryl P. Haskins, David W.
MacEachron and Kenneth Kauffman. I wish to express warmest
thanks to Suzanne Baum, who did most of the research and all
of the transcription, and to Robert W. Valkenier, who prepared
the manuscript for publication.

None of those mentioned, nor the Council itself, bear any responsibility for the opinions expressed in the book. The blame
for them rests entirely on the author.

"Lies I never never tell, but the truth not to everyone," said
Paolo Sarpi, a seventeenth-century Venetian friar who defied the
Pope. That is not a bad motto for diplomats. However, an effort
is made in this book to tell the truth to everyone, at least what
is relevant to the insecurity of nations.

Charles Yost

Venice
June 1967

Contents

PART I

The Disorganization of
Twentieth-Century Society

CHAPTER 1

The Breakup of the Old Order

Introduction

The relations among nations in the twentieth century are as critical to the security of men and women leading simple private lives as were the relations between man and nature throughout his primitive history, between rulers and subjects in pre-democratic societies, and between varieties of religion in the sixteenth and seventeenth centuries in the West.

During the last hundred years science has gone far toward conquering hunger and disease, toward making the fruits of the earth as readily and abundantly available to all as they reportedly were to Adam and Eve in the Garden. If permitted, it will doubtless go much farther in coming decades. Yet the conduct of international relations continues hardly to differ from that among Greek city-states of the fifth century B.C. or their Italian counterparts of the Renaissance which, inspired with genius though their people were, soon ended in self-destruction and prolonged subjection.

We hear a great deal these days about national security. Yet rarely in the history of civilization have people been fundamentally so insecure. A "national security" which fails to protect, which may indeed jeopardize, the common security of its citizens is a contradiction in terms, a misuse of power. Yet this is the condition of citizens of the most powerful nations.

What are the reasons for this paradox? It is the thesis of this book that this question cannot be answered merely by an examination of the foreign policy of states during this century, by a weighing of power, arms, alliances, resources, and diplomatic behavior, by an analysis of the doctrines, declarations, and apologia of statesmen and foreign offices. The reasons run far deeper.

They relate to the nature of man, to the character and passions of leaders and led, to their faith and dogmas, to the disruptive impact of science on human society, to the organization and disorganization of economic and political life in modern times, to the exorbitant and preposterous nature of weapons, to the disorientation and alienation of artists and intellectuals. All these factors account in some part for the international anarchy, and all must be taken into account in devising prescriptions for overcoming it. In our age of specialization, however, such a comprehensive view of any field of human affairs is rarely sought and even more rarely found.

In the words of the U.S. Secretary of Health, Education and Welfare, John W. Gardner, "Very few of our most prominent people take a really large view of the leadership assignment. Most of them are merely tending the machinery of that part of society to which they belong. The machinery may be a great corporation or a great government agency or a great law practice or a great university. These people may tend it very well indeed, but they are not pursuing a vision of what the total society needs. They have not developed a strategy as to how it can be achieved and they're not moving to accomplish it."

This stricture applies to most of those who conduct foreign relations in most governments. Not only do they not take sufficient pains to gain a comprehensive view of the *whole* situation, but the spectacles through which they look at their chosen part of it are likely to be colored and distorted. They see the world as it was or as they imagine it was in their youth, or as some body of cherished doctrine makes them think it ought to be, or as resentment caused by some personal or national humiliation convinces them it must be, or as it was briefly stabilized by some successful diplomatic combination of one or two decades ago, or as it might be if all governments and leaders behaved "responsibly," by which is meant the way the statesman speaking would like them to behave.

Despite sophisticated communications and other modern techniques, despite innumerable international conferences, despite national and international bureaucracies swollen to vast proportions, foreign relations continue for the most part to be conducted in a hurly-burly of hasty encounters, bringing forth most often only platitudes, expedients, or stalemate. Nothing less scientific, efficient or even rational could be imagined. It is little short of amazing that from time to time progress is actually made.

Men have never been able to perfect their organization in large societies nor, most of all, the relations between such societies as they did organize. Still, there have been periods when a substantial stability over wide territories was achieved, either through centralized empires (Roman, Chinese, Indian, British) or through a predominant cultural unity (Europe in the Middle Ages, the world under European hegemony in the eighteenth and nineteenth centuries) which blurred disparities and held conflict within tolerable limits. The twentieth century, however, has already witnessed a shattering breakup of empires, a convergence of revolutions in faith, science, politics, and economics, a failure to adjust to the consequences of these revolutions, a failure to organize and integrate the new ecumenical society they require, a failure to check the spiral of conflict among nineteenth-century political entities equipped with twentieth-century weapons.

The purpose of this book is to examine what lies behind these failures and how they might be overcome, what accounts for the disorganization of twentieth-century society and where to start stabilizing it. We shall begin with a glance at the first forty-five years of this century in order to evaluate the breakup of the old order which occurred so swiftly and disastrously during that time.

We shall then in Chapter 2 turn to an analysis of the underlying factors which brought about the breakup, which still keep our society in turmoil, but which paradoxically also incorporate the main elements of a new order. First, we shall try to estimate, since everything we do begins with our own nature, the degree to which our biological inheritance may or may not bind us to our current fratricidal behavior. Second, we shall look at the faiths—

nationalism, democracy and communism—which stir and sway the masses in our day. Next, we shall examine the ambivalent impact of science, which has given men for the first time a secular option between heaven and hell but for the most part disavowed all responsibility for the choice. Then, we shall take note of the role of the intellectuals, particularly the artists and writers, in foreshadowing, reflecting and aggravating our confusion of mind and soul. Fifth, we shall take account of the technological solution of the problems of economic production and distribution, of the divergence and convergence of modern economic systems, and of the vastly uneven application of the technological solution by all such systems. Sixth, we shall deal with the complexity and bureaucratization of present-day government, whether democratic or authoritarian, and its failure in most cases to provide either internal or external security for its citizens. Finally, in this treatment of underlying factors, we shall examine the preposterous escalation of arms and violence that characterizes international relations at the very time when such escalation is both more destructive and less necessary than ever before in history.

In Part II we shall illustrate the consequences of all these factors in three specific areas of postwar history: first, the challenge of the Soviet Union and the response of the West in Europe from the Moscow Conference of 1943 until the present time; second, challenge and response from a number of directions in the power vacuum of East Asia from the defeat of Japan to the latest war in Vietnam; third, the crises of liberation, development and modernization among the sixty new nations of the world, the intrusion there of the East-West conflict, and the portents of an even more profound North-South conflict. In each of these cases we shall particularly emphasize the inherent instability of the present system of relations among sovereign nation-states, the especial virulence which the magnification of weapons and the multiplication of states adds to that instability, and the law of disproportionate response to miscalculated challenges, which seems so often to govern the conduct of foreign affairs by both democracies and autocracies.

In Part III we shall sum up and draw conclusions. We shall recall how the convergence of underlying and immediate causes of insecurity among nations could within the next decade or two result either in a nuclear war wholly destructive of our civilization or in such a proliferation of parochial, archaic, and savage nationalisms as to bring about the same end by slower stages. In contrast, we shall suggest how it might be equally possible, with the technology now at our disposal or impending, so to order human affairs as within a few decades to make the earth a veritable paradise. Finally, plotting out a more probable middle course between these two extremes, we shall try to lay down some guidelines to a more rational conduct of international relations, to a more profitable association between East and West, to a more fruitful reciprocity between North and South, most of all to a drastic reduction in the insecurity of nations, first, through the control and ultimate abolition of weapons of mass destruction, later, through the evolution of a new international order which would correspond politically to the intrinsic global unity which science and technology have already imposed.

Let us now begin, however, with the breakup of the old order, which has made a new one necessary.

Prelude to War

Rarely in history has a civilization presented such a display of strength, magnificence, and promise as did that of the West at the opening of the twentieth century.

The Industrial Revolution had multiplied astronomically the availability of resources, and goods poured from the machine in a dazzling abundance. Wealth and comfort beyond the dreams of the Caesars or the Caliphs embellished the homes of the upper middle class of London, Paris, Berlin, and New York. Superior sophistication in seafaring and weapons had from the fifteenth century enabled Europeans gradually to extend their dominion over the globe so that by 1900, with China prostrate and India subjected, there was literally only one power center of any significance, Tokyo, outside of Europe and North America. There seemed no bounds to the prosperity and progress that these victories over men and things were likely to bring about.

The triumphs of the West, moreover, were of mind as well as of matter. Beginning with Copernicus and running through

Descartes to Darwin and Freud, a brilliant succession of scientists, philosophers, and humanists had overthrown superstition and, almost in spite of themselves, brought in the age of reason and licensed diversity. In spite of themselves, it may be said, because the consequences of such license were not what most of them had intended. As William McNeill has remarked: "The political diversity of Europe thwarted the heart's desire of nearly all the intellectually sensitive men of the time [the sixteenth-seventeenth centuries] by making impossible the construction of a single authoritative, definitive, and (as almost everyone also desired) enforceable codification of Truth. Yet, ironically, the failure to construct a world-view commanding general assent was the great achievement of the age."

It was this failure which had permitted the flowering of both science and dissent and ultimately of an open society based on both. Government of the people by expanding minorities of the people had even begun in a few countries to revive the forms and substance of democracy which had been dead for two millennia. But these intoxicating elixirs, as the Greeks also found in their own way, are bought at a price; and by 1900, at the very height of the triumph, Western society was already being called upon to pay the piper. It was beginning to find, or at least to feel, that reason, self-government, technology and mass production were not enough.

Science, it began to appear, had shut down the Garden of Eden and was threatening to do likewise to the City of God. The Earth was only one of a trillion stars and man only an unusually clever ape. Religion and philosophy were being relegated to the role of optional avocations.

At the same time, even the rich new flood of the good things of life, while it benefited far more people than ever before, benefited far fewer than seemed either just or necessary. It began to be claimed that since labor produced everything of value, those who labored most and were least privileged should own everything. Class lines stood out more glaringly and intolerably as exploding prosperity made them more pervious, and those who rose to the top of the heap were denounced as "malefactors of great wealth."

National antagonisms within the favored region, moreover, were mitigated neither by reason nor by wealth. Indeed the more "the people" (that is, the new middle-class) wrested power from the kings and aristocrats the more proud they became of their national attributes, the more possessive of their national dominions, and the more jealous of their neighbors. It was soon demonstrated that professors can be more chauvinistic and bellicose than noblemen or even generals. Progressively through the nineteenth and early twentieth centuries the atmosphere of Europe became poisoned by parochial hatreds between one language group and another and the Concert of Europe, which had preserved a precarious peace since Waterloo, split into two fortuitous but irreconcilable alliances.

These toxic elements were reflected in the "far-out" art and literature of the period, which provided perhaps the best, if most melancholy, barometer of the real state of the civilization that to most observers seemed at the apogee of success. An odor of decay, a vibration of anguish, a cry of revolt, arose from many of those most sensitive to the meaning of the *Zeitgeist,* from Dostoievski, Nietzsche, Shaw, Conrad, Dreiser, from Van Gogh, Cézanne, Picasso, Matisse, from Stravinsky and Schönberg. Disorientation of spirit, disintegration of form, dissonance of sound prophetically characterized the arts some years before they erupted into the general consciousness.

Meanwhile the average man of all classes—for the most part still caught up in the narrow drudgery of farm, factory or shop, dimly conscious of the vistas of liberation and affluence opening before him, repressed by the conventions and discriminations of a rigid society—oscillated between boredom, disgruntlement, and a factitious excitement aroused equally by domestic scandals or a rival nation's seizure of an African oasis. The wanton state of mind which as a consequence prevailed was that which in August 1914 set most of the men in Europe marching with gusto to Armageddon under the impression that they were promenading to Berlin, Paris, St. Petersburg, or Vienna.

A great many books have been written about the causes of World War I. The diplomatic maneuvers that were its immediate occasion would seem almost too frivolous and trivial to recount again, were it not that their disastrous dénouement has determined our history ever since. Moreover, they are a most exemplary study on how *not* to conduct foreign relations.

The essential characteristic of the war was that, in contrast to World War II, it was unplanned and unmotivated. It arose out of the matrix of a dynamic but still essentially primitive international society. Despite a whole mythology to the contrary, the Kaiser did not want war, the Czar did not want it, the eighty-year-old Emperor of Austria did not want it. A few officials wanted revenge for past defeats, some hoped for bloodless diplomatic victories, a few were ready to risk a small quick war in the interests of imperial survival or imperial prestige.

As noted above, the primary revolutionary force in the nineteenth century was nationalism, associated with liberty and democracy when it was suppressed but often intolerant and tyrannical when it was triumphant. Nationalist ferment had spread from the France of the Revolution through Germany and Italy, and, by the end of the century, to Eastern Europe. It brought about the partial unification of the German and Italian peoples and fatally undermined the multinational Ottoman and Hapsburg Empires. The attitude of the statesmen of the day toward this process was to capitalize on it when they could, to come to terms with it when they had to, but under no circumstances to admit or to plan for its peaceful accomplishment.

In the process of its unification Germany committed the colossal blunder of seizing, for strategic reasons, a segment of the French national domain, Alsace-Lorraine; the error, forced on Bismarck by his generals and his Emperor, perpetuated the enmity between the two countries, caused one to dream of revenge and the other to fear reprisal, and destroyed whatever chance there was of re-establishing a Concert of Europe. Russia's traditional pretensions to Constantinople and emotional sympathy with the Slavs subject to the Ottoman and Hapsburg Empires caused it actively to encourage the forces of disintegration first in one and then in the other. These two major elements of instability and tension drove the four Great Powers most concerned, Germany and Austria, Russia and France, into military alliances, one pair against the other.

Britain at first held aloof in traditional "splendid isolation" and, neutral between the two alliances, provided some restraint on both. However, her own imperial excesses, particularly in Egypt and South Africa, gave rise to such general repugnance and condemnation that the Conservative government decided during the Boer War, in a tragic miscalculation, that Britain could no longer stand alone but must join one or the other of the two alliances. An approach to Berlin produced a foolish but obdurate insistence on a formal treaty of mutual defense, for which Britain was not ready; an approach to Paris, on the other hand, was met with Gallic sophistication and resulted in a modest entente based on a division of the spoils of Egypt and Morocco and on purely "informal" military planning. Though Britain's choice had balanced on a razor's edge, a few years sufficed to make her a committed ally of France (with whom she had almost gone to war in 1898) and an implacable enemy of Germany (to whom she had almost allied herself in 1902).

Between 1904 and 1914 the two alliance systems went through at least five major and traumatic crises arising (1) from Germany's clumsy insistence "in shining armor" that she share more generously in the colonial spoils which Britain and France had long been collecting and that, in addition to the best army in Europe, she also have a substantial navy; and (2) from Russian machinations on the Bosphorus and Russian-inspired "wars of liberation" against the Turks and the Austrians. Entirely aside from the merits of the particular issues, by 1914 the effect of these repeated crises, wherein each side suffered one or more humiliating setbacks, was to raise national tempers and tensions to such a point that, while neither side had gained additional security from previous victories, neither was prepared to tolerate further defeat.

Yet there was not the slightest idea that a major war was imminent or what it would mean if it came. No government or statesman made a serious effort to improve the system or even within its framework to provide for orderly consultation, negotiation, or cooling off. When the heir to the Austrian throne was assassinated by a Serbian in 1914 the Austrian government concluded that unless Serbia was "punished" and Russia thereby restrained, the heterogeneous Austro-Hungarian Empire would inevitably fall to pieces; it therefore determined to risk a quick preventive war. Solicited for support but not informed of Vienna's exact intentions, the Kaiser gave his famous "blank cheque," because he was shocked by a royal murder and because he feared Germany would lose its only reliable ally.

As Austria proceeded with its pressure despite a large measure of capitulation by Serbia, Russia mobilized not only against Austria but against Germany as well, because her generals claimed that prior partial mobilization would disorganize subsequent general mobilization if the latter became necessary. Yet it had long been understood among military men that, since Germany could not be expected to wait while Russia's immense armies were assembled along her frontiers, a German declaration of war would certainly follow a Russian order of general mobilization.

France, also fearful of "losing" an ally, declared her unequivocal support of Russia; Britain, though almost wholly preoccupied with an incipient North Irish rebellion, made meager efforts to restrain Germany and Austria but none to restrain her own allies; Germany, too late and in vain, urged Vienna to draw back. Mobilization followed mobilization, and within little more than a week after the Austrian ultimatum, the armies of all the Great Powers of Europe were marching with the wildest enthusiasm into a suicidal war of unprecedented magnitude.

Two World Wars

A fledgling member of Parliament, aged twenty-six, had the following to say to the House of Commons on May 13, 1901: "In former days, when wars arose from individual causes, from the policy of a Minister or the passion of a King, when they were fought by small regular armies of professional soldiers, and when their course was retarded by the difficulties of communication and supply, and often suspended by the winter season, it was possible to limit the liabilities of the combatants. But now, when mighty populations are impelled on each other, each individual severally embittered and inflamed, when the resources of science and civilization sweep away everything that might mitigate their fury, a European war can only end in the ruin of the vanquished and the scarcely less fatal dislocation and exhaustion of the conquerors. Democracy is more vindictive than Cabinets. The wars of peoples will be more terrible than those of Kings."

The speaker was Winston Churchill, who had recently fought in the Sudan and been a war correspondent in South Africa. His prescience, however, was not shared. Soldiers of each side expected the same rapid success in battle that they had had in war games; financiers and economists were confident war would end by Christmas for lack of money and resources. The Kaiser said to the departing troops in August: "You will be home before the leaves have fallen from the trees." French President Poincaré told French legislators in a New Year's address in 1915: "I do not doubt that by next year, at this time . . . we will be celebrating the establishment of peace. . . . "

Of course, they were wrong. They underestimated the heroic pigheadedness, the pathetic docility, the passionate rancor of mankind. The war went on in the incredible, savage, sodden, gutted, rat-infested trenches for four years, three months, and eleven days; 10 million died in battle (over a million casualties in one long ghastly battle on the Somme and 700,000 in another in the same year at Verdun); a generation of the best young men of Britain, France, Germany and Italy (the real "lost generation") was wiped out and those nations morally and intellectually impoverished.

The agony of that life in the midst of death was expressed by the soldier-poet Edmund Blunden, who wrote:

> The more monstrous fate
> Shadows our own, the mind swoons doubly burdened,
> Taught how for miles our anguish groans and bleeds,
> A whole sweet countryside amuck with murder;
> Each moment puffed into a year with death.
> Still swept the rain, roared guns,
> Still swooped into swamps of flesh and blood,
> All the drabness of uncreation sunk,
> And all thought dwindled to a moan, Relieve!
> But who with what command can now relieve
> The dead men from that chaos, or my soul?

As George Kennan wrote forty years later: "The indirect effects of that war—its genetic and spiritual effects—were far more serious than people realized at the time. We can see, today, that these effects penalized victor and vanquished in roughly equal measure, and that the damage they inflicted, even on those who were nominally the victors, was greater than anything at stake in the issues of the war itself."

It is tragic and appalling, but healthy and true, to realize with the benefit of hindsight that all those valorous and dedicated young men died in vain, that they did not "make the world safe for democracy" or fight "a war to end war," that it would have been far better for their countries, their families, and their civilization if they had lived instead of died, if they had not fought at all. Indeed, it is only insofar as we realize that they did die in vain, and why, that they may in the end prove not to have done so.

The war ended in a series of peace treaties that have been much criticized. Their territorial provisions were, however, not unduly punitive, were based on the respectable principle of self-determination, and had in fact been substantially carried out on the ground by the peoples concerned before the peacemakers ever set to work. It is all very well, and true, to say that it was a mistake to break up the Austro-Hungarian Empire, which provided a large and harmonious economic unit in Southeast Europe, but the Empire fell apart spontaneously in November 1918 along nationalist lines.

The economic clauses of the peace treaties, however, particularly those of Versailles, were not only oppressively punitive but wholly unrealistic, as Keynes pointed out at the time. It was impossible to transfer from vanquished to victor the enormous reparations demanded without ruining the finances of the former and the domestic industries of the latter. Consequently, the first five postwar years were exacerbated and wasted in simultaneously attempting to squeeze out of Germany more than was wise or possible and to maneuver French and British public opinion into gradually cutting the bill.

The decisive and almost irretrievable error had been committed during the war and immediately after when Allied propagandists, intent on mobilizing maximum mass sanction for the enormous sacrifices in lives and treasure that were demanded, blamed the outbreak of the war exclusively on the villainy of the Central

Powers and pictured their leaders as monsters of depravity and their soldiers as Huns. Irresponsibly basing their policies on these gross distortions, French and British politicians in the period 1918–23 promised their electorates to squeeze the prostrate Germans "until the pips squeak," and proceeded to implement this statesmanlike promise (and to prove Churchill's prophecy that democracies would be "more vindictive than Cabinets") by prolonging the food blockade for four months after the war's end, denying status and respectability to the new German Republic, and intriging for the detachment of the Rhineland and ultimately occupying the Ruhr.

The consequence of these misbegotten policies was to provoke a runaway inflation in Germany which ruined the middle class, to discredit utterly in the minds of the German people the young Republic which the Allies should have done everything to foster, to exacerbate in every possible way the humiliation of German nationalism, to install Hindenburg as President only seven years after the war, and to prepare the ground for Hitler.

In the meantime, partly from deep-seated and legitimate causes but partly through one of the tragic accidents of history, the liberal Russian Revolution of March 1917 was rapidly overtaken and captured by a band of sophisticated and adroit political conspirators, proclaiming an all-embracing, seductive, and allegedly scientific doctrine and led by a prodigious but power-infatuated genius. I shall comment on the doctrine in Chapter 2; here it is sufficient to note that the Revolution gave rise, first, to a military crusade which was temporarily stopped at Warsaw in 1920, second, to an evangelical Diaspora, half political, half conspiratorial, which is still going forward, and third, to a new variety of religion and autocracy inside Russia which carried on both the reactionary and the progressive traditions of Ivan the Terrible and Peter and Catherine the Great. However, despite the Cominform, the substantial Communist parties in Western Europe and even the abortive intervention in China and Spain, Stalin opted for "revolution in one country" after Lenin's death, and the Soviet Union turned its attention and energies primarily inward until June 1941.

In Europe as a whole during the brief period from 1924 to

1930, when the worst of the devastation had been repaired, the rancors of war seemingly appeased, and a superficial economic prosperity restored, statesmen endeavored to bring back a semblance of stability to the riven continent. The Dawes and Young Plans decently interred reparations (though unhappily not the war debts to the United States). France wove a tissue of alliances around Germany but, under the enlightened leadership of Aristide Briand, permitted her re-entry into the community of Europe and the League of Nations. The Germans seemed almost reconciled, if not to Versailles, at least to their Republic.

But, as Simone Weil was to say later, "when misfortune bites too deeply, it creates a disposition toward misfortune, which makes people plunge headlong into it themselves, dragging others along with them." Misfortune had bitten too deeply, particularly in Central and Eastern Europe, to permit easy recovery, and unhappily the New World, which had sought to isolate itself politically, came in to upset the precarious balance of the Old. The fragility of free enterprise in its traditional form, manifested in the Great Crash of 1929 and the ensuing Depression, soon communicated itself to a barely convalescent Europe; its banks went tumbling down in the wake of the Credit Anstalt; Britain and a score of others, culminating in the United States, went off the gold standard; six million were unemployed in Germany and three million in Britain, and the common man in nation after nation lost faith in his rulers and their creeds.

The political consequences were to discredit both enlightened and unenlightened moderates throughout the Continent and to spawn, sanction, and invigorate the most rabid forms of extremism. A collective madness seized Europe for the second time in the century. As Mirabeau said about an earlier revolutionary period, *"Quand tout le monde a tort, tout le monde a raison."*

The arts reflected the general dilapidation and foreboding of the time. While producing some of the great works of modern literature, writers anxiously described themselves as belonging to a "lost generation," though they were in fact those who had survived. As Ernest Hemingway wrote many years later, "In those days we did not trust anyone who had not been in the war, but we did not completely trust anyone." They felt their generation had been told too many lies and asked to die under false pretenses. The world, to sensitive persons, had come to seem too horrible to be entirely real or tolerable. Kafka showed the average man befuddled and condemned without a hearing by a soulless and enigmatic bureaucracy. Faulkner, still unemancipated from an earlier post-bellum society, wrote in a nerve-wracked idiom which his contemporaries found congenial and prophetic. Picasso, commemorating the Fascist destruction of a Spanish village, did so in the inhuman forms he judged expressive of a general alienation from civilization. In the 1930s the smell of a burning fuse was in the air and mankind waited anguished and impotent for the explosion.

After the Fascism of the mountebank in Italy came the Nazism of the cunning madman in Germany, a display of barbarism and asininity unexampled in modern history. Their example was soon followed in Spain, Rumania, Hungary, Slovakia, and elsewhere. The reaction of the Soviet government was to purge most of its founding fathers and generals and to execute or imprison millions of others, in many cases on grounds of traitorous commerce with the Nazis, shortly before Moscow itself concluded a pact of eternal friendship with Berlin, which as it turned out lasted two years. The reaction of the Western democracies was for some time to turn their backs and deny that a serious problem existed.

The causes of World War II are far easier to discern and to judge than those of World War I. The victors of World War I failed to make peace until too late, until most of the defeated had been alienated, corrupted, and put back into uniform. Because they felt that it had brought them neither justice, wellbeing, nor security, neither butter nor guns, the Germans repudiated their Republic and committed their fate to a megalomaniac who had written a frank account of his ambitions which nobody believed. Britain and France, because they were exhausted and emasculated from the war, because they were uncertain whether the greater menace was Germany or Russia, because they had chosen leaders of narrow mind and will, yielded to Hitler all they had denied to the Republic. They failed to stand firm until they had lost most of their allies in Eastern Europe and their adversary was convinced victory was easy and certain.

Meanwhile in the Far East in the first third of the twentieth century two quasi-modern powers had emerged from the ashes of old empires. The Japanese had brilliantly modernized their industrial, military, and bureaucratic apparatus but had left their feudal ideals and appetites unreconstructed. First among peoples of color to set back white imperialism, they were unable to forego imperialism themselves. China, in its own eyes still the world's greatest civilization, had been prostrate, continuously humiliated, and progressively dismembered for seventy years. In 1911 it rid itself at last of its imperial regime and began the process of modernization. Another two decades were required, however, before it showed signs of creating a viable national government; perceiving which, the Japanese rapidly moved in to destroy it. War came in the Far East because the Japanese were technologically precocious but spiritually archaic, because the Chinese were still temptingly disorganized but beginning to revive, because the Europeans were wholly preoccupied with their own disorders, and the Americans just strong enough to challenge but not to deter Japan.

Of World War II it is pertinent at this point to say only the following. Unlike World War I, which was fought almost exclusively in Europe and the Near East, it embraced the world. There was massive conflict everywhere except in the Western Hemisphere, and that was heavily involved. Slaughter was just as stupendous as in World War I but its incidence was different, far less in Western Europe, far more in Eastern Europe (including 20 million Russians and 6 million Poles), far more in Asia, primarily China and Japan. For the first time in modern war as many, perhaps more, noncombatants as combatants were killed, many by weapons but probably even more, slave laborers, neglected prisoners of war, subjected civil populations, by starvation and disease. Another feature was the calculated extermination of 6 million men, women, and children of a particular so-called race, the Jews.

The sort of utter physical devastation which in World War I was largely restricted to the battlefields of northern France was now generously distributed among cities all over the globe, from

Warsaw, Rotterdam, and Dresden to Manila, Chungking, and Hiroshima, wherever the bomber airplane was able to penetrate, as well as throughout European Russia and much of Germany, where vast armies fought back and forth yard by yard.

Altogether it is fair to say that never in history was a war at the same time so extensive, so destructive, and so barbarous. The fact that on this occasion, in glaring contrast to 1914, the war was necessary to save men and nations from hideous forms of tyranny had profound political and spiritual consequences, but it did not lessen the devastation, mitigate the subsequent disorder, or bring back the dead.

One of the lessons of World War II is that dictators, bent on territorial expansion and prepared to use military force to achieve it, will be emboldened rather than deterred by concessions or "appeasement." One of the lessons of World War I is that nations not seeking war or conquest can easily slip into confrontations of prestige from which neither side can escape without concessions or "appeasement," yet which, if resolved by resort to arms, can inflict damage on both victors and vanquished, "greater than anything at stake in the issues of the war itself." Perhaps the most critical dilemma of modern history is the decision to be made whenever a confrontation arises—whether the lesson of World War I or the lesson of World War II, or neither, applies to the case in point.

It is our main argument, however, that neither the disorganization of twentieth-century society nor the international confrontations which are among its most ominous symptoms can be understood merely by reviewing diplomatic history. Social disorganization and international anarchy arise from a series of underlying compulsions, some carried down through several centuries, others emerging from the scientific revolution of the last hundred years. In Part II we shall return to an account and assessment of the three great confrontations which followed the breakup of the old order. For that account to be intelligible and the assessment valid, however, we must first delineate the environment, the creative and destructive forces of the times, from which these events took shape. We shall begin with a few remarks about the fundamental nature of man, with a view to determining at the very outset whether, as Heraclitus said, "man's character is his fate," whether in fact he is doomed by ineradicable instincts and uncontrollable emotions to estrangement, war, and anarchy.

CHAPTER 2

Underlying Causes of
National Insecurity

The Relevance of Human Nature

The greatest impediment to a peaceful world is not communism, capitalism, imperialism, nationalism or Maoism, but simply human behavior. In the foreign policies of nations it is necessary, in the very first instance, to take account in both leaders and peoples of the factors of passion, frustration, and habit which spring from deep instincts and emotions, which are not subject to rational rebuttal, and which are the most resistant to modern realities. All too often these factors, rather than the professions of statesmen or the rationalizations of state papers, are those which decide between "hawks" and "doves," between peace and war.

Fortunately, however, human behavior is not necessarily synonymous with human nature. The latter we assume to be fixed, or at least evolving and adapting very slowly through many generations; the former is remarkably malleable. Otherwise, there would be no possibility of civilizing either children or savages, though both are almost equally amenable to civilization and to corruption.

One of the great revelations of modern science was Freud's explanation of the deviousness of human nature, of the dark complexities of man's inner life. Before Freud it was possible for sincere, honorable and intelligent men to believe that both their domestic and their political tyrannies arose from the purest of intentions and were designed entirely for the good of the individuals or the masses they abused. Since Freud we are all aware that a weird congregation of psychological trauma preside over almost every public and private act of men and women, and that the motive we ascribe is more likely than not to be a rationalization of our cunning conscience. Robert Frost was only being candid when he has one of his characters say: "The temptation to do right when I can hurt someone by doing it has always been too much for me."

Human nature, as the theologians have long remarked, is a strange combination of vileness and innocence. Obviously, the individual has to be egotistical in order to survive. Egotism tends, however, to burgeon into all sorts of extravagances of pride, vainglory, pugnacity, heroism and sublimation, which, like a peacock's plumage, have little to do with survival, salvation or adaptation. Pride, vainglory, and pugnacity have of course always played, and continue to play, a conspicuous and sinister part in the fantasies of rulers, the delusions of democracies, and the persistence of war in human affairs.

What most concerns us here in an appraisal of the insecurity of nations is the degree to which these characteristics are fixed in human nature and inevitably determine relations among men in organized societies. So humane a philosopher as William James, while earnestly seeking a "moral equivalent of war," concluded that "our ancestors have bred pugnacity into our bone and marrow and thousands of years of peace won't breed it out of us."

On the other hand, some zoologists have found in their study of animals only five indispensable requirements: nutrition, reproduction, social relations, sleep, and care of the body surface. As one of them, Sally Carrighar, remarks: "When they have been able to fill these instinctive needs without fighting, they showed no aggressive drive and no distress of the central nervous system because an innate urge was being denied expression." While there may be some doubt whether human nature is much better than animal nature, there seems no good reason to believe it is worse, or that men are more instinctively and compulsively aggressive than animals.

Darwin's doctrine of the "survival of the fittest," which in fact described the process of natural selection by which useful mutations are naturally preserved, has been distorted to mean that only the most ruthless exponents of "tooth and claw" can survive. The coral polyp, the earthworm, the gorilla, and the elephant would seem to contradict this theory. Actually, of course, the term, "survival of the fittest," is to a considerable extent a tautology; everything living must be at least momentarily fit; what survives longest will have proved to be fittest; we have no way of knowing what that will be, except that it will probably not be anything massively self-destructive.

An eminent naturalist, Konrad Lorenz, has recently had a considerable popular success with the book *On Aggression,* which explains in fascinating detail both the value and limits of what he calls "aggression" in animals and its origin and obsolescence in men. The term "aggression" as he uses it is somewhat misleading: as applied to animals, it would in fact come closer to what the layman calls self-defense; as applied to men, it would coincide with that extravagance of egotism we have called pride, vainglory and pugnacity.

In the case of animals, for example, he describes what Robert Ardrey has called "the territorial imperative," whereby animals or groups of animals, including fish and birds, stake out claims to a piece of territory that they fiercely defend against invasion by others of their own species. Such behavior supports the survival of the species since it helps to reduce "nutritional competition" and assure a sufficient hunting ground and food supply to each individual and group.

Moreover, Lorenz points out that in this competition among animals or birds of the same species, actual combat, particularly combat to the death, is very rare. Usually a show of force, the flaunting of certain colors, screeching, hissing, fluttering of wing, or snarling and baring of teeth suffices to drive off the trespasser. When combat does ensue, it is likely to be limited to relatively harmless butting, snapping, or locking of horns, a stylized and inconclusive simulacrum of battle. In Sally Carrighar's words:

"Any intruder, fighting on ground that belongs to another, seems to lose courage. In order to win, most animals act as if they need to feel that their cause is right."

Among animals, therefore, a benevolent nature has instilled checks and balances in the operation of "aggression" so that it does not jeopardize the survival of the species. Among men, however, the contrary is true. Their "aggression," individual or national, is only occasionally limited to ritual; there rarely seems to be consensus among them, particularly among nations, as to whose cause is just. Precisely among those creatures in whom "reason" is supposed to dominate instinct, it may have made instincts only the more stubborn by providing an instrument for their rationalization and verbalization.

Konrad Lorenz has an evolutionary explanation for this paradox. "It is more than probable," he writes, "that the destructive intensity of the aggression drive, still a hereditary evil of mankind, is the consequence of a process of intra-specific selection [selection by competition within and among a single species] which worked on our forefathers for roughly forty thousand years, that is, throughout the Early Stone Age. When man had reached the stage of having weapons, clothing and social organization, so overcoming the dangers of starving, freezing and being eaten by wild animals, and these dangers ceased to be the essential factors influencing selection, an evil intra-specific selection must have set in. The factor influencing selection was now the wars waged between hostile neighboring tribes. These must have evolved in an extreme form of all those so-called 'warrior virtues' which unfortunately many people still regard as desirable ideals."

There is, of course, considerable difference of opinion as to the extent to which these "warrior virtues" actually arise from instincts derived from natural selection, or are rather derivatives of the psychological trauma which Freud exposed, or are merely the consequence of the successive indoctrination of each generation with the same myths and standards of honor and glory. No doubt all three elements play their part.

The sources of group or national aggressiveness in the frustrated psyche of leaders and masses have been explored by many psychologists and social scientists. E. F. M. Durbin and John

Bowlby argued almost thirty years ago that "war is due to the expression in and through group life of the transformed aggressiveness of individuals." They invited attention to the inclination of human beings to blame failure and frustration in their own activities on scapegoats, to take out such frustrations on innocent bystanders, or unconsciously to transfer accumulated hostility from a parent, for example, to a political leader or a foreign nation. In this sense the frustrations of the Germans in and after World War I produced the Nazi movement and World War II, the personal frustrations of Lee Harvey Oswald the assassination of President Kennedy. The aggressiveness in these and similar instances arose not from any innate elements of human nature but from pressure of the environment so demoralizing that the national or individual psyche could not cope with it in healthy fashion and took refuge in psychosis and transference.

A careful Dutch student of psychological behavior in World War II, Joost Meerloo, applies the same analysis not only to psychotics but to all of us. "Every war is a dramatization of man's inner war," he writes, "the externalization of his inner conflicts. Man feels temporarily relieved of tensions when there is outside trouble in the world. He can postpone finding a solution to his own conflicts as long as the outside world offers a more stirring emotional drama in which he can play a role." And further along in the analysis: "The less inner strength and security a group possesses, the more aggressive it will be. Collective hatred is coupled with internal weakness. It is motivated by the hidden fear about the group's emotional stability, inner cohesion and collective existence." Such is usually the origin of both right- and left-wing extremists' obsession with "conspiracies."

Dag Hammerskjöld remarked: "Fear motivates much of human action. It is our worst enemy and, somehow, seems to taint at least some corner of the heart of every man." Fear and anxiety find themselves compounded in a century wherein at least 60 million human beings have been slaughtered in organized fashion by other human beings and the possibility of nuclear annihilation hangs over everyone.

All the elements of the human psyche which stimulate pugnacity in man, whether products of heredity or environment or both, may undoubtedly be aggravated or assuaged, conditioned constructively or destructively, in early childhood. The display of love at the critical moment, expressed in fondling and in solicitude, or its absence, may determine in human beings or in animals the difference between a relaxed and sociable individual and one who all his life will be withdrawn or aggressive.

The great French biologist Jean Rostand says: "I think that we can demand a great deal of man if we do not begin by maltreating him and disheartening him when he is a child." It is not merely a question, however, of refraining from maltreating and disheartening the child. The child's mind is an enormously sensitive recorder; it is moved much more by example than by precept; it has a candid and even brutal logic of its own which cuts through adult pretence. Adults, therefore, should scrupulously and invariably exercise both justice and compassion in the company of children, if these are the qualities they wish to instill.

There is a little poem entitled "Crow Box" by a modern American poet, Herbert Scott, which reads:

"Come with me," my grandfather said,
"We are going to check the crow box,"
Then he took me by the hand and we walked
down to where the lane becomes a ravine.
There on a post was a crude little box
and I had to climb three rungs up the fence
to see the yellow chick enclosed.
"But won't it die?" I asked.
"Bait, my son, one life for ten;
each thing in the proper perspective," he said.

Three mornings I carried oats in my pocket
and water in my hand, to check the crow box,
until the black bird was trapped
and its neck wrung like a chicken's.
An old red hen hatched the next baby chicks
in safety, by the catalpa tree,
in the high woods,
and I took four of her brood
behind the woodshed
and cut off their heads.

What could be more logical—and more corrupting? If Grandfather can offer up an innocent chick to the black bird and then wring the black bird's neck, why then birds' lives are men's toys and I can try what it's like to cut off chicks' heads. And if men can shoot bad men and I can decide what men are bad, why then. . . . Bertrand Russell claims, perhaps extravagantly, that "Wars are due, in the main, to the insane and destructive impulses which lurk in the unconscious of those who have been unwisely handled in infancy, childhood and adolescence."

As to adolescents, Konrad Lorenz notes that there comes a critical moment in their lives when they become physically and psychologically ripe for revolt against the social norms of the "old" society of their parents. The direction of this revolt, toward sterile delinquency or constructive new departures, rests on a hair. As Lorenz puts it: "There probably is, at that time of life, a definite sensitive period for a new object-fixation, much as in the case of the object-fixation found in animals and called imprinting. If at that critical time of life old ideals prove fallacious under critical scrutiny and new ones fail to appear, the result is complete aimlessness, the utter boredom which characterizes the young delinquent. If, on the other hand, the clever demagogue, well versed in the dangerous art of producing supranormal stimulus situations, gets hold of young people at the susceptible age, he finds it easy to guide their object-fixation in a direction subservient to his political aims. . . . The instinctive need to be a member of a closely knit group fighting for common ideals may grow so strong that it becomes inessential what these ideals are and whether they possess any intrinsic value."

The substance of the matter is that we have not yet learned how to adapt our inherited emotional drives to the new environment, which we have ourselves created. Some aspects of that environment still demand the exercise of "warrior virtues," and those unwilling to apply them risk subjection and dishonor. Yet the exercise of those same "virtues" in the new environment easily becomes disproportionate and inhumane, and those applying them risk brutalization and extinction. This is the essential paradox of our times.

There may be some consolation in the conclusion which

emerges from our analysis: that, whether or not "warrior virtues" have been bred in us over forty thousand years, there is little reason to believe they are a basic requirement of the human spirit. They are merely one means of serving, when certain conditions exist, what *are* basic requirements—nutrition, reproduction, sleep, bodily care, social relations. As these conditions change and we approach in our times a state in which those requirements can be peacefully met, all rational basis for instinctive aggression fades away.

This conclusion does not mean, as we have so tragically seen, that the aggressive urge fades simultaneously. On the contrary, it finds all sorts of respectable pretexts on which to feed and fatten. Human nature, while not inherently aggressive, has through many generations of intertribal and international warfare become fixed in patterns of provocative and melodramatic behavior that are very hard to break. These patterns, which we still take for granted and indulge with a great show of self-righteousness, have been overtaken by events, particularly scientific events, and called into question. But we are not yet ready to admit that to ourselves or to tell it to our children.

Having examined the plasticity of man's nature, we proceed to an appraisal of his beliefs and institutions, particularly of their compatibility with his security and survival. After all, man has unique capacities to balance his special vices. He can reflect, he can recall, he can learn from experience; his whole conscious and subconscious life is governed by ingeniously discriminated feedback. He can apprehend and identify with the emotions and concerns of other men, he has peculiar interests and aptitudes for living in close association with his fellows, he has developed social life to a high pitch of organization and sophistication. Thus, there is a fair prospect that, if his beliefs can be made rational and his institutions practical, his nature will prove no insuperable infirmity and his aggressive drives can, before it is too late, be contained and sublimated.

Old and New Faiths

Men cannot live happily or healthily without profound and passionate beliefs of some kind. "Reason," which since the eighteenth century has provided for increasing numbers an acceptable substitute for religion, involves, even when clothed in agnosticism or atheism, a quasi-religious view of physical science that almost equates it with faith and morals. Spiritual nihilism, on the contrary, is so unsatisfying as to be self-destructive, creating on the one hand apathy and demoralization or on the other a hunger so wild that only violence can relieve it. Such was, mixed with other elements, the aberration of the Nazis. It was at least in part because of the spiritual confusion and emptiness which marked the end of the nineteenth century that so many new religions sprang up in the twentieth.

At mid-century the traditional religions continue to have hundreds of millions of adherents. There are some 950 million Christians, 450 million Muslims, 400 million Hindus, and more than 150 million Buddhists. Many of these millions continue to profess and to believe, some even to observe and to propagate, the tenets of their creeds. For example, there are approximately 125 million church members in the United States. Their influence on national attitudes is not inconsiderable and colors national policy, often with Christian rhetoric, occasionally even with Christian forebearance and commitment. Such wise spokesmen of the churches as Pope John XXIII, Paul Tillich, Reinhold Niebuhr and Eugene Carson Blake have been doing what they can to adjust and reconcile the spirit of man to the modern predicament. Their prayers and preachings awaken a more heedful response as the need and anguish increase.

While less affected by changing times, Buddhism, Islam, and Hinduism continue to exert on their adherents promptings of spirituality and compassion. Each has its historic and particular virtues which, on the ground where they have flourished for centuries, continue to offer men alternatives to brute force and circumstance. Obstacles to change in many instances, they shore up old values until new ones have matured.

Yet even a sober and sympathetic appraisal of the traditional religions cannot claim that the world is any longer deeply moved by them. They serve more often as an anchor than a rudder. Individual lives in substantial numbers are no doubt still dedicated to them, but they do not today inspire and direct the great mass movements which give an epoch its distinctive stamp and seal. They do not speak with tongues of fire.

Probably a majority of the younger generation, in particular, sees little relevance to their world or their problems in persistently supernatural dogmas that are irreconcilable, in their opinion, with reason and science. Indeed, as a distinguished British sociologist has suggested, there is serious danger in continuing to try to anchor morality to obsolete cosmologies and theologies. "Our present failure, in a scientific age," writes Lady Barbara Wootton, "to disassociate morality from remarkably improbable dogmas must be counted as one of the most vulnerable features of contemporary society. If the next twenty years does not see general recognition of a purely secular morality, we must not be surprised to find that moral standards have been emptied away along with the Christian bath water."

Perhaps it is just as well that the old religions no longer speak with tongues of fire. Christianity, Islam, and Hinduism have in their time displayed quite enough fanaticism and mutual butchery. They now have to compete with new religions which are as infatuated, bigoted, and self-righteous as were the old ones in their youth.

Arnold Toynbee, a most comprehensive observer of civilization as well as a firm believer in Christianity, asserts that the religion of mankind today is nationalism. "Midway through the twentieth century of the Christian Era," he writes, "the Western society was manifestly given over to the worship of a number of idols; but, among these, one stood out among the rest, namely, the worship of the parochial state. This feature of Post-Modern Western life was a terrifying portent on two accounts; first, because this idolization was the true, though unavowed, religion of the great majority of the inhabitants of the Westernizing world, and secondly, because this false religion had been the death of no less than fourteen, and perhaps of sixteen, of the twenty-one civilizations on record."

Whether or not one looks at nationalism from Toynbee's Christian angle of vision, any examination of the conduct of relations among mankind in these times must certainly take it into account. There seems little doubt that nationalism currently commands the highest loyalty among most men except those, still a minority, who have given their allegiance to even newer and more secular dogmas. For the most part men will no longer die for Christianity or Islam, not to mention their city, their philosophy or their race; but very large numbers of them will readily die for their country. Why this should be so, why men who would once willingly lay down their lives for Athens or Florence but not for Greece or Italy should now consent to do so for the latter but not for the former, why Russians and Americans should feel essential identity with all inhabitants of vast and recently united conglomerations while Swiss, Lebanese and Gambians should feel such identity only with those a few score miles around them, is fascinating, baffling and typically human. It may be fortuitous and irrational, but it is a fact. The underlying humor of this sentiment was suggested by Rudyard Kipling when he wrote:

> All the people like us are We
> And everyone else is They
> And They live over the sea
> While We live over the way
> But—would you believe—They look upon We
> As only a sort of They.

Whether nationalism is rational or religious or neither, it would seem with all its implications and consequences still to be, as it has been for the last two hundred years, the most significant element in modern civilization. Any individual anywhere in the world who has emerged from old-style barbarism thinks of his nation as having an existence just as real and concrete as his own. The first thing that clusters of people released from domination by other people do is to set up a nation-state, whether or not they ever had one before, and to join the United Nations, an act which symbolizes their national identity, equality, and respectability.

The fact that some which do so are very small clusters indeed, only a few hundred thousand in certain cases, and have neither the experience, the resources, nor the infrastructure to govern themselves with the sophistication appropriate to their new dignity is a source of embarrassment to older and larger nations, but one which the latter cannot safely avow without undermining the "right of self-determination" and the "sovereign equality" on which ultimately, except for naked power, their own claim to status and dignity depends. Indeed, their attitude toward new nationalisms is highly ambivalent and expedient: they deplore the appearance of any which might threaten their own but welcome warmly that of others which weaken their rivals; they praise and foster federative movements among their friends but hail as "polycentrism" the resurgence of separate nationalisms among their enemies.

The world of 1919 had some 50 nation-states; the world of 1968 has more than 130. More are on the way. The process seems self-generating and self-perpetuating. Patriotism, when it is high-minded, self-confident but self-critical, dedicated to human values, heroic in crisis, steadfast in defeat, generous in victory, can be and often has been among the noblest expressions of the human spirit. Its pathological development, however, into a warrior ethos appropriate to tribal groups armed only with swords and spears, into a secular religion, into a profusion of geographical bits and pieces, could easily be the cause of decisive disaster.

So indeed could another modern religion which also claims to be in the highest interests of humanity. There is no doubt that Marx was genuinely outraged and in large part inspired by the very real evils of nineteenth-century capitalism. The appalling conditions under which men, women, and children worked and lived in early Victorian England and subsequently on the Continent and in America are bluntly portrayed in the novels of Dickens and Zola; similar conditions have existed more recently in Asia and Africa. They seemed at the time fully to justify a revolt of the "proletariat," that is, of those who suffered most from them. Through the century after the publication of the *Communist Manifesto* succeeding waves of outraged intellectuals, across Europe in the late nineteenth and early twentieth centuries, in China in the 1920s, in other underdeveloped countries after World War II, turned first to the doctrines of Marx and then to the techniques of Lenin, seeking to seize power in the name of the proletariat and, for so they honestly intended, to end the exploitation of man by man. Their astonishing success by mid-century in dominating the Eurasian land mass from the Elbe to Hanoi, comparable to Islam's spread from Persia to Spain in less than a hundred years, testifies to the timeliness of their message and the ingenuity of their techniques.

Fortunately or unfortunately, Marxism and Leninism were shot through with technical and moral fallacies which vitiated their aims wherever they triumphed and undermined their prospects wherever they did not. Marx's labor theory of value, on which his whole political superstructure was erected, while morally justifiable, was economically immature. The pathetic claim that his doctrine was "scientific," while conferring on it some of the enormous prestige which science enjoys, introduced such rigidity into its application that his disciples, when confronted with the problems of power, were obliged either to persist in proven folly or to resort to tortured and inadequate "deviations." Moreover, like most religions in their early stages, communism sought to impose on ordinary men and women a degree of austerity and self-denial which could hardly be transmitted beyond one or two intoxicated generations.

On the moral side, however, in a shattering demonstration of the fact that means determine ends, the sins of communism were even more egregious and fatal. In the opinion of Bertrand Russell the Marxists made two major mistakes: (1) they imagined that "the only undesirable form of power over other human beings is economic power," ignored the equally corrupting characteristics of political and military power, and conferred on state officials all the authority, and more, previously vested in capitalists; and (2) they supposed a political movement largely motivated by hate could produce a stable and satisfactory state of affairs, but soon found that the momentum of such a monstrosity could be maintained only by constantly finding or inventing new enemies.

One is led to wonder how a movement so contaminated with economic fallacy and moral corruption could dominate for decades two of the greatest and most populous nations and could continue to hold a fascinating appeal to many young people in nations, particularly new ones, which it does not dominate. A partial answer is that no political movement, even the most extreme, entirely practices what it preaches and that in the Soviet Union and its erstwhile satellites, though not yet in China, the "New Class," which has inherited the privileges of the aristocracy and bourgeoisie, is more interested in manipulating their system into workability than in maintaining its pristine purity. More fundamentally, however, what accounts for the persistent mastery of communism where it is in power and its continuing appeal elsewhere is its quality as an organized and militant religion, opportunely claiming a scientific rather than a supernatural sanction, appearing with a promise of earthly salvation in an era of cultural disintegration, confusion and anguish.

A narrower and more personal faith which emerged after the two world wars was Existentialism, which did endeavor to grapple with the awesome problems man had in these times created for himself. This credo sought to confront the twin terrors of chaos and freedom by a heroic posture wherein the lonely individual, admitting that it was the abuse of freedom which had created chaos, assumed the responsibility single-handedly for confronting and mastering both. As its high priest, Jean-Paul Sartre, put the case: "Man is nothing else but that which he makes himself. That is the first principle of existentialism. . . . When we say that man chooses himself . . . we also mean that by choosing for himself he chooses for all men. For in effect, of all the actions a man may take in order to create himself as he wills to be, there is not one which is not creative, at the same time, of an image of man such as he believed he ought to be. . . . Our responsibility is thus much greater than we had supposed, for it concerns mankind as a whole." While this philosophy had elements of nobility, in that it emphasized the exemplary and universal character of each man's individual choices to a generation which had shifted responsibility to single-minded leaders, it was at once too demanding and too literary to have a sweeping impact, particularly after the conditions which had immediately generated it, the occupation of Europe by the Nazis, had passed.

In a certain sense, if the old faiths have not rediscovered the voice with which to make themselves decisively heard, if nationalism is too parochial, too archaic and too belligerent to be tolerable as a religion, if communism is neither moral nor scientific enough to survive without transforming itself, the only surviving candidate for a modern faith may be science itself. Despite the fact that this conception seems to involve almost a contradiction in terms, since for the last hundred years faith and reason have been so often contraposed, it would not be difficult to argue that physical science is the primary faith of modern man, in the broadest sense. This conception, together with the impact of technology on the whole of civilization, is of such possibly decisive significance in the relations among men and nations that we turn to it next.

The Relevance of Science

The scientist Max Born, in looking back over modern history, recently remarked: "I am haunted by the idea that this break in human civilization, caused by the discovery of the scientific method, may be irreparable. Though I love science I have the feeling that it is so much against history and tradition that it cannot be absorbed by our civilization. The political and military horrors and the complete breakdown of ethics which I have witnessed during my life may not be a symptom of an ephemeral social weakness but a necessary consequence of the rise of science —which in itself is one of the highest intellectual achievements of man. If this is so, there will be an end to man as a free, responsible being. Should the race not be extinguished by a nuclear war it will degenerate into a flock of stupid, dumb creatures under the tyranny of dictators who rule them with the help of machines and electronic computers.

"This is no prophesy, just a nightmare. Though I have not taken part in applying scientific knowledge to destructive purposes, like making the A-bomb or the H-bomb, I feel responsible. If my philosophy is correct, the fate of the race is a necessary consequence of the constitution of man, a creature in whom animal instincts and intellectual power are mixed."

Whether or not we draw such ominous conclusions as Born does, we must admit that technology, in all its aspects and consequences, is the most conspicuous, perhaps the decisive, phenomenon of our times. In any consideration of the relations among nations, whether we speak of warfare, of population, of communications, of the development of resources, of domestic stability as a factor of international equilibrium, we come up against technology as, together with human nature and nationalism, one of the three great governing powers.

It is hardly necessary to mention the innumerable ways in which, for good or ill, modern lives have been transformed by science. Most notably, the individual expectation of life itself (actually in the West, potentially everywhere) has already been prolonged to the proverbial three score years and ten and no doubt will be further extended. Yet a blind technology, like some antique figure of Fate, balances this glittering prize, on the one hand, by inventing the means of general extermination and, even more ironically, on the other, by threatening to amass on this small planet so many lives that neither its soil nor air nor space could contain them.

In another field, as has been so often noted, though still for so many so little applied, the problem of production has been solved. Techniques exist which, if population can be checked, could supply food, shelter, clothing and an endless variety of luxuries to every man, woman and child on earth. Of course, in practice, methods of keeping the machinery of production in continuous optimum operation and of distributing its output to underprivileged minorities in the West and majorities elsewhere are still of a most elementary and precarious character and would have to be vastly improved before this Utopia could be attained.

Even the partial solution of the problem of production, moreover, has had side effects which are ugly, disruptive, and ultimately perhaps unbearable. Earlier industrial machinery tied men to monotonous processes without scope for creativity or pride; the latest machinery is taking over these processes but threatens to do so at a faster rate than alternative employment, alternative means of establishing effective demand, and alternative uses of time can be devised. The character of goods produced is still determined in large measure by a kind of unnatural selection or imperfect competition in which the satisfaction of such neglected needs as environmental wholesomeness, human dignity, and education is usually subordinated to artificially stimulated demand for less needed offerings of mass production.

Unbridled industrial appetites quickly consume forests older than Christianity and pollute waters needed to sustain and refresh our grandchildren. Miraculous pesticides too loosely applied poison people as well as pests, upset ecological balances cunningly contrived over millions of years, and aggravate the growing inhospitality of our planet at the very moment when its shrinkage and crowding demands the most meticulous hoarding of its amenities.

Travel has grown fantastically rapid, the globe has seemingly shrunk in size to what a county used to be, and all the wonders of the world are available to any traveler within a matter of hours; but in consequence, wonders are becoming commonplaces, wildernesses are teeming with more tourists than wild life, travelers are exhausted and statesmen disoriented by the speed of movement from one time zone to another. An extraordinary extension of mind through machines is being carried out in the realm of cybernetics. To some, this seems to promise not only a vast expansion of social memory but a quantum jump in social purpose; to others, it appears as merely another mechanical tool for the manipulation of the many by the few. Thanks to new means of communication, wisdom and nonsense, facts and fantasy, pour into the average household in unending, unfiltered, indigestible streams. The possibilities of mass education and mass deception have been equally enhanced; whichever is best exploited will determine politics in the twenty-first century.

In this connection, too, science is producing a vast pharmacopeia of drugs for every conceivable purpose. Some of them have, others will, achieve miracles in curing physical and mental illness. At the moment, however, many of them—energizers, tranquilizers, hallucinants, soporifics, antibiotics, antihistamines, vitamins—are being distributed with a riotous latitude and irresponsibility. As a consequence, the average man is tempted by a profusion of easy escapes from the anxieties of modern life, and risks ending up with a profusion of new addictions. There is still a distinction between those who take pills to feel normal and those who take them to feel abnormal; the danger is that it might become normal to want to feel abnormal; one wonders what would happen if this came to be the case with political leaders in substantial numbers.

All this, and much more, has already happened. What science has further in store for us in the next ten, twenty or fifty years will no doubt be even more astounding and has in many cases, with a considerable degree of plausibility, been predicted. A. C. Monteith remarked that "a graduate engineer has a half life of about 10 years. Half of what he knows will be obsolete in 10 years. Half of what he will need to know 10 years hence is not available today."

Among the more plausible predictions for the next twenty years are the following. Even if receptivity to population control spreads in developed and underdeveloped countries at what could reasonably be considered an optimum rate, it will not within that time have greatly restricted absolute growth, at least in the latter area. World population in the mid-1980s is variously estimated to range from 4.5 billion to 5 billion; under the former estimate Asia might have 2.5 billion, Europe 475 million, the U.S.S.R. about 280 million, the United States about 250 million, Latin America about 400 million, and Africa nearly 500 million. Through the exploitation of already known methods, world food production might have doubled. This increase would be insufficient for the more thickly populated underdeveloped areas, unless they continue to receive massive food imports from the developed areas. Needs for water are also likely to double; the need can be met, but water will become more expensive. The exploitation of the ocean for food, fresh water, minerals, adventure and recreation will greatly increase; eventually, but probably not in this time span, the ocean may be "farmed" as intensively as is the land.

The extension of agriculture and of megalopolitan development required by growing population will change the face of the earth and will affect man unfavorably in two major respects: by restricting the space available for unspoiled nature, mountain and forest, sea and sky, wild fauna and flora, and hence for human diversion and relaxation; by continuing in the urban agglomerations to impose serious pressures and tensions on the human physique and psyche. We have not yet sufficiently assessed the consequences on individual, corporate, and international life which these pressures and tensions could have. François Bour-lière, professor of gerontology at the University of Paris, suggests: "What we have gained in a century of medical discoveries and of improvement in the standard of living, we are on the brink of losing, in the form of premature aging of some of our functions, or through psychical disturbances of varying nature."

Computers will be improved and proliferated, most of the paperwork which encumbers and employs public and private bureaucracies will be eliminated, and the lower ranks of the white-collar trades may be as decimated as unskilled labor has been. Computers will teach, they will even think; they will be available for consultation by wrist-watch radio at any time or place; to some extent they will supersede libraries; women may have robots to do their housework as men have them to do their thinking. It seems probable, however, that in the competition with computers man may still prove the fitter to survive.

The revolution in communications will continue its majestic progress. Television will dominate journalism and the TV set will become as ubiquitous as the mirror. It is even conceivable that programs will improve. Iron curtains will be overriden and everyone more and more exposed to everyone else's sales talk.

As to transportation, supersonic aircraft will be cruising at speeds up to 2,000 knots and reaching the Antipodes in six or seven hours, perhaps only slightly less time than will be needed to take off, land, and get to and from the airport at each end. Automotive vehicles will be further disciplined; they will be either excluded from cities or forced to find cleaner and quieter sources of power. Oil-producing areas may suffer the same decline many coal-producing areas already have. Railroad service for short hauls will be much accelerated and improved.

However, as TV permits easy personal contact all over the world, the need for business trips, except for unavowed purposes, will sharply decline and travel by all forms of transportation will more and more concentrate on the pursuit of vanishing space and privacy. Exploration of outer space is unlikely to bring any important material benefits to man, but may be of great psychological and political benefit by providing heroic objectives which can be held in common by all men.

During the next twenty years cures for cancer and cardiovascular diseases may be found and steps successfully taken to delay or mitigate the degenerative processes of old age. It may become increasingly difficult to find something to die of; the proportion of the elderly and conservative in the population may be expected to grow. Vital organs, such as heart, liver, and limbs, may be readily transplanted, though the source and distribution of supply seems likely to create ethical and political problems. Mental diseases may be corrected by biochemical agents; crime may be treated more rationally and successfully; and even some improvement in physical strains and in both average and exceptional mental activity may be anticipated. How well or ill these occult therapies will be used no one can say, least of all their inventors.

Finally, great advances can also be expected in the more abtract sciences. As Norbert Wiener wrote shortly before his death: "There is a general feeling that the multiplicity of fundamental particles in physics is intolerable and is bound to be replaced in the near future by a much more unified physics in which both quantum theory and relativity are to be recast."

Whether enchanted or appalled by the miracles science has vouchsafed us and those it promises, we must recognize that it has so far failed to produce a coherent world-view. As yet it has not sufficiently justified its ways to man in other than purely material terms. It is changing the world but not explaining or inspiring it.

Science exercises with fabulous proficiency techniques having immediate, seemingly expedient, though often incompatible applications; it formulates a posture vis-à-vis Nature which is alternately arrogant and humble; it asserts at one moment its exclusive competence to deal honestly with reality and classifies all other methodologies as superstition; it blandly admits at the next moment that its essential virtue lies in its not claiming to know anything definitely.

These refreshing paradoxes can be illustrated at any length one wishes by quotation from the more articulate among the scientists themselves. For example, Karl Popper writes: "I think that we shall have to get accustomed to the idea that we must not look upon science as a 'body of knowledge' but rather as a system of hypotheses; that is to say, as a system of guesses or anticipations which in principle cannot be justified, but with which we work as long as they stand up to tests, and of which we are never justified in saying that we know that they are 'true' or 'more or less certain' or even 'probable.' "

In the same vein the great physicist, Erwin Schrödinger, wrote: "In my opinion this question [whether nature is causal or acausal] does not involve a decision as to what the real character of a natural happening is, but rather as to whether the one or the other predisposition of mind be the more useful and convenient one with which to approach nature." If this is the opinion toward which modern science tends, as it seems to be, it becomes a contradiction in terms to speak of "exact sciences," except as exactitude relates to the conduct of strictly defined experiments and the scrupulously limited conclusions drawn from them.

In a similar sense, another of the outstanding protagonists of modern physics, Werner Heisenberg, has said: "Modern physics, in the final analysis, has already discredited the concept of the truly real, so that it is at the very starting point that the materialistic philosophy must be modified. . . . The elementary particles of modern physics, like the regular bodies of Plato's philosophy, are defined by the requirements of mathematical symmetry. They are not eternal and unchanging and they can hardly, therefore, strictly be termed real."

Another distinguished physicist, P. W. Bridgman, even admitted: "In the end, when . . . human weariness and the shortness of life forces us to stop analyzing our operations, we are pretty much driven to accept . . . a feeling in our bones that we know what we are doing." Thus, after three hundred years science comes full circle to Descartes, who, after formulating the strictest skepticism as to the testimony of his senses and the nature of reality, at the same time completed and vitiated "Cartesian logic" by insisting that what he felt "very clearly and very distinctly" *must* be true.

The reader is very likely to be wondering why, in an examination of the foreign policy of Great Powers, so much space is devoted to the performance and philosophy of science. The answer has already been implied. Science and technology will more and more determine the character of man's fate; scientists may, for either good or ill, eventually become our governing elite; the philosophy of science, if there is one, may become our religion; and, if there is not one, the scientific "posture" might still be the nearest we can get to wisdom in the conduct of foreign and all other affairs.

We have reported the profound skepticism and reticence to which the greatest scientists have come on the basis of the experience of the last hundred years. The rank and file, however, remain much more cocksure within their own specialty and much more indifferent outside it. Too often they resemble the occupants of a military base in an alien land, whose language, customs, and gods they ignore and despise.

This aloofness, which fortunately remains only partial, distorts human society in many important respects by applying technology without sufficient forethought and discrimination and in a fashion adapted to its own imperatives rather than to those of the humanity it is supposed to serve. As Harvey Brooks of Harvard points out: "The technology of production tends to accept as its goals values which technology alone is well adapted to achieving without balanced consideration of other, equally important goals. . . . The inclination to tackle the soluble problems first often extrapolates to the view that the more intractable problems are less important." Thus we get at the same time a tautology of aims—technology seeks what is technological—and a deterioration of values—what is technologically easiest is intrinsically best.

Then there is the question of the valuable but crushing redundance of information in each scientific field. When another great physicist, Hans Bethe, was asked, "Is there enough time in the day for the student who is going to be a professional scientist to study in other fields—the philosophical, literary, historical, political?" he replied, "Once he has specialized, usually on the graduate level, no, there is not."

Yet for all these shortcomings the world fraternity of scientists has it within its power to become a benevolent and emancipating elite which could eventually remove most of the evils now besetting mankind. It has this chance because over the past four centuries it has developed within itself certain precious and possibly decisive virtues: insatiable curiosity, cool objectivity, scrupulous exactitude, intellectual courage and honesty.

Their significance has been eloquently described by J. Bronowski: "The men and women who practice the sciences make a company of scholars which has been more lasting than any modern state, yet which has changed and evolved as no Church has. What power holds them together? In an obvious sense, theirs is the power of virtue. . . . They do not make claims, they do not cheat, they do not try to persuade at any cost, they appeal neither to prejudice nor to authority, they are often frank about their ignorance, their disputes are fairly decorous, they do not confuse what is being argued with race, politics, sex or age, they listen patiently to the young and to the old who know everything. . . . The society of scientists must be a democracy. It can keep alive and grow only by a constant tension between dissent and respect; between independence of the views of others, and tolerance for them."

In consequence, there may be gradually emerging a confraternity of scientists who, by their common disciplines, would be qualified to direct the reformation of national and international society along more rational lines. What they still for the most part lack is the will to do so, the sense of their responsibility for what happens outside their magic and introverted circles, for helping to resolve the hideous dilemmas they themselves have raised.

Evidence of the Arts

Another fraternity of great fame and power is that of the artists and writers, who by their style reflect an era and by their judgments sometimes inspire and sometimes distort it. Their fault in our times seems not to be to hold aloof from the battle but, on the contrary, to plunge in so hotly and so blindly that they often shed more blood than light. But what do art, letters and style have to do with the conduct of foreign affairs? They illuminate and to some degree determine the temper of the times, which, in turn, governs to a considerable extent what peoples and governments believe and how they behave.

The artists and writers of this century have performed their traditional function in reflecting, sensitively and starkly, the horror, the anguish, the savagery, the guilt, the alienation and the despair provoked by the breakup of the old order, the two world wars, the wholesale massacres by incineration, bombing and starvation, the archaic discriminations among races, nations and classes, and the bleak disparity between the promise and the performance of science. All these traumatic experiences had their effects upon the arts and drove artists into furious protest, bitter irony, wild extravagance, catatonic withdrawal, disintegration of form and content.

At the same time new techniques of communication and a more general vogue for culture systematically impressed on an ever wider public the trauma, the black fantasies, the agonies of the artists, which could not but to some degree infect all but the staunchest who were exposed to them. To be sure, the temper of the times also reflected a growing freedom of expression and experiment, a breaking down of old taboos, which was on the whole healthy and fruitful. Still, the most pervasive effect was one of confusion, discomposure, alienation, nihilism, a sterile alternation of violence and apathy. It was wholesome that the artists should unsettle the public mind, but they tended to do so either incoherently or frivolously. There were too few among them who had the courage or the creativity to inspire confidence and faith, to light new beacons on the hills, to nail new theses on cathedral doors. One who came closer than others to doing so was Albert Camus.

In his speech accepting the Nobel Prize in 1957 Camus said: "These men born at the beginning of the First World War who had reached the age of twenty just as Hitler was seizing power and the first revolutionary trials were taking place, who then had to complete their education by facing up to the war in Spain, the Second World War, the regime of concentration camps, a Europe of torture and prisons, must today bring their children and their work to maturity in a world threatened with nuclear destruction.

No one, I suppose, can expect them to be optimistic. I even go as far as to feel that, without ceasing to struggle against those who, through an excess of despair, insisted upon their right to dishonor and hurled themselves into the current nihilism, we must understand their error. Nonetheless, most of us in my country and in Europe rejected that nihilism and strove to find some form of legitimacy. They had to fashion for themselves an art of living in times of catastrophe in order to be reborn before fighting openly against the death-instinct at work in our history.

"Probably every generation sees itself as charged with remaking the world. Mine, however, knows that it will not remake the world. But its task is perhaps even greater for it consists in keeping the world from destroying itself . . ."

In another branch of the arts, Arnold Schönberg is usually regarded as one who revolutionized music, who broke up and discarded the old tonality and chromaticism. Yet we find him indignantly protesting: "I personally hate to be called a revolutionist which I am not. What I did was neither revolutionary nor archaic. I possessed from my very first start a developed sense of form and a strong aversion for exaggeration. There is no falling into order, because there never was disorder. There is no falling at all but on the contrary there is an ascending to higher and better order."

Yet after Schönberg, Stravinsky, Berg, Webern, Bartok, Prokofiev, musicians did seem more and more to succumb to the general dither and disintegration, to an appetite for dissonance and mere cacophony. They seized on mechanical instruments and noisemakers to try literally to pound out a new language. In a way this revolution was long overdue since symphonic and operatic repertories had become rather stale and tired by the 1960s, differing only marginally from those usually performed in the nineteenth century. The trouble was that the revolutionaries in this case went so far afield that they lost all touch with 95 per cent of their audience. Perhaps the enormous gap between the taste of the avant-garde and the taste of the public in music was filled by the prevalence of jazz, which went surprisingly far in satisfying both.

The revolutions in the arts of form and literature, however, were much more popular, much more decisive in bending and coloring men's minds. Already by the opening of the century Cézanne had broken down and reconstructed painting more completely than anyone since Giotto, whom indeed he resembled. Unfortunately thereafter, painting and sculpture tended more and more either to disintegrate or to panic. With the Expressionists they wallowed in the most clinical horrors of the contemporary scene; with the Abstractionists they withdrew into a private world of enigmatic and often meaningless form and color; with the Dadaists and their Pop and Op posterity they came to denigrate everything by dignifying triviality. The first two on occasion produced significant art, but one had only to compare the output as a whole with that of the Renaissance in Italy or the seventeenth century in the Low Countries—or indeed the nineteenth century in France—to see how far short it fell of certifying, distinguishing or inspiring a great epoch.

The most influential of them all, Picasso, who spanned the period from 1900 to the present time and went, often tongue-in-cheek, through as many styles as mistresses, explained himself to the most indiscreet of the latter, Françoise Gilot, by saying: "When I paint I always try to present an image that people don't expect and which is overwhelming enough to be unacceptable. That's what interests me. And in this sense, I want to be subversive."

In a later conversation, however, he put his finger on what had gone awry with much modern art: "The life of a society demands stability and the maintenance of certain norms, the individual must adapt himself or perish. Only the spirit of invention and an intense creative need impels man to revolt, to discover, and fully to discover himself; for that, he must little by little break the bonds that bind him to the past, to tradition, to accepted ideas. Society defends itself, knowing however that its survival depends on such men, without whom its tissues harden and it dies. Modern art is moving toward its decline, because there no longer exists a strong academic art. There has to be a rule, even if it's a bad one, because the power of art asserts itself in breaking taboos. Suppressing the obstacles isn't liberty, it's license, it's a fading away which makes everything invertebrate, formless, devoid of sense, zero."

Perhaps the most significant and refreshing contributions in the field of culture are being made these days by architecture and the decorative arts. The modern style of architecture is, at its best, clean, elegant, exhilarating and practical. It is natural and relevant to the climate of modern science and urbanism, is amenable to colorfully regional and ingeniously private variations, and resists all but the most persistent effort to make it ugly. Of course, it deteriorates like anything else when it is cheaply and carelessly mass-produced; but on the whole, if it can be taken as an omen of the future, it is a good one. Similarly, decorative styles in all sorts of materials and objects, where gay and cool abstractions can really be at home because they need only to please and not to communicate, have given more refinement and sparkle to public taste than it has had in a hundred and fifty years.

Great writers are abnormal people or succeeding generations would not still want to hear so much of what they had to say. Tolstoi, Goethe, Dickens and Balzac, each was peculiar in his own way, and no doubt so were Aeschylus, Dante and Cervantes. However, the writers of the last fifty years—and their precursors like Dostoievski and Nietzsche—have been particularly marked by horror and alienation, derived sometimes, as in the case of Dostoievski, from personal afflictions, but more often, as in the cases of Joyce, Kafka, Faulkner, Sartre, Yevtushenko and Günter Grass, simply from the air they breathed during the events of their age. This mood in literature began merely with a sense of the staleness, inconsequence, and triviality of much that had been said and written for so long but soon, with World War I, took on the somber caustic note of those who have, in reality or in imagination, looked into hell and, having been assured that it is intended only for the wicked, discovered that it is equally intended for the good.

In the second decade of the century in Dublin, at a time of revolt against State and Church, of rich national revival, and of the percolation through society of the insights of Freud, a great writer going blind, James Joyce, plunged deeply into his own subconscious. He stayed there so long he ceased to communicate with the outside world, but before that time came he revolutionized both the style and vision of twentieth-century literature.

A few years later, Franz Kafka, a lonely young man in Prague, twice alien—a Jew among Gentiles, a German among Czechs—who was portraying with eerie perception the facelessness and inhumanity of men in power, confided to his diary: "Yet I felt no certainty about anything, demanding from every single moment a new confirmation of my existence—in truth, a disinherited son."

In the 1930s one of the best young poets of the time, Dylan Thomas, was writing to a friend: "My own eye, I know, squints inward. When, and if, I look at the exterior world I see nothing or me; I should like very much to say that I see *everything* through the inner eye, but all I see is darkness, naked and not very nice."

On the contemporary scene, one of the most famous playwrights, Tennessee Williams, speaking of course for himself but in words that could also have been very properly spoken by many of his fellows at home and abroad, such as Genet or Albee or Weiss, said: "I have always been more interested in creating a character that contains something crippled. I think nearly all of us have some kind of defect, anyway, and I suppose I have found it easier to identify with the characters who verge upon hysteria, who were frightened of life, who were desperate to reach out to another person." He went on to argue, not implausibly, that these people were really the strong ones, that, for example, "Blanche was much stronger than Kowalski." But the strength of the crippled is not necessarily more legitimate or more exemplary than that of the healthy.

One may note, for example, Peter Weiss's *Marat/Sade,* in which the playwright has chosen with the utmost artificiality to exploit violence and nihilism simultaneously on three levels: the murder of a revolutionary in his bath by a woman, the dramatization of this episode by one whose name has become synonymous with delight in cruelty, the playing of this drama by the inmates of a madhouse. Such contrived exaggeration is just as sentimental as the death of Little Nell and just as unreal as *East Lynne.*

Another talented writer of the day, James Baldwin, wrote in 1962: "To be an American writer today means mounting an unending attack on all that Americans believe themselves to hold sacred. It means fighting an astute and agile guerrilla warfare with that American complacency which so inadequately masks the American panic. . . . And, finally, the air of this time and place is so heavy with rhetoric, so thick with soothing lies, that one must really do great violence to language, one must somehow disrupt the comforting beat, in order to be heard." A pertinent question was whether, if "the American panic" did in fact exist, the violence done by these writers not only to language but, more significantly, to the sobriety, confidence and purpose of their generation and the next was more likely to assuage or confirm this panic.

On the other side of the Iron Curtain the exacting discipline of fear may have throttled and toughened writers and other intellectuals. In an article in *The New York Times* Keith Botsford describes a play by an outstanding Polish playwright, *Tango* by Mrozek, in the following terms: "The play is in part an ironic attack on the illusion of liberty, on the hypocrisy that invents causes to suit man's desire for power and order. *Tango* is an attack on the twentieth century; on both East and West; on the artificialities of freedom, whether sexual, economic, artistic or political. Mrozek seems to say that twentieth-century man has neither the freedom he thinks he has nor wants that which he does possess. Instead, he argues, we get exactly the amount of freedom each of us deserves."

While the traumatic events which Camus mentioned in his Nobel Prize speech, two world wars, concentration camps, torture and prisons, the threat of nuclear destruction, could have been expected to induce horror and revolt among artists and writers, one wonders whether the prevalent failure of nerve and withdrawal, the panic and the triviality, are really excusable. What will generations looking back fifty or a hundred years from now think of our literature? How will they measure our most admired writers, Joyce, Kafka, Faulkner, Brecht, for example, against their peers of other equally troubled times, Sophocles, Euripides, Shakespeare, Rabelais, Cervantes, Bacon, Voltaire,

Goethe, Keats, Tolstoi, Dickens, Whitman? Will our descendants actually be able, in the first place, to *read* these modern authors, to struggle through the involuted style and precious mannerisms of some of them? And if they do, will they consider that they honorably represented, as it is surely the duty of intellectuals to do, the bright promise, as well as the dark experience, of their times? Will they be seen to have been boldly in the van, leading their contemporaries away from all the horrors they portrayed, or will many of them appear in retrospect merely to have been milling around in the maw of the mob, beating their breasts at the wailing wall?

The evidence of the arts as to the health of our times is melancholy. For the most part they report that the old order is still breaking up. Too few artists and writers have eyes for the elements of the new order which lie all around us; still fewer have the courage or the innocence to lend it their voice.

They have been fooled too often; they are too afraid of seeming naïve or captive or crusading; they are too easily satisfied with a protest that is only a distorting mirror of what they are protesting against. As a consequence, through failure of balance and imagination, their voice and vote too often goes in fact for the old order, to whose decay they are parasites, or to no order at all. Yet it is to their voices that ever more numerous and more impatient new generations listen most of all. Still, while they listen they must live; and if there are no convincing reports of the future, they must continue to live in the past.

But what is or might be the new order, more than the bare blessings and blights of science? We now turn to some of the more concrete factors underlying the insecurity of nations, the impact of economics, the dilemmas of government, the escalation of arms.

The Impact of Economics

It is doubtful that the character of national economies affects international relations as decisively as some political doctrines pretend.

Imperialism, "the final stage of capitalism," did not prove to be, as Lenin imagined, so desperate for markets that its proponents were obliged to seize ever enlarging domains and in the process to be drawn into ever wider and more disastrous wars among themselves. On the contrary, the role and geography of traditional imperialism have contracted vastly in the last twenty years, and the markets beyond their borders that developed countries seek today are more often those in their economic counterparts than those of the former victims of imperialism.

In a similar fashion, while the Cold War has been widely supposed to be a contest between economic systems, this has been true only in a symbolical sense, since within its own domain each system has effectively excluded the economic competition of the other. Thus far the Cold War has been much more a struggle between political systems, new faiths, military, intelligence and propaganda establishments.

There is a good deal to be said for the thesis that, economically speaking, communism is less a rival of capitalism than the somewhat crude and hasty adaptation of it to a special situation, a political device for obtaining in a few decades, at whatever cost, the economic development capitalism induced over a century or two. It is only in a relatively few cases, and in those largely for historical rather than economic reasons, that even backward nations have "chosen" communism, or had it foisted upon them. Most underdeveloped countries seem to be tending toward a mixed system that they believe is adapted to their special circumstances and seeks the best of both worlds; the internal struggle within such countries is, once again, much more between indigenous political groups seeking power, and sometimes drawing support from competing foreign sources, than between dedicated proponents of the capitalist and Communist economic systems.

In any case, there is increasing evidence that the two systems, as they feel the impact of the same imperious scientific realities, not to mention the same intractable aspects of human nature, are taking on common characteristics. Capitalism more and more circumvents *laissez-faire*, communism more and more readmits it, and all those unsystematic systems in between resist identity with either extreme. It seems reasonable to presume that henceforth the world must move, above all, toward the pragmatic, dynamic, highly automated, comprehensively coordinated economy required to supply the rising expectations of more and more numerous and sophisticated populations.

What is really interesting and important to investigate in a study of international relations is not what each economic system claims it wants, but what each really requires or does not require from the others. Here one finds, as so often when one gets away from rhetoric and dogma into the realm of reality, that the emerging problems and conflicts of interest in the economic sphere are not so much between East and West as between North and South, between developed and underdeveloped countries. However, before examining this conflict, it will be useful to note briefly some recent and impending economic changes that affect all systems, and a few that affect and fundamentally modify one system or another.

More than forty years ago John Maynard Keynes warned: "The time has already come when each country needs a considered national policy about what size of Population, whether larger or smaller than the present or the same, is most expedient. And having settled this policy we must take steps to carry it into operation. The time may arrive a little later when the community as a whole must pay attention to the innate quality as well as to the mere numbers of its future members." We have presumably not yet come to the second of these points, though we may soon, but we have certainly reached the first.

It is entirely possible, experts tell us, that within as few as five years there may be in some parts of the world disastrous famine that even an emergency mobilization of all the current food resources of the planet might not be sufficient to meet. This possibility will continue to hang over vast stretches of the underdeveloped world unless and until population growth is drastically checked and agricultural production drastically increased. The consequences of such a catastrophe, or perhaps repeated catastrophes, on relations between North and South and on the state of mind of the human race as a whole cannot be entirely foreseen but would certainly be significant and perhaps traumatic. Even aside from famine, the mere pressure of multiplying population on public and private frontiers, in underdeveloped and developed countries, will certainly create unpredictable crises and neuroses.

In a "Symposium on Morality" in the *American Scholar*, Henry A. Murray referred to "some very illuminating experiments on overcrowding in confined animal communities. Not scarcity of food or anything like that in this case, but sheer overpopulation, extreme crowdedness. The whole social system of instinctive and acquired habits breaks down. The males begin fighting, the mothers drop their young and cease to care for them, and so forth. . . . One might say that overcrowding leads to a diminution of good will among animals as well as among men. One needs elbow room for spiritual health. It is harder to act morally, let us say, under certain conditions."

It is heartening to note that men are still more tolerant of overcrowding than rats are, but the above description is already disturbingly relevant to our slums and could eventually become equally so to our suburbs. Together with pollution of the air, shattering noise, the frustrations involved in movement of any kind, overcrowding certainly produces pathological nervous strain and is conducive under varying circumstances to apathy or delinquency, to alienation or rebellion. Yet we are assured that urbanization is an irreversible trend in almost all countries, capitalist, Communist, and underdeveloped. It is a disquieting exercise to try to imagine the effects on both domestic politics and international relations of the states of mind thus created among increasingly urbanized and compacted generations.

A more wholesome phenomenon characteristic of developed societies at mid-century is the sharp rise in the standard of living reflected in the growth of the middle class. As a consequence, the traditional social pyramid is radically contracting at the base and swelling in the middle; or perhaps it would be both physically and economically more correct to describe it as resting on a new, more solid base, which is fully capable of supporting such superstructure both of wealth and poverty as public opinion is prepared politically and morally to tolerate. It is relevant to international relations that this realignment of classes, in Communist as well as capitalist states, causes more and more people to feel that they have a substantial stake in the status quo, and hence to be less ready, to the extent they have even marginal political power, to sanction radical adventures at home and abroad. Unhappily, however, for reasons elaborated in other sections, this healthily conservative tendency operates more effectively, both in democracies and elsewhere, in domestic than in foreign affairs.

The ballooning middle class includes a very wide spectrum, from nuclear physicists, ballet dancers, and engineers to millions engaged in clerical and administrative activities. The latter, like many of the remaining blue collar workers, are particularly vulnerable to the progress of automation. The present occupations of many in both groups will increasingly be taken over by machines, and hence direct purchasing power derived from this source will be greatly diminished. Expanding economies, to the extent they maintain their momentum, will be able to supply new occupations in some degree and thus maintain purchasing power the economic machinery requires. All economic systems will, however, as automation and cybernetics increasingly exercise their priority on increasingly complex jobs, be obliged, on the one hand, to expand and occupy the leisure time of their work force and, on the other, to devise for the apparatus of production, whatever its form may be, other incentives as alternatives to the purchasing power hitherto supplied by quasi-full employment.

Another consequence of the proliferation of automation and cybernetics will be the increasing requirement for education and technical skill on the part of most applicants for the sort of jobs that will be available or, at least, desirable. On the one hand, this could have a retrograde effect on the "class" structure by widening the gap between those having and those lacking higher education. On the other hand, by developing the awareness and self-confidence of a larger part of the electorate, provided education is not too narrowly specialized, it could strengthen the grasp of democracy where it already exists and develop a demand and a capability for it where it does not.

Still another consequence of the growing complexity and interdependence of operations in all economic systems will no doubt be greater attention to planning. In all capitalist states planning has traditionally been carried out in relatively discrete corporative centers, and in Communist states in a single political center, but there is now a tendency in both toward a pragmatic accommodation between the two centers. What is perhaps now most seriously needed in this respect are more effective instruments for the coordination of international monetary and commercial policies and practices.

So much for economic changes appearing to some degree in all systems. As to communism in particular, one may say that a truly, even though clandestinely, revolutionary situation exists. The governments are not about to be overthrown, but the economies, at least in Europe, are being effectively transformed. The leaders are coming to realize, though rarely as yet to admit, that it is impossible indefinitely to sacrifice the present to the future, that the goal of production should be to match demand rather than vice versa, and that for this purpose there are no substitutes over the long run for rationality, cost efficiency, and flexibility in the management of industry and agriculture. These inconvenient imperatives are obliging all Communist governments, some more, some less, to deviate from the dogmatic purity of the founding fathers. In some cases, these deviations take the form of less centralized administration and planning; in others, of freeing prices and allowing production to be guided to some degree by consumer preference and plant profit; in still others, of offering not only worker incentives but even a role for unions in plant management, of winking at a re-emergence of private sectors in agriculture or distribution, or even of grandiose and usually ephemeral reorganizations of the whole industrial or agricultural structure.

Such experiments and adaptations are not brought about without a great deal of pain and travail. They are usually heralded and punctuated by a fierce, if sometimes surreptitious, political struggle between technocrats and party officials, between administrators and theorists. This struggle, which is examined a little more fully in the next section, is roughly analogous to that which occurred during the depression of the 1930s in capitalist states between doctrinaire disciples of Adam Smith and practical politicans endeavoring to ensure that capitalism survived and worked.

In capitalist states, though economics and politics are less intimately bound together, economic changes are also occurring and are having substantial repercussions on the international scene. In the United States, for example, where the great industrial corporation or utility and the great banking institution have long been the central features of the system, a progressive and profound evolution has been going on for many years. As long ago as 1933, Adolf Berle and Gardner Means demonstrated that within the great corporation, ownership and management had been almost wholly divorced and private property therein reduced to the right to draw interest or dividends. In a more recent work, Berle pointed out: "The greatest part of American economic enterprise, formerly individualist, has been regrouped and consolidated into a few hundred non-Statist collective cooperative institutions." He went on to note a further evolution underway whereby stock control of many of the largest corporations is being bought up by pension funds, mutual funds and insurance companies, the "ownership" of which is even more diffused and the management of which is even more remote and uninhibited by those technically "owning" the business. "Free enterprise," while theoretically still unlimited, has in practice come to be circumscribed in those very extensive fields where the great corporations are entrenched or elsewhere where large amounts of capital are required. The right to start a new automobile manufacturing business, a new metropolitan newspaper, or indeed a new union in a major industry exists but is not frequently exercised.

The consolidation of production and distribution has created an economic organization of marvelous productivity, adaptability and power. Its outstanding differences from the analogous Communist organization are that (1) its managers still operate with greater independence of the bureaucrats and enjoy greater prestige and rewards; (2) its rank and file, through effective unions, exercise greater influence over wages, prices and, indirectly, corporate decisions generally; (3) it offers wider investment and income opportunities to individuals with savings. However, the role of government under capitalism, both in regard to managerial and to union decisions, has evolved substantially in the last fifty years and would now be more familiar and acceptable to Colbert than to Adam Smith.

Partly because the corporation and its managers became so powerful and sometimes so arrogant that the electorate insisted on their regulation, partly because the public will no longer tolerate politically the sort of economic breakdown that occurred in 1929, partly because the government more and more directly participates in the economy both as employer and customer, the state has emerged since the war as the governor and even to some extent the motor of the welfare society and of capitalism in its modern form. This is not the place to document the statement in detail, but even a cursory examination of the postwar history of the United States, Britain, France, Germany, and Italy bears it out. One has only to run through the American press during the last year to see vividly how strong, insistent and unremitting was the demand from the most widely representative institutions and pressure groups that the government do this, that, or the other with a view to improving the economic situation. In 1966, of 77 million persons employed in the United States, 14 million were employed by governments, federal, state and local, including 3 million in the armed forces. A further 8 million were supported in whole or in part by public assistance funds; 19 million are registered for Medicare and 22 million for Social Security. Public spending is about 20 per cent of GNP; and some industries are more than 50 per cent dependent on such spending.

The discrepancy between the munificence with which capitalism produces for private consumption and the niggardliness with which it supplies many public services is being increasingly remarked and deplored as a glaring gap in so productive a system. Probably most citizens, if they stop to reflect, would agree that schools, hospitals, public transportation, parks and anti-pollution measures are more essential to their health and welfare than much of what they buy. The impact of prejudice and poverty on a single racial group in American cities is flaring up into what approaches revolution in a country which complacently supposed it had had all the revolution it needed.

It may prove that the redressing of this balance, the planned reduction of a residual poverty that in developed capitalist states is no longer necessary and hence is morally shocking, and the consequent relative shift in the economy toward valuable public consumption will more and more preoccupy the attention and pre-empt the political energies of the populations of these states. Under such circumstances, their intense concern with foreign affairs, which has been an abnormal postwar phenomenon, might relax, though such relaxation could of course occur only if it were matched by a similar healthy preoccupation with internal problems on the part of Communist states.

This relatively hopeful conclusion, however, has to be qualified by reference to another postwar development in capitalist economies which could have an unhealthy effect. Just before he left office, President Eisenhower warned of the disproportionate role which what he called "the military-industrial complex" was coming to play in the American economy: "In the councils of government we must guard against the acquisition of unwarranted influence, whether sought or unsought, by the military-industrial complex. The potential for the disastrous role of misplaced power exists and will persist."

The situation has been further aggravated in the intervening seven years. In the United States, expenditures for national defense are now nearly 10 per cent of GNP; they are estimated at about $75 billion for fiscal 1968, as compared with about $70 billion for fiscal 1967, $46 billion in 1960, $50 billion in 1953 at the height of the Korean War, $81 billion in 1945 at the peak of World War II, and $1 billion in 1939. As President Eisenhower said in 1961: "We annually spend on military security more than the net income of all United States corporations." That statement is even more true today.

In some industries, dependence on defense is far greater than 10 per cent: in aircraft and missiles as much as 95 per cent, in shipbuilding 60 per cent, in radio and communications 40 per cent; certain cities are largely dependent on defense expenditures. Including men in uniform, defense absorbs about 10 per cent of the labor force. Probably more important, as President Kennedy estimated in an economic message to Congress in 1963, defense, space, and atomic energy programs are monopolizing two-thirds of the trained people in the country available for scientific and technical research. President Eisenhower made a closely related point in his 1961 statement: "The prospect of domination of the nation's scholars by Federal employment, project allocations, and the power of money is ever present—and gravely to be regarded."

All the consequences of this development, which is also characteristic, albeit in somewhat lesser degree, of other developed capitalist countries, cannot be predicted, but some impinging directly on foreign affairs are obvious. A great many powerful interests in these countries, over and above the military establishments, have a clear concern in maintaining military expenditures. Whether such expenditures are maintained, expanded, or reduced has of course a direct effect on the defense expenditures of other states, particularly the Soviet Union, and on the relations between East and West, between America and Asia, between Asian powers, and on general international security. While it has often and reasonably been claimed that, if substantial disarmament should ever be agreed upon, conversion of the 10 per cent of GNP involved from defense to civilian production could be carried out without economic breakdown, it is apparent that the strains and dislocations, particularly in the industries and regions most dependent on defense, would be severe. Even the prospect of a 50 per cent cut in defense expenditures to be carried out over a period of several years would be likely to send stock markets into a tailspin. Only the demonstrated intention of governments to take effective measures to meet the strain would make even this measure of disarmament politically feasible.

Recent economic changes in the so-called Third World, the underdeveloped countries, have already been alluded to incidentally and may be briefly summarized as follows. Their first strong inclination when they became masters of their own houses, for the most part after 1945, was to industrialize as rapidly and ambitiously as possible in order, over and above regard for prestige, to obtain for their people the benefits of the industrial revolution and to broaden their independence of their former masters and other developed states. Since both goals were political imperatives in most of these countries, leaders did not have too much room for maneuver if they wished to stay in power. From time to time, therefore, when the means could be extracted from their own populations or from ardent foreign wooers, they indulged in grandiose industrial projects which, if politically less harassed, they might have preferred to forego or delay. But they soon encountered four serious obstacles to this line of development.

First, the population explosion and the consequent insufficiency of food obliged many leaders to divert much, though often not enough, of their attention from industry to the reorganization of traditional agriculture and, until this could be accomplished, to find means of importing large quantities of food. Second, they found that modern industry, public services, and agriculture all require substantial corps of highly trained scientists, engineers and technicians and also at least a modest level of literacy and mechanical adeptness among the population in general, which in turn demand a far more extensive effort of education than these countries had previously known. Third was the fact that history had Balkanized most of Asia, Africa, and Latin America so that many of these countries had by themselves not even a fraction of the resources and markets required for balanced economies. Efforts to promote regional economic cooperation encountered massive political obstacles; and even the few relatively large and well-endowed states in this category had grave internal regional differences, which in some cases threatened them with dissolution. Fourth was the increasing reluctance of the developed countries, both capitalist and Communist, to supply capital and trade in the quantities required to meet even the basic needs, not to mention the more ambitious goals, of the developing countries, and in the forms the latter deemed necessary to avoid any revival of either political or economic dependence.

The overwhelming nature of these problems and deeply ingrained habits resistant to their solution slowed progress in meeting them, often to a disheartening fraction of what was required. Moreover, the accumulation and recalcitrance of the obstacles, coming on the heels of the high hopes which accompanied political independence, had a number of untoward consequences.

First was the exasperating realization that the long-sought and often hard-won independence remained, and probably for many years was destined to remain, incomplete. Even a large new state was bound to be heavily dependent on foreign trade and aid, and economic dependence inescapably imposed some limitation on political independence. Moreover, refusal of the wealthier states to supply sufficient aid, to maintain high raw material prices, to offer import preferences, combined with the shortcomings of the underdeveloped countries to prevent them from meeting planned economic targets, seriously slowed the emergence of their peoples from poverty, and added to the other factors tending toward political instability.

The combination of frustrations confronting the harassed elite in many cases provoked other reactions, such as an excited xenophobia directed primarily against developed states but occasionally also against unsympathetic neighbors, and a disillusionment with both capitalism and communism because of the insufficiency and conditional character of aid and investment from both. Another common reaction was an increasingly statist control of the economy induced, somewhat paradoxically, both by the determination to exclude the foreigner from the levers of control and by the necessity for providing the momentum which neither domestic capital, because of its absence, nor foreign capital, because of its prudence, was able or willing to supply. Sometimes, too, there was a tendency to repudiate, or at least inordinately to delay, the payment of interest and principal on loans already obtained, on grounds, often well founded, that the total debt burden was more than the economy could support or, somewhat less convincingly, that a new government or a new generation felt little obligation to meet the extravagant commitments of an older one.

These attitudes, dictated in part by the hard facts of economics, in part by the equally hard facts of human nature, and in part by long-standing mutual distrust between developed and underdeveloped countries, were to some extent tempered by the unavoidable necessity for the latter, like it or not, to seek massive external assistance and hence over the long run not to behave in such a way as to cut themselves off from it completely. Never-

theless, the balance between economic need and political imperative was often so close and the emotions engendered by the
dichotomy so intense that the latent North-South conflict threatened more and more as the century drew on to erupt through
one or more of the many faults in the thin crust of civilization
and international organization.

These were the stresses and strains, evolutions and revolutions,
which were occurring in the second half of the century inside
capitalist and Communist, developed and underdeveloped states,
and which had in varying respects and degrees substantial consequences for their foreign policies. Rationally and pragmatically
(for which in so many connections one must read—theoretically),
all countries nevertheless had limited and relatively precise real
economic needs from their neighbors and the international community. They all needed to export surpluses in order to pay for
the import of essential commodities they lacked; they needed,
each one singly or in associated groups, to maintain some acceptable and fairly stable balance between exports and imports
of goods, services and capital, including in some cases overseas
military expenditures. They needed to borrow or lend capital
and hence to ensure insofar as possible a fair and stable return
on it; they needed international monetary arrangements that
would provide the optimum degree of liquidity and flexibility in
support of international trade and investment and would successfully meet pressures on countries having temporary balance-of-
payment difficulties.

While many of the modalities of trade and investment differed
as between capitalist and Communist countries, their real needs
in these respects were not substantially dissimilar and in any case
did not provide any important economic basis for conflict between East and West. The conflicts of interest between North
and South, however, were very real and arose from sharp economic differences—primarily in rates of development and population growth, which were bound to be more and more reflected
on the political and the international scene.

The Dilemmas of Government

There is little need to argue the relevance of the character of
governments to the state of international relations. As the world

soon found, international security was incompatible with the existence of governments holding the doctrines and the ambitions avowed and practiced by the Nazis and the Japanese militarists.

One rarely encounters in international affairs, however, such candid avowals of rapacity and megalomania. We risk serious mistakes if we base our judgment as to whether a government is "good" or "bad," aggressive or unaggressive, solely on its political character. Britain and France conquered enormous empires while under democratic governments; many dictatorships of both Left and Right have, either from conviction or expediency, been cautious and conservative in their foreign policy. Still, particularly in the modern world where the risks of predatory action are so obvious, we are justified in believing that the checks and balances imposed on governments by democratic institutions and public vigilance are at least conducive to relative stability in international relations. We may therefore welcome, without exaggerating or overestimating, such limited extension of democracy as has occurred during the last two hundred years.

The principle of government by the people has during that period achieved a conspicuous success, but its practice an equally conspicuous frustration. After the American and French Revolutions, and as recently as the opening of the present century, it was confidently expected that the practice of representative democracy would irresistibly spread throughout the globe. Actually, as the final third of our century began, democratic government, in the special sense envisaged by the authors of the American Constitution and others which followed, could hardly be said to extend beyond the fringes of Europe, North America, and Australasia.

Yet lip service is now paid to democracy practically everywhere. Every government, whether or not and however elected, claims to represent all the people except supposed criminal elements and to be acting invariably in their interests. The most rigid dictatorships directed by the most exclusive oligarchies call themselves "people's democracies," and regimes barring the vast majority of the population of their country from any political activity on grounds of race nevertheless profess to believe in a representative system. The more atrocious and unjust the behavior of governments, the more ingeniously and emphatically is it claimed to be in defense of the people. Justice, law, and the rights of man are universally honored in principle, even where they are most grossly flouted in practice.

The climate of the twentieth century has in fact hardly been favorable to the flowering of democracy. In the West at least there has not since the seventeenth century been a time of such turbulence, wrath, violence and instability; such times produce, except where institutions are especially deeply rooted and well tended, regimes reflecting this immoral climate. Revolution imposed by force almost invariably overreaches itself; it affronts so many interests that it either requires dictatorship to preserve it or provokes dictatorship to reverse it.

Yet the occurrence and recurrence of great wars in the twentieth century make revolutions almost inevitable. World War I destroyed the three great empires of continental Europe, installed the Communists in Moscow, the Fascists in Rome and the Nazis in Berlin, completed the liquidation of the Ottoman Empire and commenced both the liberation and the fragmentation of the Middle East. World War II opened all Eastern Europe to the Soviets, fatally weakened the Nationalists in China, and dissolved the vast overseas empires of Britain, France, the Netherlands, Belgium and Japan. It can be confidently predicted that, should World War III occur, not a single government of a major participant in power at the beginning of the war would be in power at the end.

The revolutions of the period, as distinct from the innumerable and usually inconsequential coups d'état which also punctuated it, fell into two broad categories: those modifying in some fundamental respects indigenous regimes and those expelling foreign overlords. Most of the revolutionists of both categories claimed (though not the Fascists) and some believed (though not the Communists) that they were establishing government by the people. If, however, one surveys today those vast areas of the world where these revolutions have occurred, one finds only a few countries which are more democratically governed than they were fifty years ago and quite a number which are less so.

Government by the people is the most difficult of all political systems. Until the past two centuries, it has appeared very rarely and briefly in history and then only among small, closely knit, enlightened and fortunate groups of men. During these last two hundred years it has taken deep root in the Anglo-Saxon and Scandinavian nations, in the Netherlands, in Switzerland. Elsewhere in Western Europe and in some Latin American countries it presently seems to show strength and durability, but it has had such a checkered history there that one cannot speak with assurance of its future. In a few Afro-Asian nations peculiarly fortunate in the character and training of their leadership, such as India, Japan, Tunisia and Lebanon, it shows promise. But anywhere outside of Western Europe, North America, and Australasia it will be, under the best of circumstances, fifty years before government by the people can be considered firmly established and secure.

This does not mean that "democracy" does not exist at all outside these relatively narrow geographical limits. It means that it does not exist there in the form of representative government, periodic elections, separation of power among executive, legislative and judicial branches, two or more political parties, freedom of information and assembly, *habeas corpus* and other limitations on the authority of the state vis-à-vis individuals and property, all of which have been essential elements of the particular form of democracy evolved in Western Europe and America. Theoretically it would not seem essential that democracy—government of, by, and for the people—should be so defined and so operated. Other forms of such government are conceivable, and many eminent political leaders have sincerely claimed that their governments, being conducted for the benefit of the people and with their enthusiastic support, were clearly "democratic," even though they lacked some of the main strands of the Western pattern.

It is certainly a fact that some such parody may be the closest to democracy a prudent leader can come to quickly in a country whose population has little or no experience of representative government but has, on the contrary, a long-established tradition of violence and faction. He may honestly be moving his people in the right direction as fast as they can safely go. Nevertheless, it is only depreciating significant words to confuse intention, even if it is honest, with achievement and to call even benevolent and popular dictatorship democracy.

Revolutionaries, even after taking power, retain many of the psychological biases of revolutionaries. They have overthrown an established regime, about which an odor of sanctity had gathered; they dare not in most cases risk a free vote to validate their accession; they are far from secure in their tenure of power; they know they are considered illegitimate; they are parvenus in the society of nations and are usually made to feel so. In consequence of these psychological factors, probably three-quarters of the national governments in the world today, including the governments of some of the Great Powers, suffer from more or less aggravated inferiority complexes.

These complexes have a significant and demoralizing effect on the conduct of international relations. All the new governments are enormously sensitive; all are inflamed by the merest suggestion of patronage or criticism, imagining threats or dangers where none exist, indulging in verbal bluster to mask their fears and weakness, sometimes working themselves into a state of collective psychosis verging on breakdown. Such states of mind on the part of governments of great nations are obviously one of the elements of the modern scene most conducive to international miscalculation, confrontation, and war. A particular responsibility rests on long-established governments which should be free of these complexes to recognize and make allowance for their existence among both friends and adversaries.

The Communist leaders have constituted themselves in the countries they rule a remarkable amalgam of aristocracy, technocracy, and priesthood with an iron grip on the whole apparatus of power, totally excluding any political alternatives except as they may emerge from conflict among the rulers themselves. This is of course a very clumsy political system since it provides no reliable machinery for assuring a legitimate and peaceful succession, and hence implicitly encourages conspiracy, purge, and coup d'état.

Without going into the devious and sanguinary history of conflict among Communist rulers, it is sufficient to note that in recent years it has tended to center around a struggle between, as it were, the technocrats and the "priests"—that is, between the economic managers who are chiefly concerned with developing and using efficiently the machinery of production on which their power rests, and the party officials who are chiefly concerned with maintaining the doctrinal orthodoxy and the political apparatus on which *their* power rests. The rivalry between the two groups has to a considerable degree molded the history of the Soviet Union since the war, particularly since the death of Stalin, and has recently reached a new pitch of intensity in China. The issue in China has been complicated by a struggle among the "priests" themselves for control of the party, of dogma, of the army, and of the young.

Adversaries of communism everywhere can derive modest satisfaction from its internecine warfare because they stand to profit whichever side wins. If the balance swings toward the technocrats, their preoccupation with productive efficiency and an improved standard of living is likely to concentrate their attention at home, reduce revolutionary ardor, and make peaceful coexistence more of a reality. If the balance swings toward the priesthood, they are likely to make so many practical blunders in the conduct of the economy, not to mention foreign affairs, that they may become, whatever their intentions, a less serious threat to their external opponents.

Communism has, of course, contributed most to the instability of international relations during the last twenty-five years by its dogma of class war and world revolution, by its readiness to instigate or impose revolution by force wherever opportunity offers, and by its systematic attempt to seize power in new countries by exploiting genuine or provoking bogus "wars of national liberation." Fortunately, Communist practice in these respects, while bad enough, has for expedient reasons been much more cautious than its dogma. In Part II we shall note how the practice, and response to it, has produced confrontation in Europe, in East Asia, and elsewhere in the Third World.

Another aspect of Communist political practice which has poisoned international society, because for a time it corrupted the bureaucracies of its adversaries almost as much as its own, is its addiction to secrecy at home and espionage abroad, its exploitation of polemic and defamation, of lies and cant, of conspiracy and subversion, as the principal implements of political process and change. These vicious habits arose from reactionary elements in Russian and Chinese society and from Lenin's deformation of the Russian Social Democratic party from an instrument of modernization into one of dictatorship. When two of the greatest states so degrade themselves, they could hardly fail to infect to some degree everyone else. Police power was widely misdirected into politics, diplomacy into revolution; each embassy harbored its secret agents; government officials lost the right to privacy, dissipation, and dissent; Leninism created the mirror image of McCarthyism.

Underneath the layers of power in Communist countries, however, subterranean political evolution, despite Lenin and Mao, goes on constantly. There is an irrepressible ferment among intellectuals, writers and artists, the handling of which baffles the political leadership; its exasperated reaction oscillates between suppression on the one hand and grudging toleration on the other. At one time the intellectuals will seem almost to constitute an authorized political opposition, at another they will be swept aside by a manufactured outburst of orthodoxy. A more sophisticated dissent appears among the physical and social scientists, who are progressively less willing and able to try to contradict reality; there is, for example, recent evidence that Soviet historians and economists are coming to the conclusion that truth should be sought on the basis of facts.

A further symptom of the dichotomy in Communist society is the tendency, noted by many observers, for the more intelligent and lively-minded young people to go into the professions—science, management, and engineering—where their talents will have fuller scope, while the hitherto most rewarding and prestigious career—that of official in the party or police apparatus—is left increasingly to the plodders and the mediocrities. If this tendency continues, and naturally it varies sharply from country to country, it is bound at first to slow the evolution of the societies but eventually to tip the balance in favor of the technocrats.

In the underdeveloped countries, many of which have recently

experienced in rapid succession both national and social revolutions, the problem is usually to find an elite—that is, to sift out
from the small numbers with subordinate administrative experience and the large numbers with passionate political pretensions those able to govern, to endow them with the necessary aura
of prestige and legitimacy but with the equally necessary sense
of responsibility and service, and to preserve them from a sanguinary factionalism which they with their inexperience and in-
discipline could hardly be expected to survive. The political
answer to which new nations have for the most part come is
either a single party or a military dictatorship, with more or less
superficial trappings of democracy and with a leader displaying
greater or less charisma.

This is far from an ideal solution, but it is not a wholly unreasonable one under the circumstances. It places a very heavy
burden on the leader, and to a large degree its success or failure
depends on how competent and relatively disinterested he is.
In the absence of a leader able to build up an elite and to forge
it into an effective instrument of government, the situation is all
too often apt to degenerate into that graphically described by the
talented Nigerian novelist Chihua Achebe: "The trouble with
our new nation was that none of us had been indoors long
enough. . . . We had all been in the rain together until yesterday. Then a handful of us—the smart and the lucky, and hardly
ever the best—had scrambled for the one shelter our former
rulers had left, and had taken it over and barricaded themselves
in. And from within they sought to persuade the rest through
numerous loudspeakers . . . that all arguments should cease and
the whole people speak with one voice."

Often in new nations, when an effective civilian elite failed to
emerge, or when it fell prey to factionalism, or when the charismatic leader succumbed to megalomania and corruption, officers
of the armed forces seized power. This also was not a very satisfactory solution because the officers had not been trained for the
purpose and their instinct was to abandon, or at least suspend
indefinitely, the messy chore of accustoming the people to representative government. Still, this expedient seemed preferable in

some new countries to any of the alternatives which were currently feasible there.

Government by the military was far less excusable in older nations where, even though they were not fully developed economically or fully modernized politically, a substantial civilian elite and a growing middle class did exist, and military intervention was therefore almost wholly self-seeking and retrogressive. The participation of the military in politics was, moreover, prejudicial to international security, not so much because the military tended to be more aggressive than the civilians, but because they not surprisingly sought to build up and modernize their weaponry, thus provoking quite unnecessary arms races and aggravating animosities between neighbors which might otherwise have been more easily overcome.

The complexities of operating a democracy in the late twentieth century are indeed formidable in both new and old nations. Growth of population and area, multiplication and extravagance of information, abstruseness of technical problems demanding political judgment, all carry us farther and farther from the small community of commonsensical citizens from which democracy originally evolved. While mass plebiscites and polls (generalized and speeded by TV, telephone, and computers) make it easier for the public to express an instant opinion, they do not make it more likely that the opinion will be sober and viable. The fact that the principal economic institutions of democracies—those in which most of the population passes most of its days, the corporation and the trade union, not to mention the armed forces—are in practice governed along undemocratic hierarchical lines is also not conducive to instilling in new generations those habits of independence and sober self-assertion on which the persistence of democracy depends.

Democracies have always tended to be turbulent and factious. They seem to be no less restive now that they are so massive, so powerful, so copiously informed and misinformed. Critical struggles in democratic countries continue, and probably will long continue, between those who invoke freedom to enlarge and those who invoke it to contract the rights and opportunities of their fellow citizens. It takes several generations at least to learn that the healthiest society is one that oscillates steadily and soberly between liberal experiment and conservative assimilation, each being essential to the other.

Democracies are therefore not necessarily pacific in either internal or external affairs. In the latter they tend to be slow to stir to action but, once thoroughly aroused, correctly or mistakenly, they may act with great precipitation and, having acted, may persist long after there is any rational or proportionate objective to be achieved. It was Athens not Sparta which began and prolonged the Peloponnesian War; the autocracies bear the main responsibility for starting World War I, but the democracies prolonged it beyond the point that was needful or in their own real interest. We have quoted Winston Churchill as predicting in 1901: "Democracy is more vindictive than Cabinets. The wars of peoples will be more terrible than those of Kings."

Democratic leaders, in confronting external challenges, are likely to play out a political drama in several acts: first, they underestimate both the danger and their ability to mobilize popular support to meet it; second, compelled by external circumstance or sometimes by internal pressure, they gingerly commence a response; third, in order to mobilize the public behind them, they shift the issue onto the moral plane and undertake on its behalf a vast exercise in public relations; fourth, swept along by their own propaganda, they overreact, respond disproportionately to the actual threat, and by so doing provoke a further escalation on the other side; fifth, eventually persuaded by stubborn facts of the need to reach a realistic settlement, too late they find themselves prisoners of an uncompromising public demand, which they themselves created, for moral satisfaction and total victory.

There are other dilemmas which substantially affect the conduct of both external and internal affairs by governments of all kinds, but particularly those of large and powerful states. By the proliferation of bureaucracies and the multiplication of pressures on leaders, impediments have been introduced into the process of decision-making—impediments that are especially dangerous at a time when international crises are so frequent and potentially so fatal.

Bureaucracies are not new and have always had their vices, but in our times they have become even larger, more arrogant, and more confused. It has been estimated that the number of civil servants in the federal government of the United States has multiplied by twenty-five since 1900, from fewer than 100,000 to well over 2.5 million. A similar situation exists in other governments and of course in private corporations as well.

Parkinson's Law is too close to the truth to be humorous. Each bureaucrat wants to be a supervisor, for the prestige and income of each supervisor is often determined by the number he supervises. Revolutionary techniques in calculation and reproduction, which theoretically should permit drastic reduction in manpower, seem in fact to multiply the mass of statistics and documents and the people engaged in manipulating them. A veiled guerrilla war rages epidemically among the various divisions of the bureaucracy and can be mitigated only by elaborate systems of clearances, concurrences, and committees, which both stifle and distort the vital decision-making process on which all government and foreign policy depend.

As Henry Kissinger says so well: "The rigidity in the policies of the technologically advanced societies is in no small part due to the complexity of decision-making. Crucial problems may—and frequently do—go unrecognized for a long time. But once the decision-making apparatus has disgorged a policy, it becomes very difficult to change it. The alternative to the status quo is the prospect of repeating the whole anguishing process of arriving at decisions. This explains to some extent the curious phenomenon that decisions taken with enormous doubt and perhaps with a close division become practically sacrosanct once adopted. The whole administrative machinery swings behind their implementation as if activity could still all doubts."

This tendency is exemplified in the fascinating manner in which, for example, an international crisis in a particular area will rapidly build up a persisting momentum of concern throughout the body politic of each country involved. In each foreign office and in many universities, corps of specialists who attach themselves tenaciously and parasitically to the issue give it the appearance of life long after it should be dead. The vested interest and emotional attachment of bureaucratic factions to policies and presences in chosen areas tend to become so deep that they often long outlast any real national interest. Examples of this momentum which accumulates behind a major decision once painfully taken can be found in the multiplication of nuclear materials and missiles far beyond any conceivable practical need, or in the longevity of obsolete political nostrums like the NATO multilateral force or the sovereign independence of unviable miniature states.

These bureaucratic complexities and commitments pose almost insoluble dilemmas to those responsible for the conduct of foreign affairs. They seek to avail themselves of scientific techniques, to conduct research on the model of the social sciences, to make use of computers and scientific management, to plan rational solutions of long-range problems and of immediate issues. These laudable aims lead to a vast expansion of research and management staffs, an ever richer mosaic of specialization, a torrential flow of papers and studies, and a proliferation of committees to debate and decide among the conflicting recommendations of the specialists. Meanwhile, those responsible for the day-to-day conduct of affairs are obliged either to await the outcome of this majestic process—involving usually months of delay and often an inconclusive result—or to proceed as best they can in the traditional manner of diplomacy—that is, by an ad hoc distillation of experience, flair, prejudice, pressure, and exasperation.

This process reaches its finest flower in an international conference. The presence of people and papers, the size of delegations, press corps and baggage trains, is often so massive that the only way to conduct real business is to ignore the conventional structure almost entirely, to isolate the principals on each side for an occasional hectic hour sheltered from colleagues and press alike, and to induce them to inject into the final communiqué a few meaningful decisions among the usual platitudes. Since, however, the restricted conversations of the principals are largely consumed in preliminary amenities, compulsive monologues, polite circumlocutions and translation, and are cut short by the desire of everyone to get home as soon as possible, even such sessions are in most cases not notably productive.

Another phenomenon affecting governments in modern times—

paradoxically at the moment when dictators have become more common and the powers of presidents more extensive—is the progressive narrowing of the freedom of action of all political leaders. It has often been claimed that the influence of great men is exaggerated; Tolstoi shows Napoleon as little more than a cork floating on a sea of men and events; René Grousset, the French historian, aptly remarks that "Louis XIV had the good luck to live in the century of Louis XIV."

Policies are not devised in a vacuum but are the product of hostile interests and wills forced into a marriage of convenience. Presidents and premiers, even deified dictators like Mao, are rarely able to do what they want or what they feel needs to be done. Often they are themselves only half-aware of the sources of their policies and their inspiration. The British historian Sir Lewis Namier expresses the view: "In the end statesmen hardly ever act except under pressure of 'circumstances,' which means of mass movements and of the mental climate in their own circles."

The terrible pressure of time, events, news and people upon the modern statesman is another significant element circumscribing his freedom of action. Relentless, often trivial, information beats upon him day and night and breaks his concentration and his sleep; staff, legislators, lobbyists, constituents and visiting colleagues beset each minute of his time; the deceptively convenient aircraft tempts him to span half a dozen time zones for a ritual encounter with an equally harassed opposite number. He has little time for reading or listening to ideas not immediately pertinent to the crisis at hand, for quiet withdrawal and cool reflection, for communion with God, Nature and himself. Extreme fatigue may tend to make him think repetitively and stubbornly, to suppress creative thinking and inspire fantasies. His physical health suffers; he develops a heart condition or an ulcer (sometimes an unconscious means of escape from unbearable pressure); his nerves are rubbed raw; he becomes querulous, testy and impatient; he who of all men most needs to be calm and collected unhappily has most reason to be the opposite.

Such men must draw almost entirely on the intellectual capital native to them or stored up before they took office. If they had little at the outset, it is soon exhausted; if they came to office with a stock of obsolete preconceptions, they have little time to re-assess or rejuvenate them. All these seemingly petty impediments are relevant in the modern context not merely to the biography and psychoanalysis of highly placed individuals, but to choices between war and peace and to the survival of the human species.

One is driven by an appraisal of the dilemmas of all kinds of modern governments to revert to the question raised in the first chapter—may there not be inherent and insuperable obstacles to the security of peoples in modern times under a system which breaks them up into 130 separate sovereign states governed not by the common interests of all but by widely diverse calculations and miscalculations of 130 national interests, and which, more-over, permits and equips each of these governments to start a war, in five cases a thermonuclear war, against its neighbors or rivals?

Our examination neither of Communist governments, with their doctrinal commitment to world revolution, nor of demo-cratic governments, with their mercurial oscillation between ambition and apathy, nor of the governments of new nations, with their instability and corrupting complexes, would seem to warrant the belief that expedient accommodations among 130 of them, or even half that number, are likely to be sufficient to pre-serve the peace and ensure the survival of civilization.

These are of course the reasons why men have more and more in this century tried to create some effective international or-ganization. The more passionate has become the spirit of nation-alism, the more unbridled and sanguinary the conflicts among nations, the more insecure and anxious their citizens, the more insistent has been the demand for international peace-keeping machinery.

Woodrow Wilson was greeted as a savior in Europe in 1918 because his proposal for a League of Nations seemed to offer hope of an end to war. The League was a feeble instrument, but it might have been invigorated if the United States had joined it. As events proved, it was totally insufficient to cope with the ag-gravated nationalism and the economic collapse of the 1930s; it withered away and was promptly followed by war.

The United States took this lesson to heart by sponsoring early in World War II proposals for a much stronger international organization, which was established by the victor states in 1945. Twenty-three years later the United Nations is still alive, has increased in membership from 50 to 122, has under the leadership of three great Secretaries-General (Lie, Hammarskjöld, and Thant) played a significant part in the events of two decades, and still embodies the hopes of many millions of people throughout the world.

It has successfully conducted a number of peace-keeping operations of greater or lesser magnitude, and is still conducting such operations around Kashmir and in Cyprus. It has a world-wide economic development program and regional economic commissions in Asia, Africa, Latin America and Europe which promote and coordinate joint programs of development in those areas. It has standing commissions dealing with human rights and the status of women and ad hoc committees dealing with decolonization and a host of other matters.

The United Nations is closely associated with a large number of international specialized agencies, such as the World Health Organization, the Food and Agriculture Organization, and the International Labor Organization. It is more loosely associated with several international regional political organizations, such as the Organization of American States, the Organization of African Unity, and the Arab League. It is not associated in any way but is to some degree paralleled by several regional defense organizations or alliances, such as the North Atlantic Treaty Organization, the Warsaw Pact, the Southeast Asia Treaty Organization, and the Central Treaty Organization.

A far-flung nexus of international associations therefore embraces and to some extent binds together most of the world. The nexus is, however, very far from being a world government and very far from being sufficient in its present form to maintain international peace and security. The United Nations and all its associated and parallel organizations derive their powers not from the consent of the governed, for there are no people they govern, but from the consent of national governments, which is limited, provisional, captious, and liable at any time to be withdrawn. The United Nations, as Hammarskjöld said, reflects the world as it is. It therefore represents the modicum of authority that all or most governments have been willing from time to time to confer upon it, and reflects in its debates and frustrations the overwhelming residue of authority that national governments still jealously reserve to themselves.

The United Nations has been denied by its members, principally by the Great Powers, the right to decide, without the assent of all five of them, even that a breach of peace has occurred or, if it has, that measures of any kind should be taken against it. The United Nations has been denied standing forces to carry out such measures, even if decided, and sufficient funds for supporting such ad hoc forces as may be approved for specific emergencies. Governments still reserve to themselves, rather than channel through the United Nations, most of the funds allocated to economic development and nation-building in the Third World. The most populous of all nations, Communist China, and the three significant divided states, Germany, Korea and Vietnam, are not represented in the United Nations. On the other hand, in a destructive exaggeration of the principle of self-determination, the organization has been flooded with tiny and unviable nation-states whose meager populations have been misled into the belief that the accidents of colonialism and the bad example of Europe and Latin America should determine the political structure of Africa, Asia, the Caribbean and Oceania.

The United Nations therefore exists as the shadow rather than the substance of world government, as a creature rather than a master of 122 national authorities, as an occasional proxy rather than an established principal in the maintenance of peace and the development of international order. Nevertheless it continues to exist after twenty-three precarious years. The mold is there into which at any time the metal can be poured.

The Escalation of Arms and Violence

We are sometimes astonished that our enlightened times should still almost everywhere be plagued by violence, that innocent strollers in the streets of great cities are knifed or shot each night, that psychopathic snipers pick off presidents and ordinary folk with callous indiscrimination, that bloody riots over race, sect, class, language or nationality recur as often in so-called developed as in underdeveloped countries, that small wars are constantly in progress, and that the threat of a great one can rarely be long absent from our minds.

The phenomenon of violence, deplorable and irrational as it may be, is not so astonishing as it seems. We have noted the persistent elements in "human nature" from which violence stems and of which modern society takes insufficient account. We alluded to the inflammatory nature of modern "religions" such as nationalism and communism. We have mentioned current economic and political grievances which, too long unremedied, provoke explosions of pent-up rage. We complain of, but do little to correct, the climate of violence which pervades television, films and literature, the prestige which in the United States still protects the outmoded and anarchic "right to bear arms," and the delusions which these antisocial habits encourage and inspire.

If we take the trouble to study history, we should be well aware that even in times of high civilization—classical Greece, Renaissance Italy, seventeenth-century Europe—foreign war and civil strife were practically continuous. During the so-called long peace from 1815 to 1914, to which we look back with such nostalgia, there nevertheless occurred the Latin American, Italian and Balkan wars of liberation, the American Civil War, the three wars of German unification, the wars in the Crimea, Balkans and Far East arising from Russian and Japanese expansion, and the innumerable colonial wars provoked in Asia and Africa by the European states. It is true that warfare during the last half century has, thanks to science and to an amazing display of human savagery, become much more murderous. Prospects for the next one are of course astronomically worse.

The significant and shattering fact of our times is not that war still occurs, but that there has been a fundamental and perhaps irreversible change in its nature. This change may mean that henceforth all warfare above a certain very modest level has become so destructive of man, his works and his essential environment, that it is no longer rational or even tolerable, that the ends which men have traditionally sought through warfare can no longer be sanely pursued through these means because the means themselves defeat rather than procure the ends.

President Johnson warned in 1964: "Once upon a time even large-scale wars could be waged without risking the end of civilization, but what was once upon a time is no longer so—because general war is impossible. In a matter of moments you can wipe out from 50 to 100 million of our adversaries, or they can, in the same amount of time, wipe out 50 or 100 million of our people, taking half of our land, half of our population in a matter of an hour."

There can be argument about the exact numbers of people who would be killed or crippled by a full-scale nuclear exchange involving the Great Powers and their allies. There can be argument about the area which would be rendered uninhabitable and untillable and for how long, about the quantities of domestic animals and food crops destroyed, about the number of power plants, pipelines, railways, roads, factories, ports, hospitals, broadcasting stations, schools, libraries, government and police facilities knocked out. But there can be little question that the havoc among those states most involved, and especially among those most technologically complex, would be such that over wide areas and for unpredictable periods of time blind panic and desperate want would follow the nuclear exchange. Food, medicine and shelter would be available only to the strongest and most ruthless among the survivors; law and order would for the most part cease to exist or, where it reappeared, would be in the form of local military or vigilante dictatorship.

As Khrushchev said while he was still in power: "In the next war the survivors will envy the dead." In this connection an opinion of John J. McCloy, former Assistant Secretary of War and President of the International Bank, is worth noting: "Conjecture as to which would survive better, capitalism or communism, is simply silly. What would be left after such a war would not be recognizable as either Communism or capitalism. Such survivors as there were would have to find a new name for the primitive system by which they would conduct their struggle to recover." In the words of Sir Bernard Lovell, Director of Britain's Jodrell Bank Experimental Station: "Arguments that man would today survive such an eruption [nuclear war] are irrelevant to this discussion. Whether or not the arguments are correct now, it is axiomatic that they will become incorrect within a further decade or so of technology in its present precipitous state of activity."

Despite such repeated warnings of the consequences of the change in the nature of warfare, it curiously continues to be minimized by experts, overlooked by the general public, and subordinated by governments to the supposed requirements of national defense. There is an ever more extraordinary ambivalence between the apocalyptic warnings of the consequences of using modern weapons and the still cherished and touching faith that these weapons will bring security. Yet that faith is seriously disputed by some of the best qualified among the experts.

As Jerome Wiesner and Herbert York, former scientific advisers to the White House and the Pentagon, pointed out in an article in the *Scientific American*: "Ever since shortly after World War II the military power of the U.S. has been steadily increasing. Throughout this same period the national security of the U.S. has been rapidly and inexorably diminishing. . . . The military power of the U.S.S.R. has been steadily increasing since it became an atomic power in 1949. Soviet national security, however, has been steadily decreasing. . . . Both sides in the arms race are thus confronted by the dilemma of steadily increasing military power and steadily decreasing national security. *It is our considered professional judgment that this dilemma has no technical solution* [italics in the original]. If the great powers continue to look for solutions in the area of science and technology only, the result will be to worsen the situation. The clearly predictable course of the arms race is a steady open spiral downward into oblivion."

There is nothing startling about this statement except that it was made by two distinguished scientists who have been closely associated with the defense establishment. It is perfectly obvious to the crassest amateur that a nation like the United States, which has been protected by two great oceans and has not lost a single life on its own soil through foreign enemy action since 1815, has suffered a massive decline in national security in the circumstances described by President Johnson wherein our adversaries can "wipe out . . . half of our population in a matter of an hour." Similarly, Russia, which, though often invaded, has always by virtue of its great geographical extent been able to absorb the shock and ultimately repulse the invader, has suffered a massive decline in security when it too can lose in a few minutes an equal or greater proportion of its population and infrastructure. Moreover, in the view of Wiesner and York, there is nothing science and technology can do to remedy the situation, and whatever they might try to do would be more likely to worsen than to improve it. There are, of course, those who disagree with this conclusion and who urge on both sides the expenditure of further billions on elaborate antiballistic missile systems and shelter programs. Even they, however, admit that these costly refinements would be only marginally useful and that casualties would still be enormous.

Many would argue that the present massive accumulation of weapons *does* maintain at least relative security since it deters the other side from attacking. As Thomas W. Wolfe has said: "Men's minds are the most profitable and perhaps the only suitable target for the weapons of the nuclear age." To be sure, the threat of massive retaliation has during the past few years induced the governments, at least of the Great Powers, to exercise considerable restraint in the application of force; presumably even a Hitler would hesitate nowadays before undertaking massive overt aggression. Wars however are rarely begun so theatrically as in the scenarios played out by Hitler and Napoleon. They more often begin like the Seven Years' War with a frontier squabble in the wilderness along the Ohio River, or like World War I with the murder of an Archduke by a student, and escalate, sometimes rapidly, sometimes by slow degrees, into general conflict. It seems to be the military doctrine and expectation of the West that tactical nuclear weapons would be used in any major conventional confrontation; it seems to be the military doctrine and expectation of the Soviets that *any* use of nuclear weapons would remove all inhibitions on their general use. In 1914 it was the military doctrine of Russia that a partial mobilization against Austria alone was unfeasible, and the military doctrine of Germany that a general Russian mobilization was a *casus belli*.

There has never been an instance in history in which man has invented a new type of weapon and not used it. Of course he has never before invented such a deadly weapon. But the danger is not so much a premeditated intention to use it in a particular case as an uncalculated inch-by-inch escalation of a situation until a point of no return is reached where considerations of military exigency and political "face" suddenly seem to confront responsible statesmen with the choice between resort to ultimate weapons or grievous and unacceptable defeat. There is also the underlying danger that one side will miscalculate the intentions of the other, will read a bluff to signal a decision, and will in desperation but in error strike first. There is the further danger that, despite all the meticulous and marvelous precautions that have been taken, a fatal accident could occur, for no mechanism or procedure so far invented by man has in the long run been accident-proof. Finally, only God can ensure that someday by chance not one but two or three madmen may not be sitting at the same switch.

The difficulty is that unavowed or underrated aspects of human nature work in favor of the use of whatever weapons are available and seem most likely to be effective. The professional bias of soldiers, sailors and airmen, even when they are the most humane and responsible of men, naturally inclines them to believe that the weapons which they have spent much of their lives training to use are usable and appropriate, and that if they do not use them the other side may do so first. Just as stockbrokers in a bear market are likely to be the first to sell, so soldiers in a crisis are the most likely to urge rapid preventive or pre-emptive escalation, thus in both cases aggravating the very threat they seek to circumvent. The history of the Cuban missile crisis and of almost every other major international confrontation since 1945 bears witness that many of the military participants urged the exercise of a degree and kind of force which proved to be unnecessary and which, if it had been used, might have been fatal to both peace and victory. Soldiers, particularly when they are frustrated by their inability to "win," are the most liable to go to unprofitable extremes because of their fear of a defeat for which they might be blamed.

Soldiers are, however, by no means the only ones with this weakness. Statesmen, scientists and professors are often equally bewitched by the capabilities of glittering hardware, deluded by the dream of total victory, and intimidated by the liabilities of deadlock or failure. All of them can be as afraid as teenagers of being thought "chicken." Indeed no element in international relations is more prevalent and more dangerous than the fear of being thought weak, soft or afraid. This fear has brought on more wars than aggression ever did. All the war-gamesmen, moreover, civilian as much as military, in the boyish seriousness with which they postulate their science-fiction world, plot their strikes and counterstrikes, and solemnly parade "strategic doctrines," help to create an appearance of inevitability about an international posture that is essentially artificial, anachronistic, immoral, malignant and unnecessary.

Enough has been said at this point to signalize the taint of organized and random violence infecting the air we breathe and corrupting at every turn the conduct of international relations. Our conclusions, after the main elements of the current world scene have been laid out, will seek to show more specifically that, as long as one nation's security is another's insecurity, there will be no real security for any of them: that as long, for example, as Israel is insecure, the United Arab Republic will not be secure; as long as Pakistan is insecure, India will not be secure; as long as the Soviet Union and Communist China are insecure, the United States will not be secure. The security of each of them will be best promoted not by an addition of arms, especially nuclear arms, which will simply be cancelled out by a corresponding addition on the other side, but by reduction of arms on both sides.

Military and political strategists are fond of quoting Clausewitz. More than a century ago he wrote: "As war is no blind act of passion, but is dominated by the political object, the value of that object determines the measure of the sacrifice by which it is to be purchased. . . . As soon, therefore, as the expenditure of force becomes so great that the political object is no longer equal in value, the object must be given up." It may well be that that point has now been reached in regard to any war which would be likely to involve the use of nuclear weapons.

We shall now return to current diplomatic history with a review of the three great confrontations which emerged after 1945 from the breakup of the old order: first, the expansion of the Soviet Union into Central Europe, the response which this evoked in the West, and the partition and disorientation of Europe, particularly Germany, which this challenge and response brought about; second, the capture of China by a new sect of Communists, and the challenges and response which this displacement provoked all around its periphery, particularly in Korea, Japan, Taiwan and Southeast Asia; third, the appearance within two decades of more than sixty new nations, the crisis of modernization which at once beset all of them, and the sweeping clash of interests between North and South, developed and underdeveloped nations, which threatened to produce a new and even more universal confrontation.

I hope that the appraisal in Part I of the factors which underlie instability in international affairs will make our review of these three great confrontations more illuminating and meaningful. While we shall relate in some detail, particularly in the first two cases, the diplomatic events which were their public aspect, we shall try also to direct attention to how in each case they were influenced or determined by irrational human behavior, by the ferment of old and new faiths, by technological transformations in society, by economic progress and economic systems, by political organization and disorganization, by the revolution in the nature of weapons.

I believe the following accounts of the ambitions and stratagems of statesmen, the myopia and rigidity of bureaucracies, the passions and frustrations of peoples, will also help to show how inadequate is our present system of international relations for coping with the new physical and social environment science has created. These contemporary case histories in Part II will, therefore, serve as the groundwork for the conclusions in Part III as to what is needed to adapt the behavior of men and nations to the new realities.

PART II

Confrontations, 1945—67

CHAPTER 3

Challenge and Response in Europe

The Origins of Confrontation

In October 1943, when the tide in World War II had turned against Germany and Japan, a meeting of foreign ministers was held in Moscow at which a Four-Nation Declaration on the purpose and conduct of the war and its aftermath was agreed. The main points of the Declaration signed by Cordell Hull, V. M. Molotov, Anthony Eden and Foo Ping-sheung (the Chinese Ambassador) were:

2. That those of them at war with a common enemy will act together in all matters relating to the surrender and disarmament of that enemy. . . .
4. That they recognize the necessity of establishing at the earliest practicable date a general international organization, based on the principle of the sovereign equality of all peace-loving states, and open to membership by all such states, large and small, for the maintenance of international peace and security. . . .
6. That after the termination of hostilities they will not employ their military forces within the territories of other states except for the purposes envisaged in this declaration and after joint consultation.

In his report to the Congress upon returning home, Cordell Hull said: "As the provisions of the Four-Nation Declaration are carried into effect, there will no longer be need for spheres of influence, for alliances, for balance of power, or any other of the

87

special arrangements through which in the unhappy past, the nations strove to safeguard their security and to promote their interests."

This solemn statement to the Congress has a curious ring twenty-five years later, but Cordell Hull was neither a naïve man nor a natural optimist. He was, on the contrary, a mistrustful Tennessee mountaineer with a somber awareness of the sinfulness of his fellow creatures. He avoided public controversy in the belief that it is not useful, in his words, "to get into a pissing contest with a skunk," but he had few illusions. He made the report to the Congress quoted above because he, like President Roosevelt, was soberly and profoundly convinced that the future peace of the world depended on adherence to the principles embodied in the Declaration, on rejection of spheres of influence and balance of power, and on genuine, even if limited, postwar cooperation among the four signatory nations. It would have been surprising if he had been optimistic about its success, but it was absolutely clear that Roosevelt, Churchill and Hull all believed that the effort had to be made.

Churchill, for example, wrote in January 1945: "The only hope for the world is the agreement of the three Great Powers. If they quarrel, our children are undone." In a message to Stalin a few months later, after Roosevelt's death, he said: "There is not much comfort in looking into a future where you and the countries you dominate, plus the Communist parties in many other States, are all drawn up on one side, and those who rally to the English-speaking nations and their Associates and Dominions are on the other side. It is quite obvious that their quarrel would tear the world to pieces and that all of us leading men on either side who had anything to do with that would be shamed before history."

The main facts of the Cold War, of the confrontation in Europe between the Soviet Union and the West in the two decades following World War II, have been recounted many times. Rather than repeat them here, I shall cite a few examples, draw a few conclusions as to the real nature of the confrontation, speculate whether it might have been avoided or mitigated, and assess what remains of it.

The process of assimilating Russia to the West has been going on for more than a thousand years since the Norsemen and Christianity, separately, broke into the vast Slavic steppe. For several generations the Tartars confined the Russians to Asia and retarded their development as Europeans, to which their race, language, and religion basically inclined them. After the Tartar withdrawal, invasion and conquest came repeatedly from the West: Teutonic Knights, Poles, Turks, Swedes, French and Germans. Intermittently for four hundred years great monarchs—Ivan the Terrible, Peter the Great, Catherine, Alexander II—dragooned their people into brutal quantum leaps in the painful process of modernization. Their motives were mixed, partly to strengthen their own power over state and church, partly to prepare the country to resist Western attack, partly to "civilize" their backward environment and population.

As the distinguished historian William H. McNeill has pointed out, however, the fashion in which the process of modernization was carried out, while producing dramatic results in some respects, confirmed and congealed backwardness in others. "A profound irony, rooted in military urgency," he wrote, "blunted the force of all Russia's efforts to absorb Western skills. The Russian government could never neglect the threat inherent in an ever changing Western military technology. Yet efforts to transplant the full panoply of Western armaments to Russian soil required rapid transformation of existing social relations and practices. This, in turn, invited if it did not require wholesale resort to legal compulsion, as the shortest way to make people do what the leaders of the government found necessary. Yet, while it narrowed the technical gap between Russian and Western societies, massive use of force to compel the population at large to do what the rulers deemed necessary simultaneously widened the breach between Russia's social institutions and those of Western nations. Hence Russia's urgent efforts to imitate Western technology made full and complete assimilation of Western culture impossible."

This tragic breach was ironically widened by the very revolutionaries who wanted to bring Russia closer to the West, first the Populists who assassinated Alexander II just as he was about to promulgate a liberal constitution, then the Communists who expected their revolution to spread throughout Europe but soon found that it merely produced a "cordon sanitaire" a few miles from Leningrad. Except for the brief wartime cooperation, the breach between Russia and the West has been more profound during the past fifty years than at any other time during the past three centuries.

It is not possible to say with any certainty whether the attempt at the end of World War II to heal this breach was doomed from the outset, whether the ambitions and mistrust of a Communist regime under a quasi-Oriental dictator and the expectations of two democracies committed to a blending of legitimacy and self-determination in Europe were conceivably compatible. There is some reason to believe that, if both had been a little more patient and generous and a little more realistic, they might have come a little closer together, but whether it would have been close enough to have avoided a cold war in some form or other is doubtful.

It seems probable that a victorious Soviet Union would have insisted under any circumstances, on national security grounds which are understandable if not legitimate, in having what it called "friendly governments" in the two countries, Poland and Rumania, which geography had determined should constitute either the buffers between it and Europe or the corridors for an oft-repeated European attack upon it. Moreover, since the Soviet Union was Communist, it is hard to believe it would have considered any government of these countries to be safely "friendly" which was not also Communist-dominated. It is doubtful, therefore, whether all the long and painful negotiations to determine, first, the frontiers of Poland and, second, the composition of its postwar government, could have had any final outcome other than the one they did have.

Once the unconditional surrender of Germany was fixed as the common goal, the Red Army was almost certain to occupy the whole of Poland, the Soviet government was sure to insist on and in the end to impose a "friendly" government, the imposition of such a government was bound to seem to Britain, which had entered the war in defense of Poland, and to the United States, which was attached to freedom, self-determination and the Polish vote, an outrageous violation of the principles for which they had fought. The same considerations applied, in a slightly lesser degree because of its wartime alliance with the Nazis, to Rumania.

Yalta and "Liberated Europe"

Somewhat inconsistent charges have been filed against Roosevelt and Churchill that they sold Eastern Europe down the river at Yalta and other wartime conferences, and against Stalin that he flouted the Yalta and other agreements on liberated Europe almost before the ink was dry. These charges, which have had quite an impact on subsequent history, deserve some comment.

Neither at Yalta nor elsewhere did the United States and Britain turn over Eastern Europe to the Soviets, other than agreeing to cede to Russia that part of Poland east of the Curzon Line, northern East Prussia, and Bessarabia and Northern Bukovina. On the contrary, they exerted the most strenuous, even though on the whole unavailing, efforts to prevent Soviet domination of the area.

At the Moscow Conference of Foreign Ministers the United States and Britain were able to obtain Soviet consent to the above-quoted provisions of the Four-Nation Declaration "that after the termination of hostilities they will not employ their military forces within the territories of other states except for the purposes envisaged in this declaration and after joint consultation." At Yalta they were both astonished and delighted to obtain Soviet concurrence in a "Declaration on Liberated Europe" which provided, *inter alia:* "To foster the conditions in which the liberated peoples may exercise these rights [those guaranteed by the Atlantic Charter], the three governments will jointly assist the people in any European liberated state or former Axis satellite state in Europe where in their judgment conditions require (A) to establish conditions of internal peace; (B) to carry out emergency measures for the relief of distressed people; (C) to form interim governmental authorities broadly representative of all democratic elements in the population and pledged to the earliest possible establishment through free elections of governments responsive to the will of the people; and (D) to facilitate where necessary the holding of such elections."

The two Western governments made vigorous efforts, as soon as the Soviet armies moved into Rumania, Bulgaria and Hungary, to obtain effective representation and authority on Allied Control Commissions in those countries and, when the Commissions proved to be wholly dominated by the Soviets, protested sharply but vainly at Yalta and Potsdam. It must be admitted, however, that their case in this respect was considerably weakened by the fact that when they had earlier moved into Italy, Stalin had pressed hard for an equal or at least significant voice in the direction of civil affairs there and had designated so exalted a figure as Vishinsky as his representative on a tripartite "Military-Political Commission" set up in Algiers ostensibly for this purpose. However, neither this Commission nor the "Inter-Allied Advisory Council" established in Italy itself was permitted by the Western Allies to derogate in the slightest degree from the paramount authority of the Western military commander, General Eisenhower, and Vishinsky was shortly withdrawn from what proved to be an entirely otiose body. It doubtless gave Vishinsky considerable satisfaction subsequently to assist in excluding Western members of a corresponding commission in Rumania from any exercise of authority. As William H. McNeill concludes on this point: "Having excluded Russia from any but nominal participation in Italian affairs, the Western Powers prepared the way for their own exclusion from any but a marginal share in the affairs of Eastern Europe. No other arrangement, of course, conformed to the real distribution of military power and responsibility."

It is also worth noting in this connection that Churchill was much concerned throughout 1944 by the prospect of Soviet intrusion into Greece and Yugoslavia and proposed to Stalin a "spheres of influence" arrangement whereby British influence was to be preponderant in Greece, Soviet influence was to be preponderant in Rumania and Bulgaria, and the two were to share equally in the tutelage of Yugoslavia. The Americans blocked formal approval of this arrangement, but it was implemented in practice until the end of the war insofar as Greece, Rumania and Bulgaria were concerned and can hardly have failed to give Stalin the impression that his ambitions in regard to the latter two would not provoke serious objection from the West.

From the outset there was a wide but tacitly ignored semantic gap between what the Soviets understood and what the Westerners understood by such terms in the Yalta Declarations as "internal peace," "democratic elements" and "free elections." The Americans and British may indeed have unwittingly been laying a trap for themselves and their own public opinion by asking the Soviets to subscribe to such sweeping affirmations of Western political virtue, which were bound to be differently interpreted and differently applied. It is clear, however, that Stalin seriously underestimated both the significance Western opinion would attach to what probably seemed to him mere rhetorical window-dressing and the degree to which measures he thought essential to Soviet national security would undermine Russia's long-term relations with the West.

The heart of the problem of East-West relationship in the decisive months following Yalta and victory in Europe unfortunately lay precisely in those two countries, Poland and Rumania, where the Soviets believed the exercise of democracy in the Western sense would bring to power elements implacably opposed to them and intolerably dangerous to their security, and where the West regarded the grant or denial of such democracy to be the touchstone of Soviet intentions and of the viability of future cooperation with them. In the event, of course, the Declarations were in the Western view grossly violated by the Soviet Union in respect to Rumania and Poland within weeks of their having been accepted at Yalta. This disregard of commitments so recently and so publicly undertaken had much to do with persuading the Westerners during subsequent months that meaningful postwar cooperation was either impossible or could be achieved only on the basis of very tough, inflexible, "hard-nosed" bargaining.

In retrospect, it seems that the fatal controversy over Rumania and Poland could have been avoided only if the Soviets had inconceivably tolerated governments bitterly hostile to them, or if the Westerners had cynically agreed that the two countries should fall within an unchallenged Soviet sphere of influence. In all fairness, however, it should be remembered that only thirty years before Britain, France and Tsarist Russia had in secret treaties with equal cynicism divided up the Near East into spheres of influence; and that the United States, which maintained a long-standing sphere of influence in the Western Hemisphere, had in the forty years before World War II annexed Puerto Rico, split off Panama from Colombia in order to obtain the Canal Zone, and engaged in prolonged military occupations of several independent Caribbean nations. The trouble at least in part was once again the critical difference in the rate of "modernization" between Russia and the West: by 1945 the United States and the United Kingdom (under the Labor government) had decided that imperialism was wicked and unprofitable, but the Soviet Union had not.

What, in fact, were Soviet intentions in 1945 in regard to Eastern Europe and cooperation with the Western Powers? Unless and until Soviet archives are published, which is unlikely to occur in the foreseeable future, we can only speculate. We have expressed the view that Stalin would never have settled for less than Communist domination of the two countries, Poland and Rumania, on Russia's immediate frontiers. On the other hand, there seems to be some evidence for believing that a similar domination of other Eastern European countries may not have been originally contemplated.

In Hungary the Communist party occupied a minority position in the provisional government established by the Soviets when their armies entered the country. Moreover, in municipal elections held in Budapest in the summer of 1945 and national elections held in November, the firmly anti-Communist Smallholders' Party won sweeping majorities. A study by the Royal Institute of International Affairs described the latter election as "probably the freest general election ever held in the history of Hungary." It was only in 1947 that a government in which non-Communists were the majority was swept away by the Soviets.

Similarly in Czechoslovakia a broadly based provisional government under President Beneš was installed when the Soviets entered the country, and as late as May 1946, elections, which were admitted by all concerned to be fair and free, produced a Communist plurality of 38 per cent but a majority divided among three anti-Communist parties. The government emerging from these elections had a Communist Prime Minister and Communists or fellow-travelers in several key posts but nevertheless preserved substantial political and economic freedom in the country until the coup d'état of February 1948. It should also be remarked that from the very beginning the Soviets accepted a strongly pro-Western government in occupied Austria and even permitted the anti-Communist People's and Socialist parties to operate with relative freedom in their zone of occupation.

It is therefore by no means certain that already at the time of Yalta and Potsdam the Soviet government had determined to advance its satellite system to the borders of Bavaria, nor does it seem inevitable that the ensuing Cold War should have assumed quite the virulence and the shape which it did. Certain acts of commission and omission on the part of the United States also played some part in bringing about a confrontation of such tragic proportions.

Mistakes of the United States

One error which President Roosevelt committed was to refuse, to the greatest extent he could, to formulate and confirm postwar political settlements while the war was in progress. No doubt he did so because like most Americans he had been shocked by the spoils-sharing secret treaties concluded by the Allies during World War I, because he disapproved of the principal belligerents attempting to determine the fate of the peoples of occupied Europe before they could speak for themselves, and because he perceived that the attempt to resolve these problems while the war was in progress was bound to lead to grave dispute and hence to compromise the joint war effort.

Valid as these reasons appear, the consequence of yielding to them was the settlement of many of the issues by pre-emption and force. As Churchill so often pointed out, even the determination of military strategy solely on military grounds, or with the laudable aim of saving human lives, often meant that political objectives which should have constituted a significant reason for expending the lives were substantially lost, and in some cases that other lives were later sacrificed in a belated effort to retrieve what had earlier been abandoned or neglected.

An example of the folly of taking, on purely military grounds, decisions which had serious political consequences was afforded during the final weeks of the war in Europe, first while Roosevelt was ill and exhausted and then while Truman was still groping for the levers of command. As Robert Murphy has pointed out, there was no one in Washington during those critical weeks to make political decisions. Marshall referred them to the theater commander, and Eisenhower was concerned only with getting the war over as fast as possible and avoiding clashes with the Russians when the two armies met. It was in this ill-considered way that the fateful American decisions were taken to stop short of Berlin and Prague, which could easily, legitimately, and usefully have been reached before the Russians.

Another significant and unfortunate, though possibly unavoidable, aspect of American policy at this time was the rapid withdrawal of American armies from Europe. Already at Yalta, in what Churchill subsequently called "a momentous statement," Roosevelt announced his belief that he could not keep American troops in Europe more than two years after the war. In view of the weight which Stalin attached to military force, such an announcement cannot have been without effect on his conception of the shape of postwar Europe. In fact, of course, Roosevelt did not misread the temper of the American Congress and people who, drawn reluctantly from their isolation by Pearl Harbor, certainly had no intention in 1945 of prolonging their military presence abroad and indeed insisted on "bringing the boys home" so precipitately that the American army fell from 8.3 million persons on V-E Day to 1.9 million one year later. In a speech to the Herald-Tribune Forum on October 29, 1945, General Marshall commented: "The military establishment cannot hope to ensure the safety of the United States very much longer at the present rate of demobilization . . . in a widespread emotional crisis of the American people, demobilization has become, in effect, disintegration, not only of the armed forces but apparently of all conception of world responsibility and what it demands of us."

If, by failing to negotiate political settlements when they were in the strongest position to do so, by failing to maneuver their

military force with a view to its maximum utility in achieving political ends, and by drastically curtailing that force overseas while
it was still needed, the Americans neglected a "stick" which was
readily at their disposal, they also failed to avail themselves of the
"carrot" which might have been conducive to a pragmatic and
even-handed accommodation with the Soviet Union. When the
Yalta Conference met in February 1945, there were pending there
and in Washington three major Soviet requests for assistance in
rebuilding the economy so disastrously devastated by the Germans: (1) a so-called Fourth Protocol under Lend-Lease, which
was to cover shipments during the current fiscal year but in which
the Soviets had included about $1 billion for industrial equip-
ment and machinery, presumably in large part for postwar reconstruction; (2) a demand for German reparations to the value of
$20 billion, of which the Soviet Union was to receive half; and
(3) a request to the United States for a $6 billion credit spe-
cifically for postwar reconstruction.

Of the $1 billion sought for reconstruction in the Fourth Proto-
col only a small fraction was produced and shipped. Indeed, by
an order issued without President Truman's knowledge, all
Lend-Lease shipments were cut off immediately after V-E Day,
thus eliciting outraged protests from both Stalin and Churchill;
the order was promptly rescinded but finally and definitely rein-
stituted immediately after V-J Day in September. At Potsdam
and after, reparations to the Soviet Union from Western-occupied
Germany were scaled down to small proportions, and the Soviets
were obliged to content themselves with bleeding white their
own zone of occupation. The request to the United States for a
$6 billion credit for postwar reconstruction was never seriously
discussed and was a casualty of the mistrust between the United
States and Russia which developed rapidly after Yalta.

Insufficient attention has been paid, in assessing the causes of
the breach between Russia and the West, to the refusal of the
West to cooperate substantially in rebuilding the shattered Soviet economy or to the strong nexus of common interest and
sympathy which might have been preserved after the end of the
fighting if this experiment had been risked. As Philip Mosely,
an eminent Kremlinologist who participated in some of these

events, has concluded: "To make the cooperation stick, much
more should have been done to assure him [Stalin] of assistance
in rebuilding the Soviet economy; as it turned out, Stalin and the
Soviet people soon felt that their vast sacrifices were forgotten by
less war-damaged allies as soon as the fighting was over. That and
other policies would have required a much more integrated strategy than American policy-makers seemed capable of achieving
during World War II."

The Breach Widens

Soviet-Western relations deteriorated sharply within a few
weeks after Yalta and, despite some brief abatement during the
San Francisco and Potsdam Conferences, never recovered. The
basic cause was the radical discrepancies between the *Weltan-
schauungen* of the operators of the two systems. The immediate
occasion was the quarrel over Poland and the widely divergent
interpretations of the pertinent Yalta agreements. An important,
though not a fundamental, factor was the death of Roosevelt,
who had been present at Yalta and had a more nuanced view
of how much or how little the agreements had really meant, and
the succession of Truman, who was more disposed to see differences in black and white and who was briefed according to a
Western interpretation of the agreements as one-sided in one
direction as was the Soviet interpretation in the other.

As a consequence, in the new President's first meeting with
Molotov in Washington late in April 1945, the two statesmen
at once began to lecture each other in a fashion which unhappily
set the tone for the next twenty years. As Truman reports in his
Memoirs: "I expressed once more the desire of the United States
for friendship with Russia, but I wanted it clearly understood
that this could be only on a basis of the mutual observation of
agreements and not on the basis of a one-way street. 'I have never
been talked to like that in my life,' Molotov said. I told him,
'Carry out your agreements and you won't get talked to like
that.' " Neither party to this self-righteous conversation seems to
have entertained the possibility that the other genuinely believed
in the interpretation of the agreement which he was putting forward and that the fault lay not so much in the dishonesty of one

or the other of the signatories as in the fatal imprecision of its terms and the wide gap between what each considered essential to his political objectives in Eastern Europe.

Three months later, Truman, Churchill, and Stalin met at Potsdam. Important accords were reached, but the wartime cordiality and partnership were already faltering. While for the most part quickly grasping the essentials of the problems to which he was so new, Truman displayed, to a marked degree, customary American impatience and unwillingness to hammer out at wearisome length issues which the passage of time would render wholly insoluble. Churchill, though with a far greater sense of history than either of his colleagues, was tired, petulant, long-winded, and naturally preoccupied with the British elections. Stalin was courteous, cool, inscrutable and adroit, deferential to the President, impatient with Churchill, readily conceding minor points but keeping a relentless grip on the essentials. It was in fact a conventional international horse-trading affair, in marked contrast to the San Francisco Conference, which only a few weeks before had concluded with the creation of the United Nations in an atmosphere of sober hope.

As Herbert Feis, the distinguished historian of Potsdam and that whole critical period, sums it up: "The impulse to strive together to transform the nature and relations of nations had waned. National diplomacy was relapsing into old habits of thought and reckoning, which so short a time ago had been judged outworn and inadequate. Conflicts of desire and opinion were emerging. In the West fear of broken Germany was overcast by fear of Soviet Communist domination of Europe. In the Soviet Union brief trust in the true good will of the West was giving way to the belief that the West was bent on depriving the Soviet Union of the benefits of victory. . . ." Feis concluded his account with a sorrowful and moving apostrophe: ". . . the great nations must one and all live and act more maturely and more trustfully than they did during the months that followed the end of the war against Germany. They must invalidate the historical lessons about national behavior that were illustrated during this period. The capability of man to respond to reason—and to master their passionate purposes and fantasies—is undergoing its ultimate test."

The swift and tragic consequences of their failure to do so was displayed in a historic exchange of public statements only half a year after Potsdam. On February 9, 1946, incident to the first elections to the Supreme Soviet in eight years, Stalin made a speech at a meeting of voters of his electoral district in Moscow. On February 17, James Forrestal, U.S. Secretary of the Navy (and soon to become the first Secretary of Defense), recorded in his diary that he had asked Justice Douglas of the Supreme Court what he thought of this speech and Douglas had replied, "The Declaration of World War III." This apparently coincided with Forrestal's view, for the editor of his diaries notes, "This speech and the program it laid down came close to convincing him that there was no way, as Lippmann had hoped, in which democracy and Communism could live together. It is clear that from this time on he felt increasingly that policy could not be founded on the assumption that a peaceful solution of the Russian problem would be possible."

Indeed, this speech by Stalin has often been cited by others as a turning point, marking a decision by Stalin and the Politburo to abandon cooperation with the West and go it alone in pursuit of unilateral Soviet objectives. I confess that at one time I shared this view. Yet a rereading of the speech in the cooler atmosphere of 1967 and in fuller knowledge of Soviet history and ideology inclines me to the conclusion that this view of the speech was unduly melodramatic.

With the benefit of hindsight, the speech appears to be much more of an apologia for the past than a declaration for the future. It is primarily a lengthy justification, addressed to the Russian people, of Stalin's policy before and during the war and a claim that the survival of the Soviet system through its supreme ordeal demonstrated its fitness and virtue. "It would be wrong," Stalin declared, "to think that the Second World War was a casual occurrence or the result of the mistakes of any particular statesman, though mistakes undoubtedly were made." He cited unattributed "foreign" criticism of the Soviet social order, of the Soviet multinational state, of the Red Army, of the Five Year Plans, of agricultural collectivization, of wartime arms production and in each case replied that the test of war had refuted the criticism. To be sure, he repeated the dog-eared tenet of Marxist gospel that "the war was the inevitable result of the development of world economic and political forces on the basis of modern monopoly capitalism," which is presumably the clause taken by Western observers as a declaration of war, of irreconcilable conflict between communism and capitalism, but the whole context was clearly otherwise. It seems more likely that Stalin, by claiming war to be inevitable in a world dominated by capitalists, was rebutting criticism of himself to the effect that he had failed properly to prepare the Soviet Union for war, his domestic policies had weakened and divided the country, and his devious foreign policy failed to avert the German attack. In the whole speech he did not once speak ill of the Western Allies and in fact gave them some share of the credit for winning the war.

There are some other indications, however, that by early 1946 the Soviets may have concluded that both doctrine and opportunity coincided in warranting a limited resumption of the overt and covert campaign against the capitalist world. In the same month in which Stalin made his speech, Earl Browder, general secretary of the American Communist Party, who had the previous year been denounced by Jacques Duclos for "sowing dangerous opportunistic illusions" about "class peace in the postwar period," was expelled from the Party. Somewhat earlier, Mark Etheridge, on a visit to Bulgaria and Rumania on behalf of President Truman, found the Soviet commanders there openly claiming that Britain was finished and boasting of Soviet hegemony over all Europe east of Italy.

In the same month of February 1946, Secretary of State Byrnes was sufficiently disturbed by what was happening in Europe to warn in a speech in New York that the United States would not allow "aggression to be accomplished by coercion or pressure or by subterfuge such as political infiltration." The next month Winston Churchill in effect threw down the gauntlet in his famous speech at Fulton, Missouri, in which he declared that "From Stettin in the Baltic to Trieste in the Adriatic, an iron curtain has descended across the Continent." Stalin at once responded by denouncing Churchill as "a firebrand of war," recalling Allied intervention in Russia after World War I, and claiming that England and the United States were again demanding that the Soviet Union accept their "domination" or face an inevitable war.

In summary, Soviet policy at the beginning of 1946 probably still retained considerable flexibility. There can be no doubt that Stalin and his colleagues were ready and eager to seize inexpensive opportunities in the postwar disorder of Europe and elsewhere to install Communist regimes or increase Communist and Soviet influence. There is insufficient evidence, however, to prove that by the beginning of 1946 the Soviets had decided that it was either timely or possible to take over even the whole of Eastern Europe or, more important, that a prospect of massive Western assistance in the reconstruction of the Soviet economy might not still have persuaded them to prolong the wartime collaboration and postpone the realization of their ultimate objectives for a further period of years.

By this time, however, Western opinion and Western leaders had already been so alienated by Soviet behavior in Eastern Europe and on a whole series of other issues that they were no longer willing to offer the assistance which might have at least postponed and softened the confrontation. Already in the spring of 1945 the U.S. Congress, in approving the final Lend-Lease appropriation, had ruled out any expenditures for postwar reconstruction. No alternative was ever seriously discussed.

In another vital field as well, nuclear weapons, an early effort at collaboration soon broke down. In September 1945, just before he retired as Secretary of War, Henry Stimson proposed "an arrangement with the Russians, the general purpose of which would be to control and limit the use of the atomic bomb as an instrument of war and so far as possible to direct and encourage the development of atomic power for peaceful and humanitarian purposes. Such an approach might more specifically lead to the proposal that we would stop work on the further improvement in, or manufacture of, the bomb as a military weapon, provided the Russians and the British would do likewise."

Such a direct approach to the Soviets was seriously considered but was delayed and eventually dropped in favor of a program of control under the aegis of the United Nations. Nine precious months, moreover, slipped by before the U.S. proposal for an International Atomic Development Authority was introduced to the United Nations by Bernard Baruch with the lapidary phrase: "We are here to make a choice between the quick and the dead."

The proposal involved, on the one hand, exclusive eventual ownership by the authority of all activities relating to the production of atomic explosives but, on the other, retention of existing stockpiles of weapons while international controls were being gradually and progressively instituted. From the Soviet point of view it presumably seemed that the American monopoly of nuclear weapons and capability of nuclear blackmail were to be maintained until some problematical future date when elaborate, intrusive international machinery, of which they disapproved on principle in any case, might perhaps come into being. They countered with the proposal for an immediate agreement not to use nuclear weapons, to cease weapons production and to destroy all stockpiles, whereupon they would accept international controls. This proposal the United States of course rejected. As President Truman instructed Baruch: "We should not under any circumstances throw away our gun until we are sure the rest of the world can't arm against us."

This divergence foreshadowed the disarmament debate of the next twenty years—whether to destroy weapons and then proceed to controls or to establish controls and then destroy weapons. On this divergence and the profound lack of mutual confidence which it reflected, the effort to bottle up the dreadful genie that science had released foundered at the outset. The great opportunity was lost and has never been recovered.

Shortly after Yalta, therefore, there occurred, month by month, a reciprocal escalation of mistrust between Russia and the West. The West became convinced that Stalin had chosen this time for a vast and perhaps decisive expansion of Communist power. The Soviets may have been equally persuaded that the West, having denied them aid in reconstruction, having sought to re-establish the "cordon sanitaire," enjoying a monopoly of new and terrible weapons, was planning to mobilize, once again under the inspiration of Churchill, a second anti-Bolshevik crusade.

The Soviets, as Russians and as Communists, were profoundly, congenitally, even neurotically mistrustful of the West. The West was hardly less mistrustful of the Soviets. Most Americans had long before the war, as a consequence of the machinations of the Comintern, the liquidation of the kulaks, the great purges, the Spanish Civil War, the Nazi-Soviet Pact, acquired lasting impressions of the character and ambitions of the Soviet regime—impressions which were in some cases hopefully, in others grudgingly, suspended during the war, but which rapidly revived and intensified as a result of the postwar Soviet behavior. They deeply distrusted their erstwhile allies both as revolutionaries who proclaimed their intention of taking over the world, and as Russian imperialists who, though no doubt often subject to foreign invasions, had nevertheless through the centuries succeeded in building the largest contiguous empire over a vast conglomeration of subject peoples.

The fundamental tragedy was—and this is one of the lessons on which history has most often and most vainly spoken—that the pursuit of security on both sides multiplied and disseminated insecurity. Stalin's forcible installation of Communist regimes in Poland and Rumania, and subsequently elsewhere, while providing a territorial buffer along Russian frontiers, soon had the effect of raising up against the Soviet Union a mighty military coalition armed with horrendous weapons which could span this buffer in a matter of minutes. On the other side, counteraction by the West—by the U.S. Congress and government in precipitately abandoning their principal lever, economic aid, for fear it would strengthen a rival, by Churchill in so decisively throwing down the gauntlet at Fulton—fed the very animosity they feared and probably spurred the Kremlin to widen further the protective buttress in Central Europe.

The Cold War at Its Worst

The escalation of stroke and counterstroke continued in geometrical and disheartening progression over the next five years, indeed until after the death of Stalin. In Greece the civil war, which had seemed to be settled by an agreement among the parties in December 1945, broke out with renewed violence the next year, obviously nourished by a steady flow of men and arms from Yugoslavia, Albania and Bulgaria; and by February 1947 it was proving an insupportable financial burden to the nearly bankrupt British. Concurrently, Soviet pressure on Turkey to permit Soviet bases at the Dardanelles and to return territories yielded to Turkey in 1921, was resumed with new insistence. The immediate crisis—the threat of a Soviet breakthrough to the Mediterranean via a satellite Greece and a cowed Turkey—coming on top of the accumulation of bitterness over Soviet encroachment during the previous two years, produced the decisive American counterthrust—the Greek-Turkish aid program and the Truman Doctrine.

The Truman Doctrine was occasioned by, but by no means limited to, the situation in the Eastern Mediterranean. For the President declared to the Congress on March 12, 1947: "I believe that it must be the policy of the United States to support free peoples who are resisting attempted subjugation by armed minorities or by outside pressures. I believe that we must assist free peoples to work out their destinies in their own way. I believe that our help should be primarily through economic and financial aid which is essential to economic stability and orderly political processes." Thus, as a consequence of exorbitant and miscalculated Soviet pressure, the decisive first step was taken to reverse the anticipated American withdrawal from Europe. Even more significant was the acceptance of an open-ended obligation to assist, wherever and whenever the United States felt so disposed, "free peoples resisting attempted subjugation," a commitment which became the central and compelling feature of United States foreign policy for twenty years.

Three months later, with the offer of the Marshall Plan, the United States applied the Truman Doctrine to Western Europe in order to ensure that the Greek pattern of economic breakdown and civil war did not recur there. In May the Communists had been dropped from the French government by a Socialist Premier, Ramadier. In February 1948, the Czech and Slovak coalition governments, which, by initially agreeing to attend the Marshall Plan meeting in Paris, had shown a degree of independence unacceptable to Stalin in the darkening atmosphere of confrontation, were swept away by a coup d'état and Czechoslovakia reduced to a Communist satellite. For this naked exercise of power the Soviets also paid dearly in alienating the friends that remained to them and in paving the way for NATO.*

Another grossly miscalculated display of force occurred shortly after in Germany. It arose basically from an error of judgment on the part of all the Allies about the treatment of Germany—its division into zones and the prolongation of the occupation. It is not difficult to see in retrospect that the Allied armies, after having thoroughly disarmed and sufficiently denazified the country, should have withdrawn within a year or two, leaving a single German administration to be supervised by an Allied control agency of moderate size. In this way the partition of Germany west of the Oder, the continued presence of the Russians on the Elbe, and the communization of East Germany might have been avoided. However, the exaggerated fear of a resurgent Germany shared by all the Allies, the overrated administrative convenience of each army managing its own zone, the failure to obtain an interallied agreement on unified German reparations, and the massive mistrust among the Four Powers combined to cause them, first, to break up the country, then to stay much longer than they had intended and eventually, as between East and West, more and more to seal off their zones and to draw down the Iron Curtain.

The Western powers, unable to deal with Germany as an economic unit as they wished, unwilling long to tolerate in their zones the level of misery they found when they arrived, equally unwilling themselves to support the dead weight of a prostrate country, soon took steps to revive the economy of their zones

* It is worth noting, incidentally, in connection with the American horror of "coalition governments," which arose in large part from this and other East European episodes, that a coalition with Communists has not proved to be fatal or even dangerous *per se*, but only when it occurs within the ambit of a Communist Great Power which can eliminate the non-Communist participants without effective obstacle or reprisal. On the other hand, when the coalition government exists in a non-Communist power ambit, as in France or even in Laos, the Communist ministers can be and have been eliminated with equal dispatch and assurance.

and hence to that extent to create "West Germany." Since they
were not prepared to subject these measures to persistent Soviet
vetoes, they bypassed the Allied Council in Berlin. In futile
reprisal the Soviets walked out of it in March 1948 and immediately thereafter commenced progressively to impose the famous
"Berlin blockade," no doubt intending to force the Western
Allies to retreat behind the Elbe and leave West Berlin to its
fate. This, too, was a gross miscalculation: the airlift circumvented the blockade, the West Berliners became heroes, and the
Soviets looked ridiculous; the blockade was lifted in May 1949.
Once again, however, the impression had been deepened that the
Kremlin was determined to take whatever it could by force and
that only comparable counterforce could hold it in check.

The Czech coup and the Berlin blockade led to the creation
of the North Atlantic Treaty Organization. In the short span of
four years, Stalin and his colleagues had thrown away the opportunity for at least an uneasy *modus vivendi* with the West and
brought into being against them the most powerful peacetime
military coalition Europe had ever known. If their object was
really security and the development of controlled buffers against
an eventually resurgent Germany or an apprehended Western
crusade, their policy was an abysmal failure since they created
bitter enemies of powerful states which, though certainly unsympathetic, would have been only too happy to leave them
alone. If their object was to extend the dominion of Communist
ideology and Russian power, they did advance from the Pripet
marshes to the Elbe and the Adriatic; but in so doing they provoked a backlash which insulated the rest of Europe against
their doctrine and converted the hitherto isolated Americans
into determined opponents of their power wherever it appeared
throughout the world.

Their folly, however, was not yet at an end. In June 1950,
emboldened by what in characteristic ignorance of their adversaries they thought was a vacuum in South Korea, and probably
further stimulated by their first successful test of an atomic
bomb in August 1949 and by the concurrent triumph of the
Chinese Communists, the Russians—in an act of reckless im-
becility matched only by their installation of missiles in Cuba

twelve years later—incited the North Koreans to attack the South. This naturally and immediately provoked a military response and initiated a United States commitment to the containment of communism in Asia analogous to that assumed in the preceding three years in Europe.

The repercussions were even more far-reaching. Hitherto Stalin had extended Communist power since 1945 only through the exercise of political and police pressure where his military forces were already installed, by diplomatic pressure on such neighbors as Turkey and Finland, or by such indirect means as the infiltration of guerrillas across the Greek frontiers, the use of trade union militia and Communist police in Prague, and the manipulation of Communist parties elsewhere. In Korea, for the first time regular Communist military forces in large numbers were on the most transparent of pretexts launched across, if not an international frontier, at least a demarcation line solemnly agreed among the wartime allies. Western leaders promptly concluded that they could no longer safely assume that regular Soviet and satellite military forces would not be launched across the demarcation line in Germany or across frontiers elsewhere in Europe. The possibility of Red armies marching west to the English Channel seemed real for the first time.

These dire contingencies led Western leaders to re-assess the balance of military forces on the Continent and to conclude that, despite the NATO alliance, the Red Army was still vastly superior in numbers and arms to what the West had or could rapidly mobilize in the area, particularly with the involvement of the United States in the Far East. These facts and fears induced Western leaders further to conclude that only the prompt rearmament of Germany could assure an adequate Western defense. Some may well have reached this conclusion earlier, especially since rearmament had already commenced in East Germany. The Western governments in May 1950 had protested the appearance there of a "police force" of 40–50,000, armed with tanks and artillery and having "the character of an army." The rearmament of any Germans was a bitter pill for those Western states which only a few years before had been occupied by Nazi armies, but after prolonged debate the pill was swallowed. In

1955 West Germany became a member of NATO, and in 1957 the first German troops joined their Western European comrades on the line.

Even though West German rearmament had been provoked by their own folly, the Soviets were no doubt genuinely and profoundly alarmed by the resurrection of a German military power outside their control and almost inevitably hostile to them. The specter of a third German invasion of Russia within half a century, this time abetted and joined by a vast Western coalition, must have loomed frighteningly before them. The feverish crescendo of stroke and counterstroke, the escalation of mistrust and terror, reached a new apogee with the recovery and rearmament of Germany. From then on, genuine Western fears for its security, occasioned by the seizure of Eastern Europe and the attack on Korea, were matched by equally genuine Soviet, Polish and Czech fears of the ambitions of a revived and remilitarized Germany, aggravated by the demand for "rollback" and "liberation" on the part of prominent figures in the Republican party, which came to power in the United States in January 1953. All that remained to complete the full panoply of enmity and dread was the addition, between 1952 and 1959, of hydrogen weapons and intercontinental missiles to the arsenals of both sides.

We may pause here to inquire whether the extrapolation to Europe of the Communist military offensive in Korea was a sober and rational assessment by the West. Was there ever any real intention on the part of Stalin and his colleagues to launch the Red Army, regardless of whether it had the capability, on a march to the English Channel? It seems extremely doubtful that any such intention existed in 1950 or since.

We have alluded frequently to the caution which usually characterized Stalin's external policy from his assumption of leadership in 1924 until his death almost thirty years later. The great objects of his policy throughout these three decades were to strengthen the Soviet Union, to consolidate the Communist regime inside the Soviet Union, to establish and maintain his own domination of that regime. External objectives were secondary to these purposes and were repeatedly sacrificed to them. He rarely took what he conceived to be serious risks unless he was absolutely obliged to. It is true that he frequently and grossly miscalculated: in China in the late 1920s, in Finland in 1939, in his assessment of Nazi intentions in 1941, in his judgment of the limits of Western tolerance in Greece in 1947, in Berlin in 1948, and in Korea in 1950.

However, there was no conceivable basis in 1950 or thereafter for a miscalculation about Western determination to defend Western Europe with all means at its disposal. If a vacuum had been presumed to exist in Western Europe, as it had been presumed in Korea, the temptation to move in might have been strong, but no such presumption in Europe was rational. Only the year before a solemn treaty had been signed committing the United States, Canada, and ten West European countries to their common defense. A joint strategic plan was adopted in January 1950, agreement on a unified defense force reached in September, and a Supreme Allied Commander, General Eisenhower, designated in December. Moreover, it had just been demonstrated in Korea that the United States was *not* prepared to tolerate overt military aggression even in an area seemingly remote from American vital interest; by September the invasion had been repulsed, though the entry of the Chinese Communists was soon to expand and prolong the fighting. How could anyone in the Kremlin conceivably imagine that Western Europe could be overrun without a major war?

Nor was it really plausible to believe that the Kremlin would intentionally provoke a major war in 1950 or soon thereafter. Though it had rebuilt feverishly and well, Russia was still far from having recovered from the profound devastation of the last war. The Soviets had exploded their first atomic device the previous autumn, but they obviously were still no match for the United States in the decisive field of nuclear weapons and could not in case of war assure the cities of Soviet Europe against the fate of Hiroshima and Nagasaki.

While they undoubtedly hoped and expected in accordance with their cherished doctrine that sooner or later Western Europe would become Communist, it is doubtful that they ever had the intention of achieving this object by means of the Red Army. The exposure of the Red Army even to a devastated Eastern

Europe had proved a traumatic and subversive experience, creating grave doubts in the minds of young Russians whether the
Communist economic system was really the best in the world. The
Soviet government had felt obliged to take drastic measures to
overcome these disturbing impressions and insofar as possible
to insulate its occupation forces in Eastern Europe fiom contact
with the local population and economy. Was it likely they would
have felt safe in exposing millions of Soviet youth to the fleshpots
of a Western Europe well advanced in the process of revival under
the Marshall Plan? It seems extremely improbable.

There appear to be reasonable grounds, therefore, for suspect-
ing that, while the Kremlin made a tragic miscalculation in believing its power could be extended beyond Soviet frontiers to
the extent reached and by the means used without provoking
a perilous confrontation, the Western leaders also made a serious
miscalculation in believing in 1950 and thereafter that there was
a grave and imminent Soviet *military* threat to Western Europe,
and in erecting and maintaining in Europe so vast, expensive and
exorbitantly armed a military counterforce. Greek-Turkish aid
was necessary; the Marshall Plan was necessary; NATO was necessary; the military response in Korea was necessary. It is highly
questionable, however, whether German rearmament, at least
at the time and on the scale at which it occurred, and the subsequent extravagant dispersal of tactical nuclear weapons west of
the Elbe, were in fact necessary or wise.

This conclusion is of course drawn with the benefit of hindsight. The responsible statesmen and soldiers of the time were
under great and seemingly immediate pressure. Confronted by
repeated Soviet displays of force in Europe to which they could
not foresee an end, subject to venomous charges at home that they
had "lost China," shocked by the brutal and cynical invasion of
South Korea, dismayed by the Soviet acquisition of nuclear weapons and their own substantial inferiority in conventional forces,
they made the extrapolations and drew the conclusions we have
described.

They "played it safe" but, as is so often the case in relations
among nations, one side's safety is the other side's peril; and a
whole new dimension, not necessarily conducive to Western

security, was given by German rearmament to the confrontation in Europe. An immense panoply of force was rapidly built up on both sides of the Iron Curtain which, if our judgment that Stalin and his successors never had the slightest intention of "marching to the Channel" is correct, was excessive, to say the least. In fact, since each augmentation on one side provoked fear and augmentation on the other, and tension on both, the consequence was no doubt to reduce rather than to re-enforce security on both sides and to prolong in the heart of Europe the explosive confrontation which for many years constituted the chief threat to the peace of the world. As so many examples in history testify, nothing is more difficult to arrest than the self-generating and reciprocating momentum of military competition where the adversary's intentions are presumed to coincide with his capabilities, where the soldiers never have enough arms and men to be safe, where fear saps composure and distorts reality.

In this case the West was never able fully to comprehend the almost pathological but not wholly unfounded dread of German militarism which the Russians, the Poles and Czechs had had ground into their bones by their wartime experience. To rearm the Germans on so substantial a scale so soon after the war was to ensure a probably disproportionate military and political reaction on the other side. Rearmament also, though this was no doubt difficult to foresee at the outset, created serious and enduring political problems within the Western alliance since the Germans, once readmitted to the military fraternity, could with difficulty be denied *Gleichberechtigung*, equality in weapons and responsibility. The long and troubled history of the Multilateral Force was only the most conspicuous, the most divisive and the most wasteful of these diversions.

Even for the Germans themselves, rearmament, though it no doubt provided psychological satisfaction, was of dubious real benefit since it ruled out for many years at least the Soviet concurrence which was indispensable to any form of reunification. Encapsulation of Western Germany into Western Europe, as a part of the process of creating a united Europe, no doubt had overriding advantages. It would have been preferable to have commenced it, however, in the economic and political fields and to have held the military confrontation in Central Europe to the lowest possible level commensurate with the real danger, coolly and objectively assessed.

"Massive Retaliation"

Formulation of Western strategy and deployment of Western arms went through two phases between 1950 and 1954. In the immediate traumatic reaction to Korea, an enormous buildup of military manpower in Europe was projected; at the February 1952 NATO meeting in Lisbon a goal of 96 divisions by 1954 was approved. Whether any of the European governments participating thought this goal realistic at the time is doubtful. Certainly they made no serious effort actually to achieve it. Indeed, the fear of a Soviet invasion of Western Europe, while it did not disappear, soon abated. It was the financial burden that henceforth conditioned military policy. For example, although the British Labour government had shortly after Korea adopted a colossal three-year £4.7 billion rearmament program, one of Churchill's first acts when he resumed office at the end of 1951 was to inform Truman that the burden was too great and to call for a "strategic reassessment." The problems and reactions of other European governments were similar. The maximum number of divisions which were ever assigned to NATO's Central European Command was 27, of which well over half were German and American.

It was not only in Europe that financial stringency produced significant consequences. In its first military budget submitted to Congress in January 1954, after the Korean war had ended, the Eisenhower administration made across-the-board reductions in all force levels set by its predecessor. The first hydrogen bomb had already been successfully tested, in November 1952, and shortly thereafter tactical nuclear weapons became available. These concurrent pressures and options brought about a strategic reassessment in Washington as well as London and introduced a second phase of Western post-Korea strategy, impressively labelled "massive retaliation" by John Foster Dulles and colloquially described as "more bang for a buck."

In his speech to the Council on Foreign Relations in New York in January 1954, Dulles made the following significant points:

"It is not sound military strategy permanently to commit United States land forces to Asia to a degree that leaves us no strategic reserves. It is not sound economics, or good foreign policy, to support permanently other countries; for in the long run that creates as much ill will as good will. Also, it is not sound to become permanently committed to military expenditures so vast that they lead to 'practical bankruptcy.' . . . We need allies and collective security. Our purpose is to make these relations more effective, less costly. This can be done by placing more reliance on deterrent power and less dependence on local defensive power. . . . Local defenses must be reinforced by the further deterrent of massive retaliatory power. A potential aggressor must know that he cannot always prescribe battle conditions that suit him. . . . The basic decision [recently taken by the President and his advisors] was to depend primarily upon a great capacity to retaliate, instantly, by means and at places of our choosing. . . . That permits of a selection of military means instead of a multiplication of means. As a result, it is now possible to get, and share, more basic security at less cost."

Dotting the *i*'s and crossing the *t*'s, Admiral Radford, Chairman of the Joint Chiefs of Staff, said publicly two months later: "Our policy is to use atomic weapons if it were to our advantage to do so, and we would have to decide that at the time." Going a step farther in November of that year, Field Marshall Montgomery, Deputy Supreme Commander of NATO, declared: "I want to make it absolutely clear that we at SHAPE are basing all our operational planning on using atomic and thermonuclear weapons in our defense. With us it is no longer: 'They may possibly be used.' It is very definitely: 'They will be used, if we are attacked.' "

This change in doctrine was welcomed at the time by the European members of NATO because it relieved them of the unpleasant obligation to meet the huge force goals set at Lisbon and because it seemed to provide them, at modest cost to themselves, with an ironclad protection in the form of the American "nuclear umbrella." The posture was also convenient to the United States because it was less expensive and because it seemed a preferable alternative to committing further American ground troops at threatened points throughout the world, for instance Indochina. It was only later, when the Soviet nuclear arsenal and delivery system were more complete, that doubts began to arise as to whether it was either wise or credible to threaten to escalate every local conflict into a massive nuclear holocaust.

"Peaceful Coexistence"

It is necessary at this point to direct our attention briefly to what had been happening on the other side of the Iron Curtain. On March 6, 1953, it was announced from the Kremlin that Stalin, aged seventy-three, had died of a cerebral hemorrhage. For the previous two months he had obviously, through the fabrication of the "doctors' plot," been preparing another vast purge of the Communist party, including presumably some of his principal associates. Whether the projected purge had in his mind a substantive political purpose, to signalize some new direction in Soviet internal or external policy, or was merely one of his periodic exercises in terror to assure his own unassailable authority, is not clear. In any case he repeated the mistake made by Robespierre in July 1794 when, once too often, he threatened his colleagues with death, without being precise as to just which ones were intended. The consequence may have been that in an unwonted spasm of courage and self-preservation they all rallied against him and perhaps, though this cannot be definitely established, hastened his end.

So ingloriously, but in typical Russian fashion, ended the career of the dictator who had terrorized the Soviet Union for thirty years and most of the world for ten. He was totally unscrupulous and pathologically ruthless, enormously devious, wily and adroit, but much more a Russian autocrat than a Communist ideologue. He manipulated Marxist doctrine and the Leninist apparatus primarily to consolidate his own domination of the Soviet Union and to enhance its position and power in the world. It is probable that, despite all his horrendous crimes and errors, despite "destalinization" and the posthumous rejection of the "cult of the personality," he will eventually go down in Russian history as a great leader, because in a remarkably short space of time he lifted Russia from sixth or seventh to second place among the nations of the world, because he laid the economic, even though he sapped the political, foundations of Russia's long-delayed modernization, and because he led her successfully through the most terrible war to the most brilliant triumph of her history.

The successors of Stalin were primarily preoccupied for the next four years with settling accounts and disputing authority among themselves and with coping with the unrest inside their empire. Beria, Malenkov, Molotov, Bulganin and Zhukov marched briefly across the stage and disappeared into the grave or obscurity. At the end of the transition Khrushchev remained but, having in the process of eliminating his rivals found it necessary to destroy Stalin's reputation and denounce the cult of personality, he was obliged to operate not as an autocrat but as chairman of a not always docile oligarchy. He had to cope, moreover, with emerging "polycentrism," in some cases revolt, among the European satellites—Hungary, Poland, Rumania, Czechoslovakia, even East Germany—which, now that Stalin was gone, increasingly felt free to indulge their yearning for independence along the lines Tito had mapped out. Cracks even began to appear in the relationship with China, but more of that later.

During the first years after Stalin's death, his successors repeatedly proclaimed and for the most part pursued a policy of "peaceful coexistence" with the West. Whether this policy arose from a genuine desire to reduce tensions or was largely an expedient to maintain calm in foreign affairs while coping with post-Stalin domestic and bloc problems was never clear, though it is reasonable to suppose that both elements were present. In any case, the result was a period of relative relaxation in Europe. In October 1957, however, just as Khrushchev concluded his domestic political cleanup by relegating Zhukov to obscurity, Sputnik, the first man-made intrusion into outer space, streaked across the firmament and shook the world. The most significant first effect, coupled with concurrent Soviet weapons developments, may have been to embolden Khrushchev to revive pressure to change the status of West Berlin. He did so initially, however, within the framework of "peaceful coexistence" and in the form of proposals for negotiation.

In the meantime Western "containment" policy had also been

evolving. Despite the bold words about "rollback" and "liberation" which Republicans in the United States had tossed about before they came to office, they made no more than a rhetorical effort to bring these dreams to reality. Even when disturbances occurred in East Germany in 1953 and a full-scale uprising in Hungary in 1956, they displayed a prudent and commendable recognition of the fact that any Soviet government would be obliged to respond with force to a Western military movement over the Iron Curtain and that the consequence of such movement and response would probably be, under their own doctrine of massive retaliation, general nuclear war. If the Western deterrent was effective, so was the Eastern; the stalemate in the center of Europe was frozen fast.

Sputnik, moreover, with its demonstration of Soviet superiority both in space exploration and in long-range missiles, caused a traumatic shock to American leaders. The Atomic Energy Act was hastily amended to authorize what had been sternly refused in the immediate postwar years, the provision to the United Kingdom both of a wide spectrum of technical information and of nuclear materials for weapons use. Early in 1957 the United States had agreed to sell Britain sixty intermediate-range missiles to be operated under a double-key system. With the impact of Sputnik a similar offer was made to France in December 1957, but the last pre–de Gaulle government, which had already decided after Suez to undertake independent production of nuclear weapons, was willing to accept the offer only if the warheads would be under French control, a condition incompatible even with the amended Atomic Energy Act. IRBM's were subsequently, in 1960, installed under U.S. control in two other NATO countries, Italy and Turkey.

Meanwhile Khrushchev, despite his exhilaration with the success of Sputnik and his reactivation of the problem of Berlin in September 1958, was by no means unaware of the significance for the security of the U.S.S.R. of the stage which the development and deployment of nuclear weapons, strategic and tactical, had by that time reached. He knew that the Soviet Union was vulnerable to thermonuclear weapons delivered by intercontinental bombers or intermediate-range missiles; he claimed and probably believed that any use of the tactical nuclear weapons installed in Germany was certain to escalate into general nuclear war. In 1956 he had made the doctrinally revolutionary declaration that war between capitalist and Communist states was not inevitable. In an article in *Foreign Affairs* in October 1959, he spelled this out further, saying: "The main thing is to keep to the positions of ideological struggle, without resorting to arms in order to prove that one is right. The point is that with military techniques what they are today, there are no inaccessible places in the world. Should a world war break out, no country will be able to shut itself off from a crushing blow."

No doubt moved by such considerations but nonetheless determined to get rid of the "bone which stuck in his throat," he pushed vigorously during 1959 and into 1960 for a summit meeting and some significant agreement with the West, naturally one which would bring advantages to the U.S.S.R., presumably first of all in Berlin. The leaders of the West were equally determined that there should be no significant change in the status of Berlin, which they felt would undermine German morale, fatally weaken the Western alliance, and encourage Khrushchev to make further and even more intolerable demands.

The Americans had acquired since 1955, moreover, a deep distaste for summit meetings. They did everything they could to postpone, if possible to avoid one altogether, on the grounds that it must be adequately prepared, that it would be dangerous to raise false hopes, that it would be better not to hold one at all than to have it fail. Their real reason seems to have been the apprehension that, while such a meeting could not in the nature of things succeed, it would have to be made to appear successful, and that this seeming success of "peaceful coexistence" would make Western electorates unmanageably reluctant to support the necessary military effort and expenditure. A secondary reason was doubtless their reluctance further to enhance the prestige and respectability of Communist leaders and, in their view, diminish their own by sitting down cozily together in the full glare of global publicity.

In pursuit of delay, they were even driven to the expedient of inviting Khrushchev to the United States, a visit which proved highly educational for him and which was followed by several months of unprecedented and almost effusive Soviet cordiality vis-à-vis the West. Unfortunately Eisenhower's return visit to the Soviet Union, like the 1960 summit meeting itself, was put off for many months; in the interim several Western statesmen saw fit to announce publicly that they would make no concessions whatsoever at a summit or elsewhere. In May 1960 the U-2 aircraft was shot down over Russia, and the President publicly assumed responsibility for this aerial espionage; a few days later Khrushchev used this as a reason or a pretext to break up the summit meeting he had so long and ardently sought.

Even at the time it was suspected that an important opportunity had been bungled and lost by the West. In retrospect it seems that the penalty, a very high one, may have been the two perilous confrontations of 1961 and 1962, Berlin and Cuba. In any case, Allied behavior in 1958–60 was a classic example of how *not* to handle the Russians.

The fear of the Western leaders that a relaxation of tension, or the semblance thereof through a summit meeting, would be hollow and dangerous was both a miscalculation of imponderables and a misjudgment of their own peoples. The fact is that if tension *seems* to have relaxed, it *has* relaxed, and the new psychological climate arising therefrom makes new departures possible, whether or not other objective conditions have changed. High-level negotiations are almost always desirable, whenever they are possible, precisely because the high level of the participants puts a premium on at least partial success. However, in light of the profound hostility toward the Soviets which had taken root in Western opinion over the preceding decade and a half, it was unlikely that even partial success of a negotiation would have caused that opinion to abandon its support of necessary defense. Western governments, therefore, displayed a serious failure of nerve and judgment in obstructing the summit meeting, in announcing in advance the inflexibility of the positions they intended to take if there were a meeting, and in postponing Eisenhower's visit to the Soviet Union while he traveled about the globe to eleven other countries.

They also misread or disregarded the situation inside Russia and, most of all, the personality of Khrushchev. He was an ebullient, venturesome, volatile, vain and sensitive man, prepared to gamble on startling and grandiose new policies, equally ready to abandon them quickly if they seemed to fail. Like so many leaders of new regimes he attached particular importance on both personal and national grounds to being treated with respect, dignity and cordiality by the better educated, more polished and more secure leaders of longer established elites. It is probable that in 1958 and 1959 he had committed his prestige and authority vis-à-vis his civil and military colleagues in the Kremlin to winning some concessions in Berlin and elsewhere by a policy of negotiation and accommodation, rather than by dictate as others may have urged. It had presumably become apparent to him before the U-2 episode that the Westerners were not prepared to concede anything and that from his viewpoint the summit would be a fiasco and a disaster. The assumption by Eisenhower of personal and explicit responsibility for U-2, an admirable gesture in the American context, must have appeared to Khrushchev the final severance of the personal relationship, however fragile, he had been trying to establish with his peer, the leader of the other superpower. He reacted with the characteristic passion and violence of a rejected suitor to break up the summit before it met. For the next two and a half years his policy toward the West was governed by this same passion and violence; twice it led to the most perilous confrontations since Korea.

It is not suggested that the West could or should have surrendered Berlin or any other essential Western position. It is suggested that a more flexible, imaginative and conciliatory Western tactic during 1959 and early 1960, including cheerful and constructive participation in a summit meeting, including dignified but ungrudging cordiality toward Khrushchev himself, might have borne fruit in some partial accommodations at the summit, have preserved much longer at least a decent semblance of détente, and possibly have avoided the two fearsome confrontations.

"Testing Place of Western Courage"

In any event, following the breakdown of the summit, Khrushchev's policy veered immediately to one of passionate intransigence, to insistence that he would shortly conclude a peace treaty with East Germany and that thereafter the access of the West to Berlin would depend on the will of that regime. Tit-for-tat encounters elsewhere—a Russian setback in the Congo, an American setback in Laos, the Bay of Pigs, mass exodus of refugees from East to West Germany—further envenomed the atmosphere. At Vienna in June 1961, Khrushchev told Kennedy he would have his peace treaty, come what may, by the end of the year; at the beginning of August he raised the Berlin Wall; at the end of August without warning he broke the moratorium which had been in effect since 1958 and resumed nuclear testing.

The West, or at least the United States, reacted to these threats and acts with almost the same grimness and intensity that it had to Korea. While President Kennedy rejected recommendations that he proclaim a national emergency, he did ask for standby authority to call up reserves, tripled draft calls, sharply increased the military budget, re-enforced the Berlin garrison and, in a television address, declared: "West Berlin has now become the great testing place of Western courage and will, a focal point where our solemn commitments . . . and Soviet ambitions now meet in basic confrontation. We cannot and will not permit the Communists to drive us from Berlin, either gradually or by force." Arthur Schlesinger records that that summer he was writing to friends from the White House: "I feel more gloomy about international developments than I have felt since the summer of 1939."

At the same time, however, Kennedy rejected counsels that he refuse to negotiate, even though there seemed little he could concede. In classic and sober juxtaposition of firmness and conciliation, he made it clear throughout, despite the argument of de Gaulle that Khrushchev was bluffing and negotiations unnecessary, that he was ready and willing to talk. High tension persisted for four months until, in a speech to a Party Congress in October, Khrushchev declared that "the Western powers were showing some understanding of the situation, and were inclined to seek a solution to the German problem and the issue of West Berlin . . . [if this were so] we shall not insist on signing a peace treaty absolutely before December 31, 1961." Suddenly and without fanfare, the crisis was over.

A careful appraisal of Khrushchev's attitude since he assumed power leads to the conclusion that de Gaulle was right to the extent that Khrushchev was too profoundly aware of the consequences of nuclear war for the Soviet Union to risk it for Berlin or anything less than an absolutely vital national interest, but Kennedy was right that a combination of firmness and conciliation, which offered Khrushchev a tolerable retreat from his own ultimatum, was the sensible way to defuse the crisis. The danger of war in 1961 was probably not nearly so great as some Americans imagined; they were at least as emotional and extravagant about the issue as were their adversaries.

The second decisive test following the exploded summit meeting of May 1960 took shape in the Cuban missile crisis of October 1962. This spectacular event has been so often and so fully described that there is no need to do more here than to note both its enigmatic and its decisive character. It seems clear that Khrushchev, disappointed in his 1959 policy of partial accommodation, frustrated in his 1961 policy of intimidation, confronted, despite his display of colossal megatonnage, by a widening rather than narrowing disparity in long-range missile capacity, decided to gamble on redressing the balance by setting up medium-range weapons on America's doorstep. Why he ever imagined, in the light of events over the preceding fifteen years, particularly his own Berlin experience of the previous year, that he could get away with this reckless and stupid gamble and that the United States would not respond as it did respond—whether in fact he was sole author of the venture or was persuaded against his better judgment by others—must remain a mystery until Soviet archives are finally unveiled.

In any case, Kennedy and his colleagues once again with masterly sophistication made it immediately and abundantly clear that unless the missiles were at once withdrawn the sites would be knocked out. They confronted Khrushchev with the choice between withdrawal and initiating nuclear war, yet left him time, opportunity and excuse to withdraw, draped in decent shreds of dignity. Once again it was demonstrated that, no matter how rash and bellicose he might seem to be, Khrushchev would back away if the hazard of nuclear war seemed imminent and real. However, Kennedy himself was the first to remind the "hawks" on his own side of the narrow limits to nuclear ultimatum.

"I think there is a law of equity in these disputes," he told Schlesinger the next day. "When one party is clearly wrong it will eventually give way. . . . They had no business in putting those missiles in and in lying to me about it. They were in the wrong and knew it. So, when we stood firm, they had to back down. But this doesn't mean at all that they would back down when they felt they were in the right and had vital interests involved." Several weeks later he added: "If we had invaded Cuba . . . I am sure the Soviets would have acted. They would have to, just as we would have to. I think there are certain compulsions on any major power."

"Graduated Response"

It will be useful here to review the evolution of weaponry and strategy in these years. During the Cold War exchange which followed the breakdown of the 1960 summit meeting, while the American electoral campaign was in progress, there had come to increasing public notice the United States intelligence overestimate of Soviet capabilities which came to be known as the "missile gap." Actually, despite Sputnik, the Soviets never did lead or come close to leading in an over-all nuclear, or even missile, capability. Indeed, as we have noted, their inferiority partially accounts for their Cuban gamble. By the time Kennedy took office in January 1961, intercontinental missiles with thermonuclear warheads had been installed in both the United States and the U.S.S.R. in large numbers. Both countries were henceforth subject to enormous devastation and the loss of millions of lives at the will of the other. This arsenal, moreover, was on both sides in the process of rapid and massive reinforcement, in numbers, in invulnerability, and in deployment via submarines under the high seas.

Kennedy was as conscious as Khrushchev of the consequences of nuclear exchange under these conditions. "When that day comes, and there is a massive exchange," he said, "then that is the end, because you are talking about . . . 150 million fatali-

ties in the first eighteen hours." In his first address to the United
Nations in September 1961 he declared: "War appeals no longer
as a rational alternative. . . . Together we shall save our planet
or together we shall perish in its flames." As he became fully
acquainted during the Berlin crisis with the long-agreed Western
strategy for meeting such a crisis, which took a quantum leap
from probes down the Autobahn to massive retaliation, he remarked: "We go immediately from a rather small military action
to one where nuclear weapons are exchanged, which of course
means . . . we are also destroying this country."

Nor was Kennedy happy at the spectacle of thousands of tactical nuclear weapons, some of them five times as powerful as the
Hiroshima bomb, in the hands of lower-level commanders, even
if theoretically under his control. Here also he reached the same
conclusion as Khrushchev. In the words of one of his biogra-
phers, Theodore Sorenson: "Once an exchange of these weapons
started, the President was convinced there was no well-defined
line that would keep the big bombs out."

These reflections and conclusions, taking shape during the
early months of the new administration, were the origin of a
radical shift in United States strategy, which came to be known
as "graduated response" and "stable nuclear deterrence" and to
be associated with Defense Secretary McNamara. Nuclear weapons
and missiles were to be multiplied and rendered invulnerable to
a first strike. At the same time, conventional and counterinsurgency forces were to be reconstituted and redeployed as rapidly as
possible; sufficient airlift to ensure their mobility was to be built
up, an assortment of options was to be provided and applied
judiciously and appropriately to each situation as it arose, likewise offering options and time for reflection to the adversary. In
short, massive retaliation was to be not a first but a last resort. In
face of the increasingly invulnerable second-strike capabilities on
both sides and ever more inescapable devastation if a nuclear
exchange began, United States strategy had swung full circle and
was back where it had been at the time of the Berlin airlift and
the Korean War. As Kennedy said after Berlin and Cuba: "A line
of destroyers in a quarantine or a division of well-equipped men

on a border may be more useful to our real security than the multiplication of awesome weapons beyond all rational need."

Shortly after the Cuban crisis this new strategy was complemented in both military and political respects by the partial nuclear test ban and the accompanying détente between the Soviet Union and the West. At the end of 1962 both the Soviet Union and the United States had completed the series of massive tests in the atmosphere, which the former's rupture of the moratorium the previous year had generated. As Schlesinger reports: ". . . the President's sense of the meagerness of their results after the clamor about their necessity—all the tests seemed to have proved was the need for more tests—made him more determined than ever to bring the whole thing to an end."

He formulated this determination in his famous American University speech in June 1963, for which, together with the Cuban crisis, he may be longest remembered. "World peace," he said, "does not require that each man love his neighbor—it requires only that they live together in mutual tolerance. . . . Today, should total war ever break out again . . . all we have built, all we have worked for, would be destroyed in the first twenty-four hours. . . . We are both caught up in a vicious dangerous cycle in which suspicion on one side breeds suspicion on the other, and new weapons beget counterweapons. . . . Both the United States and its allies, and the Soviet Union and its allies, have a mutually deep interest in a just and generous peace and in halting the arms race. . . . In the final analysis, our most basic common link is that we all inhabit this small planet. We all breathe the same air. We all cherish our children's future. And we are all mortal."

"Polycentrism" in Europe

These shifts in United States policy from "massive retaliation" to "graduated response," from the arrows of Berlin to the olive branch of American University, evoked an oddly ambivalent response in Western Europe. On the one hand, the pursuit of détente was welcomed in a Europe for the most part bored with the Cold War and skeptical, except in Germany, of the reality of the Soviet military threat. On the other hand, paradoxically, the American adjustment to what seemed to it stark reality evoked dismay and alarm in some circles in Western Europe and contributed to the emerging polycentrism which had been articulated by de Gaulle but which was to some extent inherent, like that in the East, in the political and economic revival of the European nations and the relaxation of East-West tension.

For nearly two decades the defense of Western Europe had conspicuously depended on the United States, its "nuclear umbrella," its divisions positioned in Germany. Just as the citizens of the Italian city-states of the fourteenth century, having long slaughtered each other in internecine warfare, finally decided to have their wars fought by proxy by mercenaries, so it sometimes seemed that the European nations of the twentieth century, having exhausted each other in two world wars, preferred to be occupied and defended by Americans than to organize and pay for their own protection. Certainly, having a combined population larger, and an annual GNP growth rate far higher than those of the United States after their economic recovery in the 1950s, they could have financed their own conventional and nuclear defense if they had chosen to pool their resources and sacrifice some measure of sovereignty and affluence.

The time was not ripe, however, for such measure of sacrifice in either respect. Under the first shattering effect of past carnage and a seemingly imminent Soviet threat, the West Europeans did combine tentatively and partially in NATO and the Common Market. Some governments and some leaders in each country were prepared to move much farther toward unity and common defense, but there was always one or another insuperable obstacle—most of all, the two nations which had traditionally been the leaders of Europe, first the British, then the French. The former unduly delayed their psychological displacement from an empire which did not exist to a Europe which might. The French, having had bad luck in the twentieth century, decided for the moment at least, to go back to the nineteenth. European nationalism revived, welfare and development preempted national attention and national budgets; as Soviet pressure diminished, ardor for unity and common defense progressively cooled.

All these trends reinforced ambivalence toward the United States. Its military independence, its technological predominance, and its political egotism were resented and, to the extent possible, imitated. France created, and Britain maintained, an independent but (relative to the Russian) inconsequential, nuclear capability on the grounds that a United States vulnerable to Soviet missiles could not be counted on to defend Europe. Yet the tacit assumption was that the military role of a European nuclear deterrent was only to trigger the American. Actually, the independent European capabilities were motivated primarily by the intangible factor of prestige, by the pursuit of theoretical political advantage, and by the belief that only such capability confers Great Power status in the modern world.

The unfortunate fact was that the European elite governing former Great Powers could not bring themselves to admit that these states separately could no longer, by any conceivable means, maintain themselves in this category. Only Europe as a whole, whether reaching from the Atlantic to the Elbe or on to the Bug, had the capacity in the late twentieth century to be a Great Power comparable to the United States and the U.S.S.R. The United States had as early as 1950 reached the conclusion that it preferred a united Europe, even though such a Europe would be at least its peer and perhaps its rival, to the Europe of compulsively warring nationalisms which for several centuries had involved itself and much of the rest of the world in profitless turmoil. The glamor of national history and national heroes, instilled in hundreds of thousands of classrooms throughout the continent, was, however, much too strong to be easily overcome; there seemed real danger in 1967 that the psychological moment for European unity had been lost and the drift back to passionate and irrational singularity had become irresistible.

In this atmosphere the shift in United States military strategy from "massive retaliation" to "graduated response" evoked, often on inconsistent grounds, suspicion and alarm. There was fear that "graduation" might be so prolonged that either a devastating ground war might be fought on European soil or a U.S.-Soviet bargain be struck at Europe's expense. Europeans were annoyed at being asked to maintain their ground forces and conventional armament or to support more substantially the American presence at a time when the threat seemed to have diminished and when European nations were encountering economic difficulties. There was alarm that American preoccupation with Vietnam and the Far East might occasion a diversion of its attention and forces from Europe.

The NATO alliance was said to be in "disarray," but what had really happened was that the conditions which had governed its initial organization and strategy had radically changed. Fear of Russia had dictated the amplitude, fear of Germany the integration, both the positioning, of the NATO forces. Both fears had substantially diminished. Dependence on the United States for men, arms and money had governed the preponderant role it had had in the alliance. That dependence had, in proportion to the fears, also diminished, and, since it had long been resented, it began to be circumvented. De Gaulle, being boldest, frankest and most chauvinist, simply denounced it, while continuing, of course, to benefit by the American deterrent. Britain had for several years rated détente higher than deterrence and was governed in the same sense by her economic crisis, which, however, inhibited her from being seriously disagreeable to the Americans.

At the other extreme from de Gaulle's response, Germany had welcomed and fostered its dependence on the United States because it was both militarily and politically the most vulnerable of the allies, because it was psychologically the most disoriented and insecure, and because its foreign policy had inevitably the most ambitious and hazardous goal—reunification. Indeed for a time, Germany had manipulated its dependence and its dependability into a virtual veto over the European policy of the United States and was correspondingly shocked and bewildered at the slackening of American preoccupation with the European confrontation. The basic and tragic fact about Germany was that, while it had been folly to divide it, it would be even worse folly to try to reunite it prematurely, that is, unless and until an accommodation between Europe's West and East made reunification natural and tolerable. This was a fact that the German people found it hard, particularly in a Europe of resurgent nationalism, to admit even to themselves.

Meanwhile, the situation in the Soviet Union had also evolved. Khrushchev had been ousted in October 1964. He had been replaced by a dyarchy of a technocrat and a party official, both of course loyal adherents to the Marxist "conventional wisdom" and both no doubt convinced of the ultimate triumph of communism but otherwise relatively undogmatic. Brezhnev and Kosygin were preoccupied with making the internal economy of the U.S.S.R. work more effectively. By the time of the celebration of the fiftieth anniversary of the October Revolution they had made substantial progress in doing so, to a degree which both gratified the pride and whetted the appetite of their people. The new leaders, moreover, although no doubt determined firmly to maintain and continuously to improve the Soviet power position, were clearly aware of the fatal consequences of nuclear war and of the limits the arms race imposed on domestic affluence. For these reasons, presumably, they showed some disposition to permit an expanding area of peaceful coexistence.

Internally they were permitting the introduction, on a socialist base, of some elements of a market economy. The process of the embourgeoisement of a considerable segment of the Soviet population was proceeding apace, as the Chinese never tired of pointing out. Externally, polycentrism in Eastern Europe continued to develop; some of the erstwhile satellites moved even more sharply than did the U.S.S.R. toward a practical reform of their economy; others deviated boldly from Soviet foreign policy; all but Albania sought more intimate contacts with Western Europe. Most important, the Sino-Soviet conflict reached a pitch of hostility and incompatibility which, in the absence of a virtual revolution in one country or the other, seemed to exclude real reconciliation and make even temporary accommodation between them most difficult. The Soviet leaders, therefore, had good reason to seek détente and reinsurance in other directions. However, paradoxically at the same time, "stable nuclear deterrence" between the two superpowers seemed to be falling into the gravest jeopardy.

"Stable nuclear deterrence," it should be remembered, is an American phrase, which assumes an overwhelming U.S. superiority in numbers and deployment of nuclear weapons. It had never

been clear whether the Soviets would be equally content to consider such a situation "stable," whether in fact what to one side
might seem stable deterrence might not to the other seem intolerable inferiority and insecurity. As we have suggested, the deployment of missiles in Cuba was probably one expedient for reducing
this inferiority. Another expedient, perhaps decided at the same
time or perhaps later after the Cuban gambit failed, may have
been the one which only became visible at the end of 1966, the
installation of antiballistic missiles around certain Soviet cities.
This was, in light of American offensive superiority, a logical
measure in keeping with long-standing Russian defensive strategy,
and no doubt seemed from their viewpoint designed to promote
stability by deterring a U.S. attack or threat. In the complicated
equation of nuclear weaponry, however, this defensive deployment was presumed by some American authorities to reduce the
capability of the United States to respond with an effective second
strike to a postulated Soviet nuclear attack and, hence, credibly
to deter such an attack. However seriously one took this theoretical equation, the new development in the arms race again
raised the question whether there can in fact be any such thing
as "stable deterrence" in a world of massive nuclear weaponry,
rapid technological movement, hostile political systems, and fragmented political sovereignty.

Obsolescence of Doctrines

As one reviews the East-West confrontation in Europe in the
perspective of time, nagging questions keep intruding: To what
extent was the confrontation necessary? To what extent did it
serve the real interests of either side? To what extent had it
become by 1968, like the confrontation between Triple Alliance
and Triple Entente before 1914, a reflection not so much of
clashing interests as of clashing and outdated states of mind?

Certainly the regime in the Soviet Union in 1945 was fervently
committed to the "new religion" of communism, believed that
that religion would eventually become universal and that its
church, the hierarchy of Communist parties with their pope in
Moscow, would achieve world supremacy, and, having just won
a great victory and occupied a quarter of Europe, persisted in the

dogma that "inevitable capitalist wars" would promote that supremacy. It had at its disposition both the largest army and the
most extensive international subversive apparatus on the globe,
was unscrupulous in the exercise of force and chicanery, and was
led by a ruthless dictator with almost unlimited domestic power.

Equally certainly, once whatever opportunity for partial accommodation that may have existed in 1945-46 had been lost, the
Western response in the form of Greek-Turkish aid, the Marshall
Plan, and NATO was healthy and necessary. Without it, the
Soviet leaders would probably have overreached themselves even
more than they did, and the consequence would have been either
a temporary subjection of most of Europe or another world war.
The response was required not only to save Europe but to permit
the passage of time to modify the interests of the Soviet elite, to
redirect its ambitions inward, to improve its sense of both technological and international realities, to prepare it to recognize
the necessity of stability and accommodation in the nuclear age.

Although the process of evolution and education may not be
completed, it has gone far. The problem now is much less to forestall an aggression, which is no longer likely, than to halt on both
sides the momentum of armaments, doctrines and commitments
which were built up to deal with past circumstances, which are
now to a substantial degree obsolete, but which, if persisted in,
will needlessly prolong the confrontation and revive the very evils
they were devised to check.

In Part III we shall draw further conclusions from the confrontation in Europe and suggest why and how, under the
changed circumstances of the late 1960s, it must be and could be
ended. First, however, we shall examine two other contemporary
confrontations, that in the Far East and that in the emerging
South.

CHAPTER 4

Challenge and Response in East Asia

The Power Vacuum

The postwar confrontation in East Asia, like that in Europe, followed implicitly from the character and imbalance of forces which the war created. Before the war, effective power in East Asia had rested with Japan and the Western colonial empires. For a hundred years China had not controlled its own destiny. The Nationalist revival had barely begun to make headway when it was split by another civil war and driven far into the hinterland by the Japanese. When World War II ended, Japan was impotent and the Westerners, except the United States and marginally the United Kingdom, were on the verge of being expelled. An enormous vacuum appeared. Conspicuous power rested only with the United States, sprawled as a consequence of the war all over the area but eager to contract, and with the Soviet Union, once more an ambitious but enigmatic actor on the periphery of the Asian scene.

The confrontation at the outset therefore appeared to be between these two, groping gingerly and at arm's length, acting almost entirely through their respective Chinese and later Korean allies. Subsequently, as the Communists conquered and mobilized China, a more direct and flammable confrontation between China and the United States took shape. In Asia, in contrast to Europe, the United States had to bear almost the whole burden of the confrontation for the Western side.

The basic problem had been, and at the end of the war still was, the backwardness, anarchy and impotence of China. For a variety of reasons, the United States had long urged and fostered the restoration of its independence, dignity and power. In defense of China the United States had imposed economic sanctions on Japan after 1937, and on China's behalf risked the war which eventually came. In wartime conferences Roosevelt insisted from the beginning, despite the skepticism of Churchill and Stalin, that China be considered one of the "Big Four" and defended Chinese interests as best he could.

American policy was based on the belief that stability in the Far East, and insurance against a revival of a militant Japan or of militant European, including Soviet, imperialism depended on a strong and united China. Unfortunately this objective could be attained, if at all, only by immensely onerous, sophisticated and delicate measures, which under the circumstances of global war were very probably inapplicable. Yet if they could not be applied, the objective and the policy were unrealistic.

The intractable circumstances can be listed briefly. Necessity dictated a concentration of force and concern on the war zones in Europe and the Pacific, leaving relatively little for application in China. The most valuable and populous parts of China were occupied by the Japanese. The Chinese Communists, who had been fighting the Nationalists for fifteen years, held a substantial part of the unoccupied area and, being committed to a single ideology, were well-knit, dedicated, and effective. In contrast, the Nationalists were a conglomeration of democrats, plutocrats, intellectuals, warlords, landlords, loosely held together by Chiang Kai-shek, who, perhaps unavoidably, relied most on generals loyal to him, whether or not they were able soldiers, and officials loyal to him, whether or not they were honest officials. Finally, the war in the Far East ended much sooner than was anticipated and before either the Nationalist Chinese or the Americans were prepared to establish a viable order in China.

For the American policy of relying on China as the main pillar of security in the Far East to have succeeded, it would have been necessary for the Nationalist government to have been endowed immediately at the end of the war with disciplined and effective military strength and with honest and enlightened political organization. Throughout the war the United States made persistent efforts to persuade Chiang Kai-shek and his government to equip themselves in these respects, but to no avail. The essential difficulty lay in the character of the Nationalist regime. Militarily, it consisted not of a unified and inspired national army but, at the top, of a loose alliance of jealous warlords and, at the bottom, of a mass of ill-trained conscripts capable of fighting well at times against the Japanese invader but without any other moral dedication. Politically, the regime was, in theory, a nationalist party with democratic principles, but actually it was a clique of conservative oligarchs, unwilling to share their power with other non-Communist elements. Economically and socially, it represented for the most part the traditional status quo, too often administered both ineptly and corruptly.

As one of the best historians of the period, Tang Tsou, puts it: "If under these circumstances the policy of making China a great power was to serve America's self-interest, the Nationalist government had to be so transformed that it could compete successfully with the Chinese Communist party both on the battlefield and in the realms of political, economic and social reform." General Stilwell, with maddening tactlessness but persistently and honestly, tried to bring about the necessary military reorganization. He was withdrawn upon Chiang's insistence. The American Embassy circumspectly sought a broadening of the government to include non-Kuomintang but non-Communist elements favoring political and social reform. For the most part these elements were ruthlessly suppressed; when they were occasionally admitted to office, they were allowed little influence on affairs. Within the limits imposed by the Japanese occupation of much of China, substantial United States economic and financial aid was supplied. Most of it was dissipated uselessly; sizable amounts found their way into private pockets.

We may digress here for a moment to note how often in the next twenty-five years (for example, in Vietnam) the United States government was to be confronted with this dilemma in dealing with friendly governments heavily dependent on its support for their survival, hence heavily involving American prestige and interest in their success or failure, yet pursuing policies more conducive, in the American view, to failure than to success. Should the United States in such circumstances, by demanding reform and reducing its aid if need be to enforce its demands, incur the wrath of its ally and the charge of "intervention" and risk impairing, perhaps jeopardizing, the joint effort? Or should the United States, on the contrary, by accepting for the most part the judgment of its ally in regard to the latter's domestic and foreign policies, appear inescapably to underwrite them and, if they were in fact, as Chiang's proved to be, fatally unwise, thereby risk losing the whole game for both allies? Certainly, with the advantage of hindsight, we can hardly escape the judgment that in this case the U.S. government, even though it might still have failed, should have tried more ruthlessly to oblige Chiang and his colleagues to prepare themselves at whatever cost for the decisive trial of strength with the Communists. However, in those days the United States was almost wholly unfamiliar with this agonizing sort of dilemma.

A related mistake with which the United States has been charged was to have obliged China to pay a high price for Soviet entry into the Far Eastern war when actually, on the one hand, the Soviets would have come in in any case and when, on the other, their assistance was not required.

The U.S. Joint Chiefs of Staff, supported by General Mac-Arthur, argued consistently up until the very end that Soviet participation was essential in order to pin down the large Japanese forces in Manchuria while the Americans undertook the decisive and costly invasion of the Japanese homeland. This argument was a reasonable one on the assumption, derived from faulty intelligence estimates, that the war in the Far East would last for eighteen months after the close of the war in Europe and that a massive invasion of Japan would be necessary. These estimates would probably have been proven far off in any case, since the submarine campaign and conventional bombing had already by August 1945 desperately drained Japan's power of resistance, but the atom bomb rendered Soviet participation in the war useless and embarrassing.

In fact, Stalin had assured Hull in Moscow and Roosevelt in

Teheran in the fall of 1943 that Russia would enter the Far
Eastern war as soon as Germany was defeated. Nevertheless, at
the latter conference, Roosevelt and Churchill apparently felt it
advisable to offer him the bait of Southern Sakhalin and the
Kuriles and a free port under international guarantee at Dairen.
Somewhat later, Stalin told Averell Harriman the Russians would
enter the war three months after Germany collapsed but would
have to know what they were fighting for. In December he speci-
fied that this reservation meant not only the annexation of
Southern Sakhalin and the Kuriles but Soviet *lease* of Dairen,
Port Arthur and the Manchurian railways, as well as recognition
of the independence of Outer Mongolia. During this period,
however, the present author and others in the State Department
were of the opinion that, so strong would be the Soviet desire to
play a substantial role in the Far Eastern postwar settlement and
to share in the loot, that no power could keep them *out* of the
war once they could disengage from Germany.

It is impossible to know now exactly what weight Roosevelt
gave, in conceding to Stalin at Yalta essentially what he asked in
the Far East, to the importunities of the Joint Chiefs concerning
the earliest possible Soviet participation in the war, and what
weight he gave to a judgment, based on mounting friction over
the past year between Chinese Nationalists and Chinese Communists, that it was vital to the former to have a binding settlement with Stalin. Presumably, he also had in mind that when
the Soviets did enter the war, they would be able to seize from
China, if they wished, all and more than they asked at Yalta.
Harriman, who was probably better informed on the matter than
any other American, expressed the view in testifying before a
Congressional committee six years later that Roosevelt felt he
had in this negotiation at Yalta obtained his principal objectives,
not only formal Soviet agreement to enter the war against Japan
in three months but "Stalin's pledge of support to Chiang Kai-
shek, and the recognition of the sovereignty of the Chinese National Government over Manchuria." Under the circumstances
this was a substantial achievement, even though it was subsequently lost.

Just as the United States in formulating its postwar Far Eastern policy overestimated the capabilities of the Chinese Nationalists, so too it underestimated the capabilities of the Chinese Communists. It is a curious fact that this underestimate was probably shared, though on different grounds, by Stalin.

There were varying nuances in the appraisal of the Chinese Communists by responsible Americans during the war. However, both Ambassador Patrick Hurley, who was a strong supporter of Chiang, and some of the junior Embassy officers, who had lost all confidence in him, suffered under the same illusion that the Chinese Communists were not "real" Communists, but at heart nationalist reformers subscribing to the democratic principles of Sun Yat-sen.

In a conversation with Harriman in June 1944, Stalin described the Chinese Communists as "real patriots" but as "margarine Communists." On later occasions he spoke of them as "cabbage" or "radish" Communists, the latter epithet signifying red outside and white inside. It is extremely unlikely that Stalin shared Hurley's illusion about the ideological bent of Mao and his colleagues. What he probably did genuinely doubt at this time was their ability to compete successfully with Chiang. Stalin advised Mao at the end of the war, it would appear from reliable Yugoslav testimony, that "the development of the uprising in China had no prospect, and that the Chinese comrades should join the Chiang Kai-shek government and dissolve their army." According to Stalin's account to the Yugoslavs, the Chinese agreed but "went back to China and acted otherwise. . . . Now, in the case of China, we admit we were wrong. It proved that the Chinese comrades and not the Soviet comrades were right." It may be surmised as well that Stalin was hardly eager to share leadership of the Communist world with a Chinese rival and that he was not therefore unhappy to depreciate Mao as long as he safely could.

Stalin's posture, however, did not imply an intention to support Chiang any longer than he remained on top and it was expedient to do so. Indeed, as soon as Soviet forces had completed their rapid occupation of Manchuria in August-September 1945, Stalin began to hedge his bets by providing the Communists with veiled support in the form of arms and logistic advantage. Moreover, while Hurley with his customary naïveté continued to believe implicitly Stalin's assurances to him of support for Chiang, Harriman and Kennan were already warning the State Department in April of that year that his position was tactical and that he might set up a puppet government in North China at the end of the war if Kuomintang-Communist differences were not settled by that time.

Meanwhile other Americans in China, ranging from John Davies to General Wedemeyer, had also been urging a coalition government between Nationalists and Communists, not because they had any illusions about the character of the latter, but because they had serious doubts about the ability of the former to compete with them. In July 1945, just before Potsdam, Wedemeyer pointed out that "serious postwar disturbance may be averted" and the war effort against Japan reinforced "if the United States, Russia and Britain united strongly in their endeavor to bring about a coalition of these two political parties in China by coercing both sides to make realistic concessions." Already in November 1944 Davies had been reporting that, while "a coalition Chinese Government in which the Communists find a satisfactory place is the solution of the impasse most desirable to us," even under such circumstances the Communists would continue to control the territory they then held and would "also probably extend their political influence throughout the rest of the country, for they are the only group in China possessing a program with positive appeal to the people. . . . The Communists are in China to stay. And China's destiny is not Chiang's but theirs." In other words, it would seem that Davies, despite his recommendation of a coalition with the Communists as the only possibility of Nationalist survival, had already become so pessimistic about the Nationalists' prospects as to doubt whether even this expedient would do more than postpone the evil day of eventual Communist takeover.

A year later on November 20, 1945, General Wedemeyer, having observed the performance of both Nationalists and Communists for three months after the Japanese surrender, expressed to Washington grave doubts about Chiang's ability to bring stability and democracy to China. Chiang lacked able, honest advisers, was surrounded by unscrupulous men, and was loyal to warlords and officials who were exploiting their positions in the liberated provinces to enrich themselves. Wedemeyer drew the following conclusions:

1. The Generalissimo will be able to stabilize the situation in south China provided he accepts the assistance of foreign administrators and technicians and engages in political, economic and social reforms through honest, competent civilian officials.

2. He will be unable to stabilize the situation in north China for months or perhaps even years unless a satisfactory settlement with the Chinese Communists is achieved and followed up realistically by the kind of action suggested in paragraph 1.

3. He will be unable to occupy Manchuria for many years unless satisfactory agreements are reached with Russia and the Chinese Communists.

4. Russia is in effect creating favorable conditions for the realization of Chinese Communist and possibly their own plans in north China and Manchuria. These activities are violations of the recent Sino-Russian Treaty and related agreements.

5. It appears remote that a satisfactory understanding will be reached between Chinese Communists and the National Government.

It would seem probable that General Wedemeyer was not unaware of the seeming contradiction between paragraphs 2 and 3 of these conclusions on the one hand, and paragraphs 4 and 5 on the other, and that he in fact already foresaw the probable outcome of the impending Chinese civil war if the United States did not intervene in massive fashion. He went on in this same report to point out that, first, it was impossible for the Americans to assist in unifying China and Manchuria without becoming involved in the civil war and, second, it was impossible to bring about unification unless the United States supplied forces and shipping "far beyond those now available or contemplated in the area."

At the same time Admiral Barbey was reporting to the Navy Department from Chungking that, in view of the Nationalist weakness, every possible pressure must be exerted to bring the contending parties together, even if that meant confirming the Communists in control of the provinces they already held. However, Walter Robertson at the Embassy, commenting on Barbey's recommendation, expressed doubt that, even if Chiang could be persuaded to accept it, Mao would do so with the tide already running so strongly in his favor.

Such was the situation when, a week after Wedemeyer's report, President Truman dispatched General George Marshall to China with the mandate, in brief, to bring about a truce between the parties and a broad representative government in which, presumably, both would take part. Incidentally, to the extent available resources permitted and whether or not the Generalissimo cooperated in implementing the mandate, Marshall was to assist Chiang in moving his forces into north China and Manchuria, despite Wedemeyer's belief that the Nationalists could not install themselves successfully in those areas without "satisfactory settlements" with the Communists.

To achieve these purposes Marshall had, insofar as the Nationalists were concerned, only the general political leverage that had proved ineffective with Chiang throughout the war—a promise of United States loans and military advisers, and a substantial capability for transporting Nationalist troops northward. The latter, however, had to be used without much reference to the course of political negotiations if the transfer was to occur before the Communists had consolidated their hold in the north. Vis-à-vis the Communists, Marshall had only the leverage of his transport capability, such accommodation to Communist political terms as he might be able and willing to extract from Chiang (which proved to be meager), and perhaps, despite the manifest concern to keep American troops out of involvement in the civil war, some vague presumption that if the Communists proved too aggressive, these troops might eventually be used.

The credibility of the latter threat, if it ever existed, progressively evaporated as the process of "bringing the boys home" proceeded on its headlong course. The U.S. Army, which amounted to 8.3 million at the time of the surrender of Germany, fell to 4.2 million by the end of 1945 when Marshall went to China, to 1.9 million by mid-1946, and to less than 1 million a year later as the confrontation in Europe was taking serious tangible form.

Actually, even those Americans who most strongly criticized the administration's postwar China policy at no time recommended the use of American troops there other than in an advisory capacity. In the debate on the China Aid Act of 1948, Walter Judd stated in the House of Representatives: "Not for one moment has anyone contemplated sending a single combat soldier in." In the hearings on the bill, William Bullitt testified: "I do not propose that American troops be sent to China." In a debate in the Senate in 1949, Senator Knowland said: "There has never been a proposal on the part of those who are critical of the policy we have pursued in the Far East to send an army to China."

Meanwhile, Soviet policy in the Far East, without any explicit deviation from the treaty signed with the Nationalists in mid-August 1945, gradually hardened in practice through the subsequent months. The Chinese Communists were already filtering into Manchuria in early September. The Soviets certainly did not obstruct, indeed presumably facilitated, their dispersal throughout the region and their setting up of local governments. When Nationalist troops in American vessels appeared at Manchurian ports to take over from the Soviets, who repeatedly affirmed their intention to withdraw promptly, they were prevented from landing either by Soviet obstruction or by the presence of Chinese Communists already established there, and had to make costly and time-consuming detours by land. Yet the Soviet Union could not be caught in any overt violation of their treaty engagements, or indeed in any support of the Communists as substantial and conspicuous as that which the United States was according the Nationalists. Indeed a severely inhibiting factor on the Americans was the fear that, if they assisted the Nationalists to clash with the Communists, the Soviets might be provoked into abandoning their formal neutrality. Being still in military control of Manchuria, the Soviets were of course in a far better position to help their friends than the Americans were to help theirs.

The question arises why, only a few months after Stalin had been sufficiently, even if erroneously, persuaded of the favorable prospects of the Nationalists to reaffirm his recognition of their sovereignty and to sign a treaty with them, he began to shift his support to the Communists. It may have been that, faithful to

the expedient policy of betting on both horses, he was merely redressing the balance by ensuring that the Communists remained
in a strong position. It may have been that he had already begun
to perceive the underlying weakness of the Nationalists and the
possibility that the Communists, with a little timely and inexpensive support, might win. There was one external element,
however, which may have weighed in the balance and should not
be left out of account. That was the effect upon the Soviets of
United States policy toward Japan.

In May 1945, Stalin told Harry Hopkins that Russia expected
to share in the occupation of Japan. At the time of the Japanese
surrender he proposed that Soviet troops join American forces in
the initial entry into Japan; his offer was politely rejected by the
Americans. Subsequently, primarily because of the mounting
pressure for rapid demobilization of the U.S. Army, the American
attitude changed and Allied governments, including the Soviets,
were invited to dispatch troops to participate in the occupation.

By that time, however, a controversy had arisen between the
United States and the U.S.S.R. over the nature of Allied control
in Japan. The United States had in August proposed a Far
Eastern Advisory Commission to be established in Washington
to recommend policies and methods for carrying out the terms of
surrender. At the meeting of Foreign Ministers in London in
September, however, Molotov insisted on a four-power control
council in Japan to determine and carry out, on a basis of unanimity, the full range of Allied policy toward Japan. In other
words, the Soviets asked for the veto. This was unacceptable to
the Americans, who insisted that the Supreme Commander, General MacArthur, would take advice but must have full authority
to take decisions as he saw fit. Since the Americans were in control
on the ground and were supported by the British, their view
prevailed, but as a consequence the Soviets refused to participate
in the occupation or in the Washington Advisory Commission.

Shortly it became apparent, moreover, that the Soviets deeply
resented the American monopoly of real power in Japan. In a
message to Washington in mid-October, Harriman warned that
if the United States excluded the Soviet Union from what it
considered fair participation in policy-making in regard to Japan,

the Soviets would be likely to act unilaterally in Far Eastern areas they dominated. His judgment was fully confirmed in a conversation Harriman had with Stalin a few days later in which the latter charged that "the Soviet Union was being treated like an American satellite in the Pacific—a role it could not accept." Stalin went on to say that it would be more honest for the Soviets to withdraw their representatives from Japan altogether than to remain there "like a piece of furniture."

Once again, as in the case of the occupation of Italy, the United States decided that, while it could tolerate Soviet presence and advice, the authority of the American military commander to take binding decisions, even contrary to Soviet advice, could not be abridged. No doubt the case for rejecting Soviet participation on their terms was even stronger in Japan than it had been in Italy. The United States and the British Commonwealth had borne almost the entire burden of the war against Japan; effective, politically unified control of Japan seemed essential to long-term peace and security in the Pacific; by September 1945, the grave difficulty of conducting an occupation through unanimous agreement among four powers was already emerging in Europe. However, as in the case of Italy and as Harriman warned in this instance, a price had to be paid for the exercise of untrammelled American or Anglo-American authority in former enemy territories they occupied. That price was the exercise of untrammelled Soviet authority in territories they occupied.

The Soviets were no doubt as conscious as the Americans that Japan, like Germany, would one day revive and that whoever determined the orientation of the one, as of the other, might determine the destiny of the whole region. It is only reasonable to presume that United States policy in Japan was one of the factors, even if only one among several, which induced the Soviet government to follow in Manchuria a policy increasingly favorable to the Chinese Communists and hostile to the Nationalists, and incidentally in Korea a policy increasingly designed to cut off and satellize the north which they occupied. If the Russians could not share in the way they wanted in determining the future of territories under American control, they were obviously likely to exclude the United States and its allies from territories under their control and indeed, in characteristic totalitarian fashion, to do so more thoroughly and categorically than the Western Allies had done. So, in the Far East as in Europe, the Iron Curtain came down with increasing speed.

American policy-makers were faced with an impossible dilemma in the Far East immediately following the war, which they no doubt subconsciously and uneasily apprehended even though they failed to face it explicitly in all its starkness. General Wedemeyer came closest in his conclusions quoted above.

Because of their political deficiencies, despite their seeming preponderance, the Nationalists were in 1945 and thereafter unable to compete successfully with the Communists, at least in north China and Manchuria. There were only two expedients by which defeat might have been averted. One would have been the massive involvement of American forces on the side of the Nationalists. This alternative was never seriously considered by either the Democratic administration or the Republican opposition. The second alternative of encouraging an accommodation and eventually a coalition between the Nationalists and the Communists was therefore chosen, not because it was attractive but because it seemed the least of the evils. It probably never had any chance of success for the reason Walter Robertson cited at the time—that the tide was already running so substantially in favor of the Communists that they would not have come to agreement on any terms remotely tolerable to the Nationalists. Had a coalition been successfully worked out, moreover, it would probably under the circumstances, as John Davies suggested in 1944, merely have constituted a stage, no doubt a brief one, in the process by which the Communists, by either political or military means or both, took over China.

This judgment does not run counter to the view expressed in Chapter 3, that coalitions with Communists are not universally and necessarily wicked and disastrous. The postwar coalition in France is evidence to the contrary. In China, however, the balance of forces, because of the fatal shortcomings of the Nationalists, may have already by late 1946 shifted so decisively to the Communists that they would have been as victorious in a political struggle as they proved to be in the military one.

One further theoretical alternative seems never to have been seriously considered. That would have been to follow the policy, which eventually became that of the United States and its allies in Korea and Vietnam, of accepting the division of China and concentrating on the preservation and defense of the south. It is probable that this device was not seriously considered, first, because Chiang would never have accepted it or, if he had, would not have taken the necessary measures of reform in the south any more than he had in the north; and, second, because here too no doubt, as later in Korea and Vietnam, a substantial commitment of American forces would have been required to hold the demarcation line securely and over a long period of time.

So the tragedy moved to its ineluctable conclusion. For the next four years, that is, from the failure of Marshall's efforts to bring about a Nationalist-Communist coalition in 1946 to the North Korean attack on the South in mid-1950, United States policy in the Far East rested on two basic assumptions, which were set forth by Marshall as Secretary of State in a statement to a joint executive session of the Committees on Foreign Relations and Foreign Affairs in February 1948 in the following terms:

"China does not itself possess the raw material and industrial resources which would enable it to become a first-class military power within the foreseeable future. The country is at present in the midst of a social and political revolution. Until this revolution is completed—and it will take a long time—there is no prospect that sufficient stability and order can be established to permit China's early development into a strong state. Furthermore, on the side of American interests, we cannot afford, economically or militarily, to take over the continued failures of the present Chinese Government to the dissipation of our strength in more vital regions where we now have a reasonable opportunity of successfully meeting or thwarting the Communist threat, that is, in the vital industrial area of Western Europe with its traditions of free institutions."

The first assumption expressed in this statement, directly contrary to that which Roosevelt had sought to make prevail during the war, was that China had and could have for the foreseeable future neither the resources nor the political stability to constitute a first-class power and hence, even if the Communists were to win the civil war, to become a threat to the United States. This view was of course shared by Marshall's great rival, Douglas MacArthur, and in large part accounts for the miscalculation on which his fatal Yalu campaign in October-November 1950 was based. The second assumption was that the United States did not have either the military or economic resources to engage in costly confrontations in Europe and the Far East at the same time and that the preservation of Western Europe was far more vital, as well as more urgent, than the preservation of China.

As we have seen, during the years 1947–49 the United States undertook vast new commitments in Europe through the Truman Doctrine, the Marshall Plan, and NATO. In consequence, it severely restricted its commitments in the Far East and, after the Communists had completed their conquest of the mainland, would very probably have recognized them had they on their side shown any willingness for an accommodation. Secretary of State Acheson, in a celebrated speech in January 1950, drew a United States defense perimeter in the Western Pacific, closely conforming to one MacArthur had publicly described the year before, which excluded both Formosa and South Korea. In opposing and initially defeating a Korean aid bill at that time, Republican members of the House of Representatives publicly argued that South Korea was indefensible—"a Bataan without a Corregidor, a Dunkerque without a flotilla, dead-end street without an escape," in the words of one of them.

Causes and Consequences of the Korean War

Despite both major assumptions of United States policy quoted above, the great confrontation in the Far East began on June 25, 1950, and has lasted ever since. As noted in the preceding chapter, it was at least as gross a miscalculation on the part of the Communists as any which the Americans had previously made and was to have the most far-reaching and tragic repercussions in Europe as well as the Far East.

The decision to encourage and assist the North Koreans to seize the South may have been taken during Mao Tse-tung's prolonged visit to Moscow early in the year, or earlier by the Soviets alone. One cannot be sure what were the primary motives and rationale or who the primary instigator of the venture. The success of the Communists during the preceding three years in occupying the whole of China with relatively little difficulty may have emboldened both leaders to believe they could profitably continue. The withdrawal of American forces from Korea a year earlier, together with expressions of disinterest by influential Americans such as those quoted above, may have convinced Stalin and Mao that this further prize could be won cheaply.

Some authorities have argued that Stalin's principal objective in advancing to the Straits of Shimonoseki was to intimidate Japan, to deter it from prolonged association with the United States, to disrupt American plans for a peace treaty which would perpetuate U.S. military bases there and, if these efforts failed, would at least re-enforce the Communist buffer zone against a renascent and irredentist Japan. If this was indeed a motive, it would lend further weight to our central thesis of the inextricable interweaving of the threads of global relations between the two power blocs, so that one thread could not be drawn tighter, even for apparently unexceptionable reasons, without another thread, seemingly remote and unrelated, suddenly breaking under the strain.

In the event, the reaction of the United States to the attack in Korea was immediate. As one who participated in some of the critical meetings in Washington on June 25, I can vividly recall the unanimity of conviction that, if there were not a prompt and effective American military response in Korea, the credibility of Western containment everywhere would be undermined and Communist aggression fostered elsewhere. Whether or not this conviction was sound, it was passionately held and was a not unnatural reaction to the first overt military attack across a frontier or demarcation line since the end of the war. The failure of the Communist leaders to foresee that an aggression of this flagrancy and magnitude would inevitably provoke an American military response was a tragic measure of their psychological isolation and of the total breakdown of rational communication between the two blocs.

An indirect but equally momentous consequence of the Korean

attack was to persuade President Truman to order, on the very same day, the U.S. Seventh Fleet into the Formosa Strait to interdict any Chinese Communist attempt to seize the island. For some time the Communists had been preparing for an invasion of Formosa but the United States government had hitherto taken the position that it did not intend at this late date to involve itself in the Chinese civil war nor to provide military aid to the Nationalists on the island. A mixture of motives may have occasioned the instant reversal of this policy. As James Reston reported in *The New York Times* a month later: "When President Truman on June 27 ordered the United States Seventh Fleet to prevent any attack on Formosa, he had several things in mind. He wanted to localize the Korean War by neutralizing Formosa, and to minimize the political opposition to the Korean War by neutralizing Senators Taft, Knowland, Smith of New Jersey and others who had been condemning his 'hands-off Formosa' policy."

Whatever the motives, the consequences were far-reaching. The reunification of China under the Communists was halted just short of total success; a separate Nationalist government, claiming to be legitimately that of the whole of China, was preserved on Formosa, recognized, aided and protected by the United States; the latter was committed to the proposition that the Communist regime in Peking was illegitimate and probably ephemeral. This regime which controlled almost the whole of the territory and population of China was excluded from the United Nations; the Chinese and American people were cut off from practically all access to each other, and each was more and more convinced as the years passed that the other was a hostile power dedicated to its destruction. These stereotypes, which had begun to take shape during the civil war, were enormously intensified by the Chinese involvement in the Korean War and the two and a half years of bitter combat between the two nations.

This was the first limited war in which the United States had engaged since 1898 and the first inconclusive one since 1815. It was characterized by a series of miscalculations and gave birth to a series of misconceptions.

United States air and naval authorities first maintained that their arms alone would be sufficient to halt the North Korean attack; it soon proved that substantial ground forces would be required, which arrived just in time to hold the Pusan perimeter in heroic and costly combat. The U.S. Joint Chiefs of Staff considered MacArthur's plan for the Inchon landing extremely hazardous and almost certain to fail; it was carried out with brilliant success. The decision to advance north of the 38th parallel was taken after hasty consideration, partly on military grounds—that it was important to future security that the destruction of the North Korean army be completed—but more substantially on political-emotional grounds—that the aggression had to be thoroughly punished if its recurrence was to be prevented and that the opportunity should be seized to carry out the long-standing United Nations objective of reuniting Korea under a representative government.

MacArthur informed Truman at their meeting on Wake Island on October 15 that there was little chance the Chinese would enter the war, that if they did they could get only 50–60,000 men across the Yalu, and that if they "tried to get down to Pyongyang, there would be the greatest slaughter." Within two weeks, 180,000 Chinese troops were in Korea and had begun to fight the advancing U.N. forces, by mid-November 300,000 Chinese had crossed the Yalu, in early December they retook Pyongyang, by mid-December they were back to the 38th parallel, and by Christmas Chou En-lai was proclaiming a second Communist drive to reunify the whole of Korea by force. There was "the greatest slaughter," but it was great on both sides and lasted for nearly three years.

There should have been no particular surprise that under existing circumstances the Chinese Communists entered the war. Already in late August, following Senator Austin's statement in the Security Council that the United Nations objective in the war should be the reunification of Korea, Chinese propaganda began to associate China's interests directly with those of North Korea to the extent of proclaiming: "North Korea's enemy is our enemy. North Korea's defense is our defense." In September, large and conspicuous Chinese troop movements into Manchuria took place; at midnight on October 2, the day after South Korean troops crossed the 38th parallel, Chou En-lai summoned the Indian Ambassador, Panikkar, and stated categorically that if United States troops did likewise, China would enter the war. He was not believed or, to the extent he was, China's capabilities were grossly miscalculated.

Peking was no doubt impelled to intervene, as is usually the the case in confrontations between nations, by calculations in which security and prestige were inextricably mingled. Even though it was Communist aggression which had disrupted the status quo, it probably seemed to the Chinese that the military presence of the "American imperialists" on their Manchurian frontier would constitute an intolerable menace to their national security. Just as the West had calculated that, should they fail to meet and halt Communist military expansion in Korea, the Communists would be encouraged to launch similar attacks elsewhere, so very probably did the Communists estimate the consequences of their failure to meet and halt Western military expansion in the same place.

Considerations of prestige were no doubt particularly compelling to a Chinese regime which after twenty years of struggle had only just achieved power and was presumably still uncertain of holding it, which found itself prevented from completing the destruction of its principal competitor because of the Seventh Fleet in the Formosa Strait, and which was determined to restore the status of a great nation that had for more than a century been harried by both Western and Eastern "barbarians." Peking may well have concluded that if it tolerated the extinction of its Korean counterparts and the installation of MacArthur's army alongside its most vital area, its hope of reviving Chinese and establishing Communist power in the Far East would be at an end.

Similar exaggerated fears swept through Western capitals after MacArthur's November offensive was smashed, the U.N. forces driven helter-skelter back below the 38th parallel, and Seoul lost for the second time. In the United States, according to polls taken at the time, over 50 per cent of the people thought that World War III was around the corner. A general war warning was sent to all military commanders, and the defense budget for fiscal 1951 was quadrupled from $13.5 billion to $52 billion.

General Eisenhower went to Europe as NATO commander; the United States dispatched more ground troops to the Continent; plans for German rearmament, agreed to the previous September, were actively pushed.

In MacArthur's headquarters in Tokyo euphoria based on one miscalculation gave place overnight to panic based on another. On December 30 the General advised Washington that the only way to avoid defeat in Korea was to expand the war by blockading the coast of China, bombing its industrial centers, using Chinese Nationalist forces in Korea and against vulnerable areas of the Chinese mainland. His recommendation to expand limited into general war was vetoed by Washington and London on what would seem the obvious ground that the rational way to deal with hazards is not to multiply them. However, since limited war was unfamiliar and unpalatable to the American character, persistence in this course continued to generate impassioned protest and political discomfiture until the war ended.

When the tide turned on the battlefield and a new wave of euphoria appeared, there was bitter complaint that the Communist offer of truce talks was prematurely accepted and the Allied offensive halted "on the verge of victory." On this issue the Allied Commander in Korea, General Matthew Ridgway, concluded in his memoirs, *Soldier:* "If we had been ordered to fight our way to the Yalu we could have done it—if our government had been willing to pay the price in dead and wounded that action would have cost. From the purely military standpoint the effort, to my mind, would not have been worth the cost. . . . The seizure of the land between the truce line and the Yalu would have merely meant the seizure of more real estate. . . . Would the American people have been willing to support the great army that would have been required to support that line? Would they have approved our attacking on into Manchuria? On into the heart of the great mainland of Asia, a bottomless pit into which all the armies of the free world could be drawn and be ground to bits and destroyed? I doubt it."

The war ended without victory for either side. It completed, however, the process of transforming the traditional friendship of the Chinese and American peoples into almost unmitigated hostility. The latter was as artificially founded as the former had been.

The Chinese Communists were of course predisposed to hostility against a capitalist state that had done its best to thwart their coming to power. Instead, however, of taking advantage of its acquiescence in their victory to establish a relationship of accommodation and mutual restraint, they succumbed to the temptation of further conquest and perpetuated a confrontation which it would have been in their real interest to suspend.

The Americans responded in Korea with a firmness that was necessary and a restraint that was commendable in refusing to escalate what was bad enough into what was worse. They too, however, moved out of the world of reality and common sense when they committed themselves to the expiring Nationalists, not as the real masters of Formosa but as the mythical masters of the mainland, and thereby repeated the error that had cut them off from the Soviet Union from 1917 to 1933. For many years not only were almost all normal contacts denied but the two peoples —and rarely in history have there been any with less reason to quarrel—were assiduously inculcated with false images of each other, which it may take decades to correct.

Southeast Asia After World War II

For the fifteen years after the end of the Korean War, the confrontation in East Asia was to center around its southern flank, particularly the former French colonies of Vietnam and Laos. Here was the critical point at which the power and prestige of the two systems were gradually, reluctantly, almost involuntarily marshalled. Here, moreover, after the French bowed out, the United States confronted a situation radically different, bewilderingly elusive, and much more intractable than either the struggle for Europe or the conflict in Korea.

The mystery, drama and charm of Southeast Asia are still better reflected for Western eyes in the novels of Joseph Conrad than in academic studies. It is a dazzling, exuberant, incoherent mosaic of refinement and ignorance, wealth and poverty, virtue and vice, commitment and apathy. In 1939 it boasted a single independent state, Thailand. All the rest were colonial fiefs, occupied and exploited by the West. Yet ever since World War I the subversive ferment of Western ideas, nationalism, democracy, socialism, had been working under the bland imperial surface. When that surface was shattered by the Japanese, the ferment boiled over. Overnight there were eight independent states: Thailand, the Philippines, Indonesia, Burma, Malaya, Vietnam, Laos and Cambodia.

Just as in Europe under the Germans, in Southeast Asia under the Japanese the Communists had been particularly valorous and adroit. By the end of the war they were firmly anchored almost everywhere. In Indonesia they created the largest political party and twice, in 1948 and 1965, narrowly missed taking power by coup d'état. In Burma, Malaya and the Philippines they organized and carried on prolonged guerrilla warfare which taxed the resources of the new governments. In Vietnam they captured the nationalist movement almost entirely. This does not mean that all those who fought against the French in Vietnam, or even all those later fighting against the Americans, were Communists. It does mean that Ho Chi Minh and his associates, who were and are full-fledged Communists in affiliation with both their Russian and Chinese co-religionists, had succeeded in dominating that preponderant part of the nationalist movement which entered upon the war of liberation against the French in December 1946. The same Communist leaders continued in full control of the rebellion in Vietnam and its offshoots in Laos and Cambodia until their partial victory in 1954, in totalitarian command of the North thereafter, and in indirect but so far decisive control of the National Liberation Front in South Vietnam from its establishment in 1960 until the present day.

The French fought for nearly eight years bravely and expensively but in vain. Their fatal handicap was that they were never clear what they were fighting for or against. Insofar as they were fighting nationalism they could not win, as they later found even in Algeria; insofar as they were fighting communism they failed to grant enough status and power to their Vietnamese allies. They flouted the sound dictum of Mao Tse-tung: "Without a political goal, guerrilla warfare must fail, as it must if its political objectives do not coincide with the aspirations of the people and their sympathy, cooperation and assistance cannot be gained." Eventually, the French people lost the will to fight at such heavy cost for a distant and dissolving empire, and Pierre Mendès-France brought the effort to an end at Geneva in 1954. Since this curious settlement, unsatisfactory to both sides and hence inherently unstable, has profoundly affected the subsequent course of the East Asian confrontation, it deserves a few words of explanation.

Vietnam, Act I: The Geneva Accords and SEATO

The agreements negotiated at Geneva in June and July 1954 (1) laid down "a provisional demarcation line" at the 17th parallel of latitude dividing Vietnam between the contending parties; (2) provided that the forces of each side should be withdrawn behind the demarcation line and that, "pending the general elections which will bring about the unification of Vietnam," civil administration in each of the two zones should rest with the party whose forces had regrouped there; (3) forbade the introduction of additional forces or arms into Vietnam or the establishment of foreign bases there; (4) authorized civilians in either zone to move to the other (during subsequent months about 860,000 refugees, mostly Roman Catholics, moved from North to South Vietnam and about 150,000 Viet Minh adherents moved from South to North); (5) set up an International Commission composed of India, Canada and Poland, acting normally by majority vote but, in regard to "violations, or threats of violations, which might lead to a resumption of hostilities," on a basis of unanimity, to control and supervise the execution of the agreement; (6) provided for report to "the members of the Geneva Conference" (of which Britain and the Soviet Union were then co-chairmen) if one of the parties refused to carry out a recommendation of the Commission or if it could not reach unanimity in one of the stipulated cases; (7) embodied in a Final Declaration, "its conviction that the execution of the provisions set out in the present declaration and in the agreement on the cessation of hostilities creates the necessary basis for the achievement in the near future of a political settlement in Vietnam," assured the Vietnamese people that they would be permitted "to enjoy the fundamental freedoms, guaranteed by democratic institutions established as a result of free general elections by secret ballot," and declared that "general elections shall be held in July 1956, under the supervision of an international commission," likewise composed of India, Canada and Poland.

The South Vietnamese government did not sign the agreements or declaration but issued a "protest" in which it took strong exception to the rejection by the Conference of its proposal for "an armistice without division, even provisional, of the territory of Vietnam" and "the institution of a provisional control by the United Nations over the entire territory pending the re-establishment of peace and arrangements permitting the Vietnamese people to determine its destiny through free elections." The government particularly protested "the fact that the French High Command has arrogated to itself without preliminary agreement with the delegation of the State of Vietnam the right to fix the date of future elections," and reserved to itself "complete freedom of action to guarantee the sacred right of the Vietnamese people to territorial unity, national independence and freedom."

The United States also refused to sign the Final Declaration, though it issued a declaration of its own in which it affirmed that it would refrain from the threat or use of force to disturb the agreements and "would view any renewal of the aggression in violation of the aforesaid agreements with grave concern and as seriously threatening international peace and security." Thus it simultaneously disavowed the agreements and implied it would fight to enforce them. On the same day President Eisenhower issued a statement in which he pointed out that "the United States has not itself been a party to or bound by the decisions taken by the Conference, but it is our hope that it will lead to the establishment of peace consistent with the rights and the needs of the countries concerned. The agreement contains features which we do not like," the President added in an obvious interpolation in the text prepared for him, "but a great deal depends on how they work in practice."

Twelve years later, during one of several abortive attempts by the United States to induce the United Nations Security Council to deal with the war in Vietnam, the sole point on which all members of the Council could reach even informal agreement was that the Geneva Accords of 1954 should form the basis of any new settlement. This consensus, however, was merely a reflection of the extent to which the situation had deteriorated in those twelve years since now all—except those most concerned, the Vietnamese—wished to turn the clock back to an arrangement which had originally suited no one and had been accepted primarily as window-dressing to screen incompatible expectations.

The fact was that those who accepted the Geneva agreements had done so on the basis of misunderstandings and miscalculations, which were not wholly unobserved at the time but which those who did agree were willing to gloss over in order to secure immediate and urgent ends. It was significant that Ngo Dinh Diem, who assumed office in June 1954 while the French were still in charge in Saigon and the Geneva Conference was meeting, took the first conspicuously independent act of a hitherto conspicuously dependent government in refusing to accept the accords. It was the French, however, who had been fighting the war at enormous cost, who were fed to the teeth with it, and who had no intention, considering the fact that their Indochinese empire was now clearly at an end, of continuing to shed blood on behalf of the Vietnamese and the Americans. They would presumably have taken whatever honorable terms they could get and were elated to be able to settle on partition when they had feared they might have to surrender the whole country. What happened afterward was not their concern, as long as the war did not break out again.

The most serious miscalculation was made by Ho Chi Minh and his colleagues, for they might have won the whole prize had they continued fighting longer. No doubt they too were tired and perhaps fearful that the United States, which had been making increasingly menacing noises, would involve itself directly if the war continued. Very possibly, however, the decisive factor may have been advice from Moscow and Peking where the new leaders were eager, for a variety of reasons, to flesh out "peaceful coexistence" with some elements of détente, to induce the French parliament to scuttle the European Defense Community, to concentrate on urgent internal problems with which both Communist states were confronted, and perhaps most of all, having recently terminated one costly and unproductive war with the United States in Korea, to avoid being drawn into another in Vietnam.

Inherent in the accords, which indeed echoed the controversial "Declaration on Liberated Europe" agreed to at Yalta, was the misunderstanding embodied in the bland and undefined references to "political settlement," "fundamental freedoms," "democratic institutions" and "free general elections," which implied that the two parties were talking about the same things when of course, as the experience of the preceding nine years should have taught them both, they were not. While Ho Chi Minh and his colleagues were probably persuaded, rightly or wrongly, that "free elections" in the Western sense would produce a result favorable to them in the South and bring them victory there without further combat, it is extremely unlikely that they ever contemplated any sort of elections in their own half of Vietnam other than the totalitarian variety so successfully applied in Eastern Europe after 1947. Once again it was demonstrated that the use of these ambiguous terms in East-West agreements can lead to no result other than well-founded charges of bad faith on both sides.

During the final months of the war and those immediately following, the United States, alarmed that all or most of Southeast Asia might like China be "lost," moved rapidly from the wings onto the center of the stage. In a press conference on April 7, 1954, President Eisenhower used a phrase, "row of dominoes," which was destined to enjoy great favor and long life. Very serious consideration was apparently given at this time to United States air and naval intervention to save Dien Bien Phu. Vice-President Nixon, briefing newspaper editors, even foreshadowed the dispatch of American ground forces if Indochina could not otherwise be preserved. The United States had, however, extricated itself from the Korean War less than a year before, and Congressional distaste for unilateral involvement in still another Asian morass was unmistakably expressed. Churchill and Eden, moreover, were firmly opposed to any extension of the conflict, particularly just before the Geneva Conference. It was not, therefore, until the Conference was over and North Vietnam had been ceded that John Foster Dulles was able to persuade a few Europeans and Asians to set up in Asia a superficially plausible imitation of European collective defense.

In September, Australia, France, New Zealand, Pakistan, the Philippines, Thailand, the United Kingdom, and the United States signed the Southeast Asia Collective Defense Treaty and, in a separate protocol, explicitly included South Vietnam, Laos, and Cambodia in the area to be defended. In ensuing months the United States also signed a mutual defense treaty with the Nationalist Chinese government on Formosa, perfected defense arrangements with Japan and Korea, and commenced substantial aid programs to Vietnam, Laos, and Cambodia which, when the French drastically reduced their aid at the end of the year, became the principal support of those three governments.

If 1950 was the year in which the United States halted its disengagement from Asia and assumed commitment for the defense of Korea and Formosa, 1954 was the year in which these commitments were extended to a substantial part of Southeast Asia. For the nth time since World War II Communist resort to force for aggrandizement had generated in still another part of the world precisely the United States presence and commitment which the Communists subsequently were so bitterly to condemn and combat. The lapse of only a very short time was sufficient to demonstrate, however, that containment in Asia was far more complex and elusive than in Europe, that the principal objective of Britain and France in the former was not to create a military structure but to avoid recurrence of war, and that SEATO was therefore to prove to be as much a device for restraining the United States as for restraining the Communists.

"Peaceful Coexistence"

Peaceful coexistence was facilitated by the sweet reasonableness of the two principal Communist powers during the period immediately following. We have suggested some of the reasons which may have induced them to counsel Ho Chi Minh to settle for half a loaf; these reasons continued to apply after the settlement.

In early October 1954, Khrushchev and Bulganin visited Peking and concluded a series of agreements by which they extended to

China "scientific and technological cooperation" (no doubt including nuclear, which they were later to regret), and renounced the special privileges in Manchuria acquired by Stalin at Yalta. The joint communiqué issued at the end of the visit condemned SEATO, American support of the "Chiang Kai-shek clique," and the American "occupation" of Japan, but praised the Geneva Accords and the joint "examination of pressing international problems" by the Great Powers on whom the United Nations Charter "lays the primary responsibility for the maintenance of world peace." This statement concorded with the Soviet desire for a summit conference, which in fact took place the next year and at which, despite the uneasiness and skepticism of the Americans, "peaceful coexistence" was given further currency and status.

Chou En-lai meanwhile attended and captivated the first Afro-Asian Conference at Bandung which reaffirmed the famous Five Principles or "Panch Shila" that Chou, Nehru, and U Nu had promulgated in 1954. These principles were: "mutual respect for each other's territorial integrity and sovereignty, nonaggression, noninterference in each other's internal affairs, equality and mutual benefits, and peaceful coexistence."

A casual acquaintance with history should and probably did warn Nehru, U Nu, and others who joined Chou in subscribing to these principles that they are only conditionally observed by any powerful nation-state, that they are as a matter of doctrine observed by Communist states only to the degree it seems expedient to do so, and that even relatively honest acceptance of them is often based on incompatible interpretations of the terms employed. Nevertheless, Nehru and U Nu no doubt saw value in obtaining Chinese Communist endorsement of these pieties, unreliable and ambiguous as that endorsement might be. It was apparent that the principal Communist powers, for reasons of their own, were genuinely desirous of calm in the Far East, for several years elapsed before they again seriously disturbed their neighbors.

We have encountered before both in Europe and the Far East the tragic discordance in the rhythm of Eastern and Western challenge and response, arising from the fact that overaction by one side often provokes, after an interval of incubation, overreaction by the other. The United States had tardily recognized the Communist intention to unify Korea and Vietnam by force. Though one objective had been thwarted by arms and the other by negotiation, the Americans frantically assumed, just when Peking and Moscow were temporarily turning to domestic consolidation and shelving foreign adventure, that the Communist juggernaut was about to roll out in all directions. Many thought, said, and wrote that all of Indochina, even all of Southeast Asia, was already "down the drain," or at best could only be saved by desperate measures. Over the next few years, what were deemed to be the necessary measures were taken. They amounted, on the one hand, to confining and quarantining the Chinese Communists and their allies within the narrowest possible compass and, on the other, to installing and maintaining in countries outside the Bamboo Curtain, wherever American influence was predominant, true-blue, one hundred per cent anti-Communist regimes.

On only one point of doctrine was there agreement between Peking and Washington. Mao Tse-tung had written in 1949 in an article entitled "On the People's Democratic Dictatorship": "There can be no sitting on the fence; there is no third road. . . . Not only in China but throughout the world, one must lean either to imperialism or socialism. There is no exception. Neutrality is merely a camouflage." In those years, Washington was in full accord with this judgment.

We might parenthetically note the folly and short-sightedness of what came to be the common Western practice of attempting to quarantine its adversaries in the Cold War. The practice arose from a number of misapplied preconceptions and analogies: that the "merchants of death" selling contraband to both sides had involved the United States in World War I, that it is possible to coerce a powerful state or a client of powerful states by economic sanctions, that it is immoral to have any dealings with wicked people or wicked nations, that a free society can be contaminated and subverted by association with a closed society but not vice-versa, and that if you do not quite dare to use military force you should come as close to it as you can. Neither as applied to the Soviet Union nor to Communist China nor to East Germany nor Cuba nor North Vietnam has a quarantine produced the desired results. On the contrary, it has in each case, in addition to causing unhealthy recrimination between the United States and its friends, increased the dependence of the quarantined state on other Communist nations and reduced its accessibility and vulnerability to any sort of alternative influence. In assuming that a free society excels a closed one most of all in the diversity of its choices, the appeal of its principles, and the productivity of its economy, it seems strange that the policy of the free world was not more often to bring these elements as fully as possible to bear on the Communist world, rather than to restrict contact and competition so substantially to the military and clandestine spheres where Communist capabilities were most nearly equal.

Vietnam, Act II: The Reign of Ngo Dinh Diem

To return to Indochina, the French have never forgiven the United States for not having withdrawn when they did. Convinced that the obstacles they had confronted were insurmountable, the French believed it was reckless and immoral for anyone else to try where they failed. They overlooked the considerable difference between maintaining a foreign imperialism and resisting a domestic tyranny.

As a matter of fact, the policy of the Vietnamese Communist party was not only tyrannical vis-à-vis its own compatriots but imperialist vis-à-vis its Laotian and Cambodian neighbors. Through the exercise of superior force, it would have almost certainly imposed Communist regimes on the non-Communist majorities in all three countries (overwhelming majorities in Cambodia and Laos) if the United States had not immediately filled the vacuum created by the withdrawal of the French.

The United States government was, however, far from clear how that vacuum was to be filled without a direct involvement, which, besides being contrary to the Geneva Accords, was the last thing it wanted. It began by applying the formula that seemed to be working in Korea, though it had failed in China: back unconditionally a political leader who is one hundred per cent anti-Communist; train and equip a mass army to meet a mass invasion.

About nine years were required fully to expose the deficiencies in this formula. What was needed in South Vietnam politically was not anti-communism but a social mobilization of the whole people as effective as that imposed by the Communists in the North and capable of competing with them on their own ground. What was needed in South Vietnam militarily was not a conventional mass army but a dedicated force, close to the people, trained in counterinsurgency, and capable of winning the villages from the Viet Cong.

The United States inherited from the French in Vietnam not only chaos but a remarkable political phenomenon, Ngo Dinh Diem. Diem was an honest, dedicated, deeply religious individual, but the fact that he had spent twenty years in exile had combined with traits of his own personality to isolate him from his own people. An acute observer of the Vietnamese scene, Jean Lacouture, described him as "an Asiatic Philip II." "He had an attachment," Lacouture wrote, "to the ancient society of Annam—high aristocracy, closed castes, intellectual hierarchies, its cohesive families, its disdain of strangers, its hatred of China. He wanted to revive the old order, the ancient morality, its respect for the master, the rule of the closed city. But this was beyond his power."

Unfortunately, his character was correctly read among the Americans only by those who had to work most closely with him, and not even all of them. Some did, however, recommend categorically from Saigon that he be dropped or, failing that, that the leverage of American aid be firmly used to enforce policies of modernization, liberalization, land reform, and traditional village democracy. Diem moved in exactly the opposite direction.

During three years of exile in the United States, his piety and fervent anti-communism had won him the passionate admiration of the Catholic hierarchy and other influential Americans, who were less careful than they should have been about his other qualifications for governing a country as stricken and vulnerable as Vietnam. Whenever he was criticized, they reacted with indignation; whenever he was threatened, they rallied to him. As a consequence, he became more and more stubborn, inflexible, and reactionary, more and more lost touch with reality, was more and more enveloped and exploited by his outrageous family. It was the story of Chiang Kai-shek all over again.

Eventually his image became so hallowed, his self-confidence so egregious, and his political position in the United States so unassailable that he could finally and far too late be removed only by a coup d'état which Washington was obliged to tolerate. In the meantime the precious four years of peace, 1955–59, had been wasted. Indeed the peace ended because Diem's policies, which made them desperate and him unpopular, convinced the Communists, North and South, that war was both a preferable and a promising alternative.

Misguided Democracy in Laos

Another cautionary example of the wrongheadedness of preferring anti-Communist orthodoxy to broadly based political alliances was afforded in the same years by American policy in Laos. Here the governments after 1954 had included all significant political elements, and there had been a willingness from the beginning, in order to end the dissidence in the north, even to take in representatives of the tiny Communist movement if they would agree to play according to democratic rules. A coalition government on this basis was eventually set up despite symptoms of nervous prostration in Washington; it was soon dissolved through the recalcitrance and withdrawal of the Communists, but none of the dire consequences so often attributed to coalition with Communists occurred. Washington, however, resolved not to risk having its nerves shaken again, swung its decisive weight behind a small simon-pure Rightist minority, mostly military, and facilitated the establishment of a government which excluded not only the Communists but most of the moderate political elements as well. The not unnatural consequence was to bring about a revolt of those elements, to force them temporarily into a neutralist anti-American posture, to bring about a year of disastrous political and military turbulence, and thus to provide the North Vietnamese, abetted by the Soviets, with the opportunity to wrap themselves in the Laotian flag and seize about half the country.

Thus the United States once again confirmed the truth of William Blake's dictum that "you never know what is enough unless you know what is more than enough." When President Kennedy took office in January 1961, he was confronted by a quite unnecessary Laotian crisis which nevertheless threatened to result in short order either in the appearance of Communist battalions in Vientiane and Luang Prabang or the introduction of large numbers of American troops in Laos. Fortunately, neither Khrushchev nor Kennedy had any stomach for these extremes and in 1962 opted for another Geneva Conference and the establishment in Laos of another broadly based government under Prince Souvanna Phouma, whom the United States had earlier ousted. Once again the Communists were initially included but soon withdrew. The Royal government reverted to close association with the United States, and the political status quo of 1959 was more or less restored. The chief consequence of the whole fatuous operation was that several provinces previously free were now firmly occupied by the North Vietnamese.

The Contradictions of Maoism

Such were the main events pertinent to the confrontation in the Far East from the end of World War II until the opening of the 1960s. It will now be useful to pause a moment to examine how external events combined with internal contradictions to produce in Communist China in 1966–67 the extraordinary political convulsions which so astonished both laymen and experts. These convulsions were most instructive concerning the nature of Chinese communism and significant for its future conduct and relations with the rest of the world.

After the Korean War ended in 1953, Communist China had been for the most part externally passive but internally very busy. There had been in 1954 and 1958 much-publicized confrontations with the United States over the "offshore islands," Quemoy and Matsu, out of all proportion to their real importance; but the U.S. Congress had passed solemn and sweeping resolutions, Peking had backed off snarling, and the Formosa Strait had thereafter been unvexed by anything more dangerous than Nationalist raids and Communist rhetoric.

The most significant external event of the period was of course the bitter schism with the Soviet Union. It may have been inevitable from the beginning, considering that neither of the two great Communist powers was likely for long to accept, either ideologically or nationally, subordination to the other: no church can long endure two popes. In any case, the conflict reached a decisive turning point with the withdrawal of Soviet technicians and the cessation of Soviet military aid in 1960, and continued thereafter to worsen almost uninterruptedly until the present time.

At home, meanwhile, Mao Tse-tung and his colleagues began to cope in earnest with the contradictions of communism, particularly its contradictions with human nature, with the Chinese national character, with the imperatives of technology, and with the class which it itself creates. After fifteen years these contradictions remain unresolved, indeed magnified.

Lucien Bodard, a perceptive French observer, remarked several years ago: "The profound reality of China, beyond all analyses, is the immense pride of the Chinese in being Chinese. Mao Tse-tung's communism is only the deepest form of that pride." This is an exaggeration. Nonetheless it does reflect the fact that the core of Chinese character and civilization is indeed an immense pride in being Chinese, and that any regime which seems to revive China's prestige and power after a century of eclipse will enjoy great popular support on those grounds alone, whatever its other aspects. It is probable that Marxism, even among most Chinese who profess it most ardently, is only skin deep. Nationalism is certainly both a major trait and a major asset of Mao's communism. To isolate and humiliate this nationalism and the regime which embodies it only aggravates the nationalism and further alienates the regime from the rest of the world.

Other traditional aspects of Chinese character were, however, less amenable to what soon came to be canonized as the "thoughts of Mao Tse-tung." These represented a curious, almost touching, amalgam of Marxist dogma, Puritan austerity, instinctive xenophobia, and a childlike faith that "the people" can achieve miracles through the pure exercise of will, autodidactics, and manual labor. The idealized Maoist man, not wholly unlike the idealized early American, was to be a synthesis of Paul Bunyan, the Revolutionary Minuteman, the Methodist circuit-rider and the Salem witchcraft judge; as such, he was to be incorruptible and invincible. In this conception there was room for everyone except Confucius, Sun Yat-sen and, as it turned out, a large part of Mao's own hierarchy.

Three of Mao's essays written between 1939 and 1945—"In Memory of Norman Bethune," "Serve the People," and "The Foolish Old Man Who Removed the Mountains"—which the Red Guards were assiduously perusing and disseminating in 1967, read almost like the effusions of primitive Christians. Yet for that very reason Mao's communism was with difficulty compatible with the traditional realism, materialism and, when opportunity offers, voluptuousness of the Chinese people. Ground down by war, warlords, foreign invaders and domestic spoilsmen, they welcomed the austere heroes of the Long March. It was easier, however, to admire than to imitate, to assume than to maintain this posture. When the "Hundred Flowers" were briefly allowed to bloom, they did not bloom for Mao. Human nature combined with national character to generate backsliding, in which even much of the Communist hierarchy participated.

In another domain, technology, the contradictions of Maoism proved even more intractable. Despite an estimated increase of more than a third in gross domestic product between 1952 and 1957, no mean performance, Mao was not satisfied and decreed "The Great Leap Forward" by which the "foolish" old and young men were to remove mountains, that is, smelt pig iron in their back yards, communize agriculture and living habits, and lift production overnight to the level of Mao's ambition and dreams. Of course the result was a dismal disaster; it was a tribute to the doggedness and resilience of the Chinese character that total breakdown did not occur; as it was, industrial and agricultural production did not again reach 1957 levels for several years, though population continued to explode.

The contradiction was doctrinally even more fundamental and subversive. While the three great branches of the revolution were proclaimed to be "the class struggle, the struggle for production and scientific experiment," the new class of party officials, technocrats, scientists and intellectuals that these three processes engendered was, as Communists elsewhere had earlier found, essentially unresponsive to the authority, the vulgarization and the primitiveness which were the essence of Maoism.

In a sense, Mao was humane and democratic in trying to bridge the age-old chasm, China's curse in many ways, between the bureaucratic elite and the mass of peasants on whom the pompous superstructure of all regimes rested and depended. He repeatedly sought to abate the elevation, the isolation, the privilege and the arrogance which officials and intelligentsia, whether they represent an old or a new regime, so easily assume in organized society. He commanded them to return to the people and work in the fields and factories; he rejected the superiority of science over human purpose; he wrestled with those, no matter how exalted, who questioned his thaumaturgical interpretation of Marx; he castigated, circumvented and purged his own party apparatus; he discriminated against the sons of the privileged; he forbade the formation of the "new class." In effect, he sought to hog-tie the future and carry the "Long March" on forever.

The "thoughts of Mao Tse-tung" combined with a struggle for power among the top-most echelons of the party to produce in 1966 and 1967 a huge explosion inside China. So hard-fought, relentless, and unprecedented was it that Mao and his lieutenants had to close the schools and mobilize the students, not against capitalists and imperialists but against the Communist apparatus itself. When this mobilization only compounded the confusion, the army had to be called in to correct it, sometimes by force. Even the army, like the Party, split and clashed. Workers, peasants, bureaucrats, intellectuals, soldiers, students, all elements of the population, were dragged willy-nilly into this bizarre, bloody and colossal religious war.

What would be the outcome of this latest and most prodigious illustration of the inclination of a revolution to eat its own off-spring could hardly be predicted. Would Mao succeed for a time in his defiant attempt to preserve the purity of the revolution and, by the convulsive mobilization of the masses, to assimilate to them even the new bureaucracy? Would the army, with or without his consent, with or without participation of the party bureaucracy, establish a new and quite different order? Would Mao, in one way or another, be overwhelmed by the inertial forces of human nature, national tradition, modern technology, and the political structure he had himself created? Would the mandate of heaven be withdrawn from the regime as a whole and China once more break up into hostile fragments dominated by warlords?

As suggested in another connection, foreign adversaries of Chinese communism could, even if civil war were averted, take comfort from Mao's crusades. The more "Great Leaps Forward" were attempted in industry and agriculture contrary to expert advice, the more slowly would the Chinese economy develop, the more unmanageable would become the pressure of population, the less alluring the Communist example to other underdeveloped peoples, and the less capable would Chinese industry be of supporting a modern military establishment. The more the Chinese army concentrated on preparation for fighting a "peoples' war" according to the gospel of Lin Piao (a guerrilla struggle of country against town based on the special experience of the Chinese civil war), the more irrevocably Peking cut itself off from the Soviet military and technical assistance, the less of a threat to the rest of the world would be the Chinese armed forces and the more they would be compelled, whatever their ambitions might be, to follow a defensive strategy. The more intellectuals were denigrated and creative thinking censored, the more Red Guards were diverted from the schools and universities to the field and public squares, the more learning was confined to the "thoughts of Mao Tsetung," the less would the next generation be capable of coping with the real problems of the modern world and the less exemplary and powerful would be the China of tomorrow.

Realists like Chou En-lai presumably did not lose sight of these facts and persistently but subtly sought, without losing the charisma or the confidence of Mao, to keep the party together in a viable course. The army too, though far from united, tended nevertheless to intervene on the side of order and practicality. It seemed probable that for a people basically as practical as the Chinese, a flight from reality as comprehensive as Mao's could only be temporary. Eventually, painfully, equivocally, slowly, the Chinese government and people would edge back to policies and techniques that work and that in the course of time would re-establish China as a great power. For the time being, however, the already immense problems facing China were compounded and its weight in its neighborhood and in the world substantially diminished.

That a realization of this unpalatable fact must have forced itself upon the rulers of China is suggested by the almost unvarying prudence which since 1953 has characterized their foreign policy, as distinguished from their rhetoric. Indeed it must be intensely humiliating to Red Guardsmen and other ardent Chinese to be told of the numerous occasions on which American aircraft and vessels have violated Chinese territory, of the tightening military "encirclement" of China by the United States and its "feudal" allies, and particularly of the outrageous and prolonged "aggression" of the United States against China's neighbor and friend, North Vietnam—without there being any effective response whatsoever on the part of their supposedly virile and indomitable government.

In 1962 Chinese armed forces did enter India. It is significant, however, that in this single instance of offensive military movement outside its frontiers Peking chose an adversary which, though large, was militarily weak, a spot where substantial military response by the adversary would be extremely difficult, and an issue, a frontier dispute, on which the Chinese case was not without merit. Nevertheless even here, though psychological warfare was revived during the India-Pakistan conflict in 1965, further military action has been carefully eschewed.

Some critics addicted to historical parallelism have taken Lin Piao's famous article of September 1965 to be both a candid revelation of Chinese Communist intentions and a declaration of war on the world, along the lines of Hitler's *Mein Kampf*. Other perhaps more meticulous analysts have found in it a relatively assuring reaffirmation of the Maoist theses: first, that the ultimate Communist triumph is to be won, not by war among great powers with sophisticated weapons, but by peoples' guerrilla wars, by unspoiled rural against effete urban areas following the Chinese pattern; and, second, that each insurgent people must expect to fight and win its own war of this kind without other than marginal help from outside. The fact that Chinese Communist aid to embattled Vietnam at their very gates has been of this limited character lends weight to the belief that, while they will no doubt foment revolutions far and near wherever they cheaply can, there is as little likelihood that they will in the foreseeable future march their armies to Bangkok and Rangoon as that the Soviets will march to the English Channel. Indeed, historical experience with the malignancy of religious conflict suggests that, if these two armies march at all, they are more likely to move toward rather than away from each other.

It would, however, be a fatal error to assume that, because of all these inhibiting factors, Communist China will either in the short run submit to what it would consider intolerable national humiliation or in the long run behave differently in regard to the affairs of its region than other revolutionary or imperial great powers have in regard to theirs. Peking has a huge army; despite its internal convulsions it continues to develop nuclear weapons with alarming speed; it is keenly ambitious to restore China's traditional power and prestige; it is dedicated to a revolutionary creed which is inherently and violently evangelistic. If and when it is able sufficiently to master its internal political, economic and technological problems, if by then it has not moderated its revolutionary zeal or recovered its sense of reality, if at that time there exists a military and political vacuum around its periphery, it could become what it is not yet, an appalling menace to the peace of the world. So persuaded were Kennedy and Macmillan of this potentiality—and of the relative temperance of the U.S.S.R.—that in discussing the appointment of a new NATO commander in 1963 the Prime Minister could say to the President, only half jokingly, "I suppose it should be a Russian."

The first conclusion to be drawn from this set of contingencies should be the urgent necessity for the rest of the world to reestablish and multiply contact and communication with the Peking regime and, to the extent it will permit, with the Chinese people in order that both may come to know the modern world as it really is. The foundation of a rational relationship between China and the rest of the world, as between Russia and the West, as between one human being and another, must be intercourse and understanding. Nevertheless, until those human elements can reassert themselves over theology and arrogance, the appearance of a tempting political and military vacuum around China's peripheries must still be sedulously avoided. It is imperative, however, that measures for this purpose be strictly defensive, that they not be so extreme as to provoke the very excess they are designed to curb—for example, a massive Chinese involvement in Vietnam—and that they move steadfastly toward an indigenous regional framework within which China can be at first contained but eventually embraced.

Japan and India

The pillars of any such regional framework would eventually have to be Japan and India, the other two East Asian great powers. (The Soviet Union may perhaps play a part but will not fit readily, if at all, into the regional framework.) Neither Japan nor India is, however, psychologically prepared to play such a role at the present time.

Japan is economically developed and politically united enough to do so. Indeed her recovery from the collapse of 1945 is among the miracles of modern times; she is already far stronger and stabler than China in all but a military sense, and before long may become the third industrial power of the world. Yet Japan is still severely inhibited by the trauma created by her imperial intoxication and its shattering rout. She is still far from ready to play any significant military role, and is indeed still diffident about trying to assume political leadership of those nations she so recently conquered. Many of them might still object to her trying to do so. While this diffidence is in some ways inconvenient, it had perhaps better be respected by Japan's friends, who were impelled prematurely to hustle a still disoriented Germany into a substantial military posture, which has been somewhat double-edged for it and for them. The Japanese are an enormously talented, highly disciplined, but still profoundly insular, passionate and repressed people. It would seem prudent to leave their military genie in its bottle, where they still prefer it, but to encourage their fullest participation in the economic development and political organization of their region.

India, after China the largest, the most civilized, and in general the best endowed of all the underdeveloped countries, is still overwhelmed by problems of fantastic magnitude—by a debilitating and uncertain climate which has always been her curse, by a bursting population, by a penury of food and education, by an anachronistic burden of caste, custom and sanctimoniousness, by regional, religious and linguistic antagonisms, by an unhappy coexistence of political faction and social apathy. The elite is so preoccupied and encumbered with these internal enigmas that there is little prospect India could soon play the role in Asia to which her past and, one hopes, her future entitle her. To the partial extent she can, she should be encouraged to do so.

Such, in rough outline, is the character of confrontation in East Asia in 1968. Before summing up, let us glance again at Vietnam, which has become, through one of the strange and illogical ironies of history, the bloody fulcrum on which converge and press the paramount forces of the twentieth century.

Vietnam, Act III: 1959–67

Beginning in 1959, after four years of relative and misspent tranquility, violence and terror reappeared on a considerable scale in South Vietnam. Assassination of officials, village chiefs, teachers, doctors and others of the elite became endemic and substantial; Diem's suppressive measures against Communists and all other opponents of the regime were multiplied; guerrilla activity revived in particularly disaffected parts of the country.

By September 1960, although there were then only about 5,000 guerrillas in the field, Diem's brother Nhu was telling journalists that "the second Indochina war has begun." That same month a Congress of the Vietnamese Communist party meeting in Hanoi demanded the liberation of the South; in November an almost successful revolt of his own paratroopers revealed how fragile was Diem's position; in December the "National Liberation Front" of South Vietnam was formally established. The coincidental revolt of the dispossessed "neutralists" in Laos permitted North Vietnamese seizure of the critical area through which the infiltration route, the "Ho Chi Minh Trail," was opened to the South.

Although 1960 was the year in which Khrushchev resumed the Cold War in Europe, there is no evidence that the revival of the war in Vietnam, any more than its concurrent revival in Laos, constituted either an element in a world-wide "Communist offensive" or a local manifestation of Chinese "expansionism." At the time Peking was still bogged down in the backwash of the disastrous "Great Leap Forward." Furthermore, this was also the year in which Khrushchev withdrew his technicians from China and the Sino-Soviet split, though still concealed, was in fact confirmed.

A plausible and sufficient explanation of the revival of the war would seem to be: that an inevitable objective of governments of both parts of divided countries, particularly the stronger of the two, will be to reunite their countries; that Ho and his colleagues never wavered in their intention ultimately to extend their political system to their southern compatriots, among whom many partisans of that system remained after 1954; and that Diem's Bourbonism and unpopularity gave them the opportunity, his persecution of their adherents the incentive, to choose this moment to renew their attempt. Like their Korean co-religionists ten years before, they seriously miscalculated the reaction; though, like them again, had they had to cope with their compatriots alone they would have succeeded.

There was, however, a very significant wider issue involved. A favorite expression in Communist dialectic and propaganda has long been "wars of national liberation," into which rubric they artfully compress not only genuine national revolts against foreign masters, such as those in Indonesia and Algeria (though not of course those in Hungary and Tibet), but also basically any Communist-inspired or supported insurrection against a non-Communist government, no matter how nationalist, independent and sovereign the latter may be. Even so magnanimous a statesman as Adlai Stevenson had become convinced, after four years' experience with African, Asian and Latin American crises at the United Nations, that such wars constitute, only second to the existence of nuclear arsenals, the gravest threat to the peace of the world in the 1960s. He thought it of the utmost importance, as his last speeches bear eloquent witness, that the Communist powers be persuaded that the prosecution of "aggression by proxy" in the guise of "national liberation" is profoundly incompatible with "peaceful coexistence."

Here, however, one encounters a dilemma: since Communists have never yet come to power in any state except by civil war or coup d'état, and since they argue with some cogency that their adversaries will never permit them to do so otherwise, they can hardly be expected to abandon readily or soon what they conceive to be their only means to power. The practice of parliamentary democracy, to which they have been constrained in Western Europe, has not yet and perhaps never will provide them proof to the contrary. The dilemma therefore persists and remains a principal threat to the peace.

In this context, since the Communists falsely classified the renewed conflict in South Vietnam, as they correctly had the earlier one, a "war of national liberation," it could not be dealt with as a wholly isolated phenomenon. The Americans long and sincerely sought to limit their involvement. As late as September 1963, President Kennedy was saying of the Vietnamese in a television interview: "In the final analysis, it is their war. They are the ones who have to win it or lose it. We can help them, we can give them equipment, but they have to win it, the people of Vietnam."

At that point Kennedy could still contemplate the possibility that the war might be lost. At that point there were still only 16,000 American military men in Vietnam, and they were there simply as "advisers," not for combat. At that point, and for more than a year thereafter, it would still have been possible for the United States government to have concluded that South Vietnam was too hopelessly contaminated, too thoroughly permeated by the Viet Cong, too politically backward and unstable to be redeemed without disproportionate expenditure of force. It could have reached a further conclusion, like that of the Truman administration in the case of all the Eastern European countries except Greece, that South Vietnam should be abandoned and the line of containment drawn elsewhere—for example, at the Annamite chain of mountains between Vietnam and Laos, rather than at the 17th parallel.

Both sides in the Vietnamese confrontation, however, made

their critical decisions in a spirit rather of heroic knight-errantry than of cold calculation. As so often happens in prestigious international trials of strength, the participants gradually, compulsively, almost inadvertently raised their stakes until both were so deeply committed they lost control. In 1964 Hanoi, smelling victory, began to infiltrate its regular military forces into the South; by the middle of the year the United States Military Command estimated that there were about 4,000 of them there; by mid-1965 there were 10,000, plus about 160,000 Viet Cong guerrillas. In the early months of 1965 they brazenly and bloodily attacked American installations; it seemed they might soon drive the demoralized South Vietnamese from the field.

As Ho and his friends should have foreseen and as occurred in Korea, the Americans refused to tolerate the extinction of their ally. The number of American troops in Vietnam rose from 20,000 at the end of 1964 to 175,000 a year later, jumped to 375,-000 by the end of 1966, and were scheduled to rise to close to half a million by the end of 1967.

Early in 1965, unwisely selecting a time when the Soviet Premier was visiting Hanoi, the United States began aerial bombing of the North, mistakenly expecting, despite the experience of Korea, that this would cut off the flow of men and arms to the South, hoping also, despite the experience of World War II, that it would cow Hanoi into suing for peace. The vanity of these hopes and expectations was soon and repeatedly revealed. According to U.S. Department of Defense estimates, infiltration from North to South rose from no more than 1,000 a month in mid-1965 to about 7,000 a month by mid-1966, bringing the combined Viet Cong and North Vietnamese strength in the South at the end of 1966 to about 275,000. By 1967, confirmed and probable infiltration had fallen off to about 4,000 a month (another 2,000 were estimated as "possible"), but it appeared that this reduction was due less to United States interdiction than to Hanoi's choice and that it did not substantially affect the total of Communist forces active in the South.

By that time much of the rest of the world was persuaded, rightly or wrongly, that only if the United States *stopped* bombing was there any prospect of negotiating peace—a view held all the more passionately as the bombing escalated through 1967. As month succeeded month and year succeeded year, each side persistently and implausibly imagined that a little more infiltration or a little more reinforcement, a little more terror or a little more bombing, would permit it to "win"; each more and more doggedly conceived that it could not afford to "lose."

At least two significant points had, however, been established, which should have been instructive to each side. The Communist powers had been shown, whether or not they digested the lesson, that the United States was not prepared, at least in areas where it was clearly committed, to tolerate the triumph of "wars of liberation" in the Communist sense of the term without an application of force which would be extremely painful to those carrying on the war, and would be, moreover, contrary to the manifest interest of the Soviet Union, if not of China, in a growing measure of peaceful coexistence. On the other side, the United States had been shown, whether or not it digested the lesson, that even a very small country can, with sufficient will and modest means, carry on a guerrilla war of such magnitude and indomitability as to pin down indefinitely a substantial part of the military power of the world's strongest state and to thwart, through a whole series of unforeseen repercussions, many of its most admirable and critical objectives at home and abroad.

A third lesson, applicable to both sides but in 1967 still digested by neither, was the hazard of drawing sweeping and indiscriminate historical parallels. Ho Chi Minh and his colleagues argued that they were justified in resorting to force, as so many others had done in the past, to "liberate" and unify their nation. They ignored the distinguishing fact that theirs had been divided, even though provisionally, by solemn international agreement, that an effort to reunite by force a similarly divided country, Korea, had brought on one war, and that military efforts to reunite others, Vietnam or Germany, were likely to bring on worse ones. In the same way the United States government argued that it was justified in responding to the challenge, as it had done in Korea, by the exercise of whatever degree of force it unilaterally deemed necessary, ignoring the distinguishing fact that, for many reasons, world opinion and much of its own drew a sharp distinction between the cases of Korea and Vietnam. This distinction was in some measure borne out by the clearly subordinate role of China in both the origin and conduct of the Vietnamese war. One consequence for the United States government of its failure to digest this lesson was a traumatic and ominous division in American opinion and a serious threat to the prospects of the Democratic party and all its domestic programs.

A fourth lesson, also applicable to both sides, was that in the modern world there is less and less leeway for the solution of international problems and conflicts by force of arms. Most now agree, in principle though unhappily not yet in strategic planning, that nuclear arms are inappropriate and counterproductive for the settlement of conflicts. The Communists, however, particularly the Chinese, still cherish the illusion that guerrilla wars will in many cases be advantageous. By developing an elaborate "counterinsurgency" capability, the United States military establishment has been endeavoring to prepare itself to meet such threats wherever they might arise. The Vietnamese war has revealed, on the one hand, that guerrilla war even in an area where it is widely supported can be contained but, on the other hand, that the expenditure of force, resources and political assets necessary to do so even in one area may be seriously out of proportion to what a single state, even a very powerful one, may find it expedient in the future to expend.

President Johnson deserved the gratitude of his country and the world for imposing, despite persistent pressure from his military advisers and mounting exasperation of American opinion, significant though elastic restraints on the conduct of the war, which could otherwise so easily have escalated into much wider, more costly and more calamitous conflict. Still the United States was caught in what seemed in some ways the most agonizing dilemma of its history. Every nation, even the strongest, has a limited span, both of usable physical resources and of applicable political energy. If too much of both is absorbed in one problem, such as the war in Vietnam, too little will be left for others equally or more compelling, such as the shame of the cities. This was a part of the dilemma. Another was that, after so vast an involvement and so solemn a commitment, the United States could not simply withdraw from Vietnam; yet for a variety of reasons it could not expect, in any decisive sense, to "win" the war. As President Kennedy said, only the Vietnamese could do that; the United States could only, for as long as its public opinion would permit, keep them from losing.

Often in great contests between nations, between armies, between revolutionary and conservative forces, their collision by seeming chance polarizes at a particular spot, frequently not of paramount intrinsic importance but around which nevertheless gradually accumulate more and more force, more and more passion, more and more intransigence. The origin is usually a miscalculation by one side that the spot is especially vulnerable or the adversary indisposed to react there; the reaction is likely to be redoubled because the challenge seems especially flagrant. Against the will of both sides, they become inextricably entangled and bound together at a point actually remote from their primary concern; unwilling to avow their misgivings and dismay lest they be thought weak, they fight stubbornly on, each publicly demanding the impossible of the other, each secretly groping for an accommodation that will not be intolerable. Meanwhile the poor people involved suffer stoically, hopelessly and for the most part uselessly, since their suffering has little effect on the warriors. So it was in Korea until at last a point of common weariness, disillusionment and grudging rationality was reached at which both sides were willing to swallow peace without victory. So in the end it will probably be in Vietnam.

For the time being, the latent, potentially prodigious confrontation between the United States and China was adjourned. China was absorbed in its internal convulsions. The United States was preoccupied with the war in Vietnam, which it wisely did not want to expand. Yet both seemed mesmerized by their expectation of inevitable conflict. The Americans were convinced the Chinese intend, when they are strong enough, to seize and dominate all of East Asia and, in the meantime, to foment revolution there and everywhere. The Chinese were convinced the Americans intend, when they can find or fabricate a pretext, to attack and destroy them and, in the meantime, to surround them with an ever tightening ring of military power.

In fact, the United States has no intention to attack, though its fears could in time inspire one; and China, for the present, has no capacity to expand although its fears, as much as its ambitions, could in time cause it to create one. It behooves both to cast off, as the United States has recently shown signs of doing, the theological rigor and exaggerated fears of the past and by much more active measures of contact and communication begin to create a more rational relationship, based on interest rather than emotion, which would lead away from an unnecessary and calamitous conflict.

CHAPTER 5

The Crisis of Modernization and the North-South Confrontation

The Neglected Billions

Until a few years ago historians generally ignored the two-thirds of the world's people who live in Asia, Africa, and Latin America. They were discounted either as docile subjects of European empires, as degenerate offspring of extinct civilizations, as backward country cousins, as "little brown brothers," or as "lesser breeds without the law."

Since World War II these 2 billion people have recaptured control of their continents and re-entered history. China with 700 million people, while still convulsed by revolution, has recovered vitality and pride and will eventually recover power. India with 500 million, Indonesia with 100 million, Pakistan with another 100 million are free, obstreperous, prodigious and stretched almost to the breaking point. Latin America, after long hibernation, with a population grown from 120 to 250 million in the last thirty years, is also moving from the era of coup d'état to the era of revolution. Africa, another 300 million, could claim only three independent countries in 1939 and now boasts thirty-nine. Altogether, since 1945, there are sixty newly independent nations on the globe, and the population of Asia, Africa, and Latin America combined has grown from 1.5 billion to 2.5 billion.

Almost every country in each of these continents, having suddenly emerged from the eighteenth or nineteenth century into the twentieth, is undergoing a traumatic crisis of modernization. The question in each of them is whether it can cast off an old structure and create a new one adapted both to modern technology and to the special character of its people, whether it can within a short span of years evolve not only a new society but a new soul.

The task is compounded by three confrontations, which in the liberated and developing countries coincide with the crisis of modernization and with each other. The first is the residual confrontation with "Western imperialism." It is manifested, in the case of recently liberated nations, in the ambivalent, love-hate relationship with the former colonial power whereby the new nation at the same time resents as neocolonialism any vestigial presence of the ousted master, no matter how mutually useful, and yet proudly displays his culture and insistently demands his help. This obsolete kind of confrontation and this ambivalence are also found to some extent in areas which have long been free, such as Latin America, and others which have not been formally colonized, such as Eastern Europe, in their relationship with the dominant Great Power of the region, the United States and the U.S.S.R. respectively.

The second kind of confrontation is of course the reverberation in the Third World of the contest between West and East, between permissive and totalitarian societies, which has been described in the preceding two chapters. Intrusive competition between the two power blocs tends politically to distort and economically to accelerate the process of modernization in the underdeveloped world. Where it takes military form, it may distort and accelerate geometrically, or it may go so far as to ravage and retard.

The third confrontation, still provisional and incoherent, is that between North and South, between all or most developed countries, capitalist, socialist or Communist, and all or most underdeveloped countries. This impending confrontation also tends to be predominantly, though with some reassuring exceptions, between people with white and people with colored skins.

If the human race is wise, it will spare itself this third confrontation while it still can. But if the North continues to be greedy, complacent, and callous, and the South becomes ravenous and desperate, this one could be the most universal and the most calamitous of all.

The Revolution of Rising Expectations

"To know how to free oneself is nothing," said André Gide; "the arduous thing is to know what to do with one's freedom."

The most conspicuous recent happening in the underdeveloped world has been liberation from colonial domination, the appearance of sixty new nations in two decades. Political freedom is, however, to some degree only a superficial manifestation of the much more profound and consequential underlying phenomenon which has been aptly labeled the "revolution of rising expectations." These expectations are political, social, economic, racial and cultural, as well as national, and together they may set all, as they have already set part, of the world afire. In fact it is probable that many of the national structures in which this revolution is now emerging will not be able to contain or survive it.

The common man of the poor country often has a per capita annual income of little more than $100, sometimes less. In past centuries he never had more and never expected more. In the past he never had anything to say about his government, except the government of his village and perhaps of his tribe; he never expected to have anything to say about the rest. In the past he lost half his children in their infancy and was likely to die himself well before his prime; neither he nor they had any education other than in his craft and custom. There had rarely been reason to expect it could be otherwise, except for the handful who with tooth and claw fought their way to the top of the heap.

In recent decades this poor Asian, African, Latin American, particularly if he is an urban dweller but to some extent wherever he lives, has seen with his own eyes and has been told by his new leaders that those iron disabilities are no longer necessary or legitimate. He has seen the ubiquitous white man, master, trader, tourist, living in casual, seductive opulence; he has gathered from the white man's movies, magazines, and advertisements that elsewhere this opulence is shared by almost everybody; he has observed at home that it is increasingly accessible to the fortunate or unscrupulous among his compatriots. He has found that he and his children need not die so soon or live so miserably, that they can have water in their fields, light and radio in their huts, that they can learn to read and drive a car, that they can influence government by voting, rioting or fighting, that they can even sit behind a desk and tell their erstwhile peers to go to hell.

These are intoxicating discoveries, particularly for the young people who make up more than half the population of poor countries, and most of all for the students who in some of them, because of the dearth of trained people, constitute almost a new governing class. These insistent expectations, moreover, are not easily or soon appeased. As Robert Heilbroner points out: "Economic development in its early stages is not a process of alleviating discontent. Initially it is a cause of deepening it."

The burden of the discontent falls in the first instance on the new political leaders who assumed the responsibility for the new freedom, who have almost invariably promised too much, and who even if they have not, cannot conceivably deliver a fraction of what is expected and demanded. Yet whenever they do not deliver "enough," whatever that may prove to be in each case, they risk being vilified, crucified, destroyed. Some meet their inability to deliver bread by providing circuses—political excitement, ideological nostrums, mass delirium, fratricidal or xenophobic witchhunts. Yet here too the new statesman is caught between the upper and nether millstones, for unless he can produce a constructive as distinguished from a symbolic mobilization, unless he can break the cake of rural custom and apathy, his political circuses will eventually bring about a Thermidoran reaction against himself without more than momentarily containing the sea of rising expectations.

The social, economic and political obstacles to solid achievement are indeed appalling. In many underdeveloped countries, including the largest, population is still expanding faster than resources; desperate efforts succeed only in keeping standards of living at current pitiful levels; birth control, while at last admissible, is still stubbornly resisted and will at best take some years to have a perceptible impact. Even though diets are grossly inadequate and food supply is falling even farther behind population, agriculture remains the most hidebound of human pursuits and the most recalcitrant to revolution. Basic infrastructure, the roads, electric power, and irrigation that is indispensable to all development, is the most difficult to finance because it is so massive and its return so slow and so oblique. Already suffocating cities are flooded with the human surplus of the countryside, which in the rudimentary state of industry finds no employment and squats sullenly in shantytowns.

Three-quarters of the population in many countries are illiterate and half of those of school age are still denied schooling. What schooling there is, after the elementary grades, tends to be academic rather than practical, classical rather than technical; the same bias persists in the rare universities which produce a superfluity of lawyers attracted to politics and an insufficiency of engineers and agriculturalists willing to dirty their hands. A consequence is white-collar unemployment and unrest over and against a dearth of technicians required for development; of those fortunate enough to study abroad, some return with indigestible alien doctrines and many do not return at all.

Economic development, political democracy and national identity are each inhibited by the backwardness and inertia of the rural masses and by the arrogance and dilettantism of much of the elite. The traditional gap between masses and elite impedes effective and necessary social mobilization. In Communist countries the inhibiting factors are dealt with by the regimentation and intoxication of the masses, by the extinction of one elite and the fabrication of another; but the regimentation tends to loosen and the intoxication to wear off; either the new elite devours itself or it acquires the vices of the old. Elsewhere the problems of social mobilization and transitional political form are met by more or less ingenious improvisations: parliamentary systems representing in fact only tacitly allied new and old elites, single-party dictatorships with or without elements of democracy inside the party, charismatic leaders manipulating a single dominant party or maneuvering agilely among several competing parties, military leaders moving into a political bedlam as the only force strong or neuter enough to maintain domestic order and national identity, usually at the cost of prolonging social stagnation. None of these expedients has succeeded, or could succeed, in overcoming quickly the terrifying complex of problems with which the new countries are faced.

If too many indigenous leaders fail to meet these problems, whether from lack of means, will, or wisdom, the anger of the deprived 2.5 billion—all too soon to be 3 billion or more—is likely to be deflected to the peoples of Europe and North America whose aid and markets, it will be passionately believed, hold the keys to the kingdom of heaven but which are being callously, cynically and intolerably withheld.

Intrusion, Alignment, and Nonalignment in the "South"

The policies of the developed and underdeveloped countries toward each other are often equally confused, ambivalent and fantastic. In the case of the former, intrusion alternates with indifference, conspiracy with fraternization, and humanitarianism with self-righteousness—a description that applies to both Communist and Western states.

The Communists acquired from the writings of their prophets an oversimplified view of the evolution and vulnerability of the Third World. After the Russian and Chinese Revolutions had contradicted the Marxist thesis that capitalism would first and most easily be overthrown in highly industrialized states, doctrine swung to the other extreme and held that the "colonial" or "rural" areas, which were assumed to comprise the whole world outside Europe and North America, were all ripe for revolution. Stalin cherished this view at one time, and Lin Piao still does.

In accordance with standard Leninist practice and as occasion offered, the Soviet Union since the 1920s and the Chinese comrades since the 1950s have been giving a push to the "wave of the future." The extent to which they could do so has often been exaggerated by their Western adversaries, but they have on the whole been as assiduous as their resources and local circumstances have permitted. Their activities have ranged over a wide gamut: the fraternal celebration of Afro-Asian solidarity, massive military and economic aid, the "higher education" of the youth of Asia and Africa, the promotion of revolution through Communist parties and their protegés, the instigation and support of "wars of national liberation."

The behavior of the West toward the Third World has been equally diverse and ambivalent. Sometimes former colonial powers are so disgusted with what seems to them the incorrigibility or the insolence of their erstwhile charges that they cut them off completely, as the French did with Guinea. More often, particularly if they have important economic interests in the liberated country, they seek to maintain a significant, though preferably not too expensive, influence there.

The United States and, to a lesser extent, some European countries and Japan have not only promoted traditional private investment in those parts of the Third World where private investors can be persuaded to go but also have, either bilaterally or through international agencies, made available vast amounts of economic aid of every conceivable kind to poor countries everywhere. While statistics are debatable, among other reasons because of varying definitions of "aid," it seems safe to say that since World War II the United States has extended to underdeveloped states economic aid worth at least $45 billion, and Europe and Japan have given aid worth about $30 billion.

It must be admitted, however, that just as the Marshall Plan was politically viable only as a response to the threat of Communist seizure of Europe, so the lion's share of Western aid to underprivileged countries has been prompted by Communist ambitions and practices. Indeed, thus far the confrontation between East and West has unhappily been the main governor of all "Northern" policy toward most of the Third World. In stimulating the participants, the confrontation has of course profited the underdeveloped states by vastly increasing both economic and military aid over what they would probably otherwise have received. But there is an all too close resemblance between the recent history of parts of Asia, Africa and Latin America—unwisely turned into arenas of the Cold War and wracked by their own revolutions—and the turmoil in the Greece of Thucydides or the Italy of Machiavelli.

There has been an extravagant rivalry between the Cold War protagonists in the more conspicuous and politically sensitive aspects of economic development. There has been an unhealthy stimulation of the tendency of new countries, like old, to engage in arms races against each other, through the competitive provision by East and West of expensive and unnecessary military assistance. Still more disruptive has been the underground warfare waged between the clandestine organizations of the participants in the Cold War and their local clients, aggravating in these already turbulent regions the techniques of conspiracy, subversion, purge, assassination, and coup d'état that had been so ruinous to Greece and Italy at the height of their glory, to Tsarist Russia through most of its history, to the Soviet Union in the heyday of Stalin, and to Mao's China at the present time.

Necessarily the underdeveloped countries have built up certain antibodies for coping with these formidable intrusions. We have already mentioned the anticolonialist animus which operates so severely against the West, often long after any reason for it has passed.

There was originally in underdeveloped countries a rather innocent receptivity toward Marxist socialism because many of their leaders had been attracted to it in their student days, because it was the enemy of the "imperialist" bogeymen, because socialism of some sort seemed inescapable for countries with so little private capital of their own, and because Russia and China seemed such impressive examples of poor countries that had lifted themselves by their own bootstraps. While some residue of these impressions obviously remains, and of course some is justified, the original ardor has substantially cooled. The achievements of the Soviet Union and particularly of China look today considerably less relevant and attractive than they once did. Even more disillusioning has been the experience of newly independent governments with Communist machinations involving the indoctrination against them of their own students, subvention of their political opponents, and the organization of coups d'états and guerrilla wars.

As previously noted, these Communist excesses, in certain cases the fact or threat of overt armed aggression, have caused some underdeveloped countries on the peripheries of Russia and China to enter into military alliances with the West and have introduced there a conspicuous and persistent Western presence for which the Communists have no one to blame but themselves. One country remote from the Communist sphere, and only one, Cuba, has reacted in the opposite sense but for much the same reason. Castro's communism, insofar as it has external origins, is less an ideological conception or a pro-Soviet inclination than an impulsive backlash to an excessive and discriminatory intrusion by the United States.

For the most part, however, the Third World has responded to the encroachment of the Cold War by what it calls "nonalignment." A profound skepticism has grown up concerning the purity and disinterestedness of the lofty ideals advertised by all protagonists in the war. A tendency, maddening to dedicated Cold Warriors, cynically to equate the policies of both sides has become manifest. The preferred tactics of most of the Third World is more and more ostentatiously to stand aloof from East-West confrontations of all kinds and even reluctantly to attenuate goals of their own, such as United Nations peace-keeping, if these become the subject of major controversy among the Great Powers. Emphasis is placed more and more on clearly identifiable national interest, and on whatever degree of intramural solidarity among underdeveloped states, regional, continental or universal, can be expediently hammered out from time to time. None of this, of course, inhibits most of these states from maintaining relations of varying degrees of cordiality with both West and East or, more important, from using either an uncommitted posture to extract the maximum amount of aid from both or an indecisively committed posture to inflate constantly the aid demanded from one or the other.

The intrusions of the Cold War into the Third World and the distortions thereby produced follow certain simple, easily distinguishable patterns. Overt military intervention or persistent armed insurrection inspired by one Cold War protagonist usually causes the nations attacked to ally themselves with or to seek military assistance from the other. Thus in the Far East, South Korea and South Vietnam allied themselves bilaterally with the United States, Thailand and the Philippines joined SEATO, Laos associated itself closely with the United States, and Malaysia with the United Kingdom; in the Near East, Turkey joined NATO and CENTO, and Iran CENTO. A few countries, even though subject to persistent insurrection, such as Burma and Cambodia, judged it safer, because of their proximity to China and their pessimistic estimate of the future of their region, to persist in nonalignment.

Nations of Asia and Africa more distant from the Communist periphery were basically anchored to nonalignment but drifted expediently in one direction or the other, depending on accidents in their history or inclinations of their leadership. Several which had had especial difficulties in liberating themselves from their European masters, such as Algeria, Indonesia, Guinea, Mali, leaned predominantly though not conclusively to the East for longer or shorter periods. Other factors caused a similar response elsewhere. The creation and patronage of Israel by the West induced an eastward bias in Egypt and Syria and from time to time in Iraq. A dictator's dreams of glory in Ghana, an excess of neocolonialism in Congo Brazzaville, territorial disputes with Western-oriented neighbors in Somalia, proximity of Tanzania to vestigial white domination in Rhodesia, Mozambique and South Africa, brought about similar expedient affiliations with the East in those cases.

On the other hand, Afro-Asian states which had experienced inordinate, even if clandestine, Communist intrusion, or states apprehensive of neighbors which had become to some degree Communist clients, took refuge in circumspect associations with the West. Such a reaction was manifest in Cameroon, in Morocco, in the Ivory Coast and other neighbors of Ghana and Guinea, in Saudi Arabia, Jordan and occasionally Lebanon, which felt themselves threatened by Soviet-armed Egypt. The former Belgian Congo gyrated wildly, first reacting against what seemed an excessive residual Belgian presence, then against an excessive Eastern orientation by Lumumba, then against fragmentation promoted on the one hand by Tshombe and on the other by rebels armed by radical African states, then once more against a too predominant Belgian interest. Other states, reacting to overzealous and clumsy intrusions, also dramatically readjusted their orientation. Indonesia swung about several degrees as a consequence of a misfired Communist coup; Algeria and Ghana overthrew their Leftist dictators; Guinea expelled first Easterners and then Westerners. Pakistan allied itself solidly with the West for support against an India which seemed under Soviet protection, but drifted toward Peking when the West, in response to China's attack on India, rallied to India's support. The relapse of the Near East into open war in 1967 warrants a few specific remarks about that region.

After World War I, many of the Arabs felt defrauded of their liberation from the Ottoman Empire by the imposition of British and French "mandates" on Palestine, Iraq, Syria and Lebanon and by the maintenance of British power in Egypt. Most of these vestiges of imperialism were removed, voluntarily or involuntarily, shortly after World War II, but they were replaced, in the Arab view, by the enforced introduction of Israel into their midst and the exile and impoverishment of a million Palestine Arabs.

The creation of Israel was regarded by the Arabs as merely a new manifestation of Western imperialism, particularly since most of the early Zionists were European with a European attitude of superiority and even arrogance vis-à-vis the Arabs. The presence of a million refugees in Arab countries kept the issue fresh and burning; the three stunning Israeli military victories in 1948, 1956 and 1967 were deeply humiliating to the Arabs and, while reducing their power, magnified their resentment.

Israel, a mere 2.5 million souls surrounded by 50 or 60 million hostile Arabs, felt obliged, rightly or wrongly, to seek security through military power and close association with the West, particularly the United States. The alternative of compromise and accommodation with its Arab neighbors, which might or might not have been possible, was never really tried. Israel's association with the West eventually drove many of the Arab states into corresponding association with the East, though intra-Arab vendettas from time to time disordered this pattern. Both sides, supplied and emboldened by their Western or Eastern patrons, rejected all concessions that were not forced on them, equipped themselves with great quantities of ever more sophisticated arms, allowed emotion and fear, more than real interest, to govern their policies toward each other, and every decade went again to war.

Because of their associations and commitments, Great Powers were always liable to be drawn in, and a tragic Near Eastern confrontation to become a disastrous global one. The extravagant arming of the Near Eastern states by their respective patrons steadily aggravated the fears of the former and the involvement of the latter. The events of June 1967, a war which was inherent in the festering stalemate but which neither side sought at the time, yet which automatically ranged the United States and the Soviet Union against each other, illustrated once again the perils of strong states conferring on weaker ones, to which they are committed but which they cannot control, the power to start "domino" confrontations and risk "domino" wars. The lesson of 1914, when Russia placed its fate in the hands of Serbia, Germany of Austria, France of Russia and England of France, has not yet been taken to heart.

Another shopworn lesson of the events in the Near East is that military victory is all too likely to generate, not a climate of peace, but more insatiable expectations among the victors and more insatiable resentment among the vanquished. It is still as unclear as ever how long either the Great Powers or the peoples of the Near East themselves will tolerate this endless sterile conflict, which frustrates the legitimate expectations of all in the area and jeopardizes the security of everyone elsewhere.

Latin America constituted a rather special case. The central feature of intra-hemisphere relations continued to be the ambivalence of all the rest of it to the enormously preponderant United States. On the one hand, the Latin Americans feared Yankee domination and abhorred Yankee intervention; on the other, they sought and welcomed fraternal association and manageable aid and investment. Relations were complicated, first, by the crisis of modernization and of rising expectations and, second, by the extension to the hemisphere of the East-West confrontation. The first produced a new magnitude of social ferment, a new crop of insurrections and, in response, the Alliance for Progress, the impact and success of which are still far from certain. The second exacerbated the crisis, disaffected much of Latin America's university youth, established an expensive and unreliable but prestigious Soviet satellite ninety miles from the United States, provoked successful American interventions in Guatemala and the Dominican Republic and a disastrously unsuccessful one in Cuba, unsettled the inter-American security system, threatened to trigger a nuclear war, and created an enduring trauma inside the United States.

The overriding consequence of these intrusions and responses in the Third World over a period of twenty years was to raise the cost of intrusion to both sides and enhance the popularity of nonalignment. Communist military intervention, even in the veiled form of "wars of liberation," proved increasingly costly and counterproductive. American military interventions, while they might succeed in their immediate purpose as in the Dominican Republic or be welcomed by those threatened with Communist expansion in East Asia, provoked a widely hostile reaction, which seemed likely to deepen the more such interventions occurred. A serious question already exists whether political gains at the point of intervention may not be more than outweighed by political losses on a regional or global front. On the other hand, Soviet efforts to capitalize on the hostility to such intervention by seeking sweeping condemnation of it from the U.N. General Assembly were to some degree thwarted by the insistence of most members on inserting into the draft resolutions, before adopting them, clauses also and equally condemning the forms of indirect intervention to which the Communists are prone. It was more and more clear that the Third World was going to be less and less willing, to the extent it could help itself, to tolerate any form of intervention.

Similarly, military alliances embracing underdeveloped countries tended to wither away as and when the pressure which had generated them relaxed, or sometimes even when it did not. This was the fate of both CENTO and SEATO. Farther away from the Communist periphery, an American endeavor in the late 1950s to organize a regional system in the Near East under the Eisenhower Doctrine never got off the ground—indeed, played a part in provoking in several countries violent spasms of national self-assertion, which in turn involved the United States in the unnecessary landing of marines in Lebanon. Repeated Sino-Soviet endeavors to muscle in on Afro-Asian and nonaligned groups in order to manipulate them against the West were on the whole equally abortive and eventually foundered on the shoals of Sino-Soviet rivalry.

In the bright dawn of liberation the new countries were plunged not only into a "neocolonial" confrontation, partly imaginary, and the backlash of the East-West confrontation, all too real, but also into a sea of internal troubles. We have noted those that proved too much for Ngo Dinh Diem, that prevent India from playing the role to which her size and civilization entitle her, that swept the unhappy Congo in six years from Lumumba to Kasavubu to Adoula to Tshombe to Mobutu, and that toppled Ben Bella and Nkrumah from their high seats. In addition to the latter three upheavals, the military swept the civilians from power in Egypt, Pakistan, Burma, Syria, Indonesia, Nigeria, Sudan, several French African and a considerable number of Latin American states, and were prevented from doing so in Kenya, Tanzania, Uganda, and Gabon only by the solicited and timely intervention of the former colonial power.

These are only the most conspicuous of the almost innumerable coups, countercoups, and convulsions in the Third World, some peaceful, some bloody, some shifting only the cast on the political stage, some changing fundamentally the theme and purpose of the national drama. Most of them arise from the impossibility of satisfying in a short span of years even modest expectations that have been raised by liberation and technology, from the absence in most of these countries of both politically sophisticated and technically trained elites, and from the Niagara of social problems engendered by sudden, unplanned and often involuntary modernization.

Finally, political order and morale in the African states were profoundly disturbed by the survival in the southern part of the continent of the last considerable remnants of true colonialism and of white minorities not only governing but oppressing black majorities. The black elites of the rest of the continent considered these survivals to be such an intolerable affront to their dignity that their energies were heavily preoccupied and their relations to Western states substantially warped by persistent but frustrated efforts to bring these outrages to an end.

The "North" Reassesses Its Role

The experience of twenty years with the complexities, extravagances and frustrations of the Third World induced in both East and West an "agonizing reappraisal" of their role there, the outcome of which was still by 1968 in gravest doubt. Certainly Moscow, and even to some degree Peking, must have lost many of its illusions about the ardor and speed with which the underdeveloped nations would fall into the arms of communism. The balance sheet of these two decades showed one Communist regime, North Korea, which had been set up during a Soviet military occupation; one, North Vietnam, which had captured the national liberation movement against a colonial master and had established itself in that guise; and one, Cuba, which had come to power in conventional Latin American fashion and subsequently, more to spite the Yankees than for any ideological reason, taken on Communist trappings. Out of 90-odd nations in the Third World, that was all—just three.

Moscow and its East European allies, if not Peking, also became more uncomfortably aware as time went on of the expense of subsidizing the insatiable military establishments and Five Year Plans of undependable Asian and African "friends." The U.S.S.R. alone extended economic aid in the amount of over $6 billion in the period 1954–67, including, to give one unproductive example, about $375 million to Indonesia. Popular opinion in the Soviet Union and Eastern Europe found these burdens excessive for states which are themselves still less than fully developed and whose consumers are only just beginning to savor the benefits of decades of self-denial.

Two serious aspects of international relations also affected the Communist attitude toward the Third World. One was that East-West confrontation there, if carried beyond aid programs and clandestine byplay into revolutionary action, tended to face the Communists with an uncomfortable dilemma. The West's command of most of the world's lines of sea and air communication and its superior logistic capability meant that it could much more easily and rapidly apply preponderant power at any threatened point. The Communist leaders were thereupon obliged, if they had sparked the confrontation, either to abandon their local clients and withdraw ignominiously or to escalate the episode to the strategic level and threaten general war. Neither alternative was attractive, and only in the case of Cuba did they resort to the second. Indeed, Communist governments, in contrast to the United States, have very rarely dispatched their military forces outside their own territory or that of their immediate allies. (In revolutionary situations adjacent to their borders, such as Greece, Korea, and Vietnam, the Communist powers did not suffer from the same logistic disabilities and could fight either directly or by proxy, without themselves posing a strategic question.)

Finally, and this was a countervailing element, the Sino-Soviet split vastly complicated the equation by causing a passionate intramural competition between the two powers both for the allegiance of Communist parties everywhere and for influence with nonaligned governments. The Soviets therefore felt obliged to play a more active role in East-West competition in some parts of the Third World than they might otherwise have done. Of course, the external failures of the Chinese in 1965 and their internal crisis of 1966–67 tipped the balance heavily, though perhaps temporarily (for the Russians are after all a white people), in the Soviet favor.

The West, also moved by some of the same considerations as the Soviets, engaged in the mid-1960s in a reappraisal of its attitude toward the Third World. It is never easy to persuade parliaments and taxpayers to spend large sums of money over a long span of years for the benefit of foreigners. In many ways it was most remarkable that the West had been willing during the period 1945–67 to give or lend, bilaterally or multilaterally, in cash or in kind, economic aid to underdeveloped nations in the impressive sum of approximately $75 billion.

As we have noted, however, this huge and commendable effort

was neither as philanthropic nor as self-denying nor as sufficient as was often claimed. Insofar as the United States was concerned, most of the aid was extended in the belief that it was required to compete successfully with communism in the underdeveloped countries, to develop there sufficient economic and political stability so that Lin Piao's dream of a revolutionary Third World engulfing the West would not be realized, and hence essentially to protect the security of the United States. Much of U.S. aid was in the form of agricultural surpluses, which, as long as they lasted, it was in its interest to get rid of. Much of American and most of European aid was, moreover, in the form of currency or credit expendable only in the donor country (where prices incidentally were often higher than elsewhere) and hence profitable to the economy of the donor as well as of the recipient. Finally, much European aid, particularly French and British, was supplied to their former colonies primarily with a view of maintaining prestige and influence there; other European "aid" was provided under such onerous credit terms that it became in fact, to the extent it was repaid, a profitable commercial transaction.

Although the U.N. General Assembly in designating the 1960s as the "Development Decade" called on all developed countries to contribute annually during that decade 1 per cent of their national income to economic aid to less developed countries, few developed countries ever complied with that injunction. Indeed, their aid during this decade tended to show a proportionate decline at the very time that their national income was rising substantially. For example, although total U.S. economic aid (according to OECD data) rose from $3,530 million in 1961 to $3,730 million in 1965, this was an actual decline, as a proportion of national income, from 0.83 per cent to 0.67 per cent. Meanwhile, Congressional appropriations for the Agency for International Development averaged $2,423 million in fiscal years 1961–63 and only $2,219 million in 1964–66. The fiscal 1967 appropriation was even lower, at $2,143 million. Of this amount, the United States was planning to spend $525 million, nearly one-quarter, for economic aid for Vietnam, which did not help the other underdeveloped countries. It seems almost certain, as this is written, that U.S. economic aid in fiscal 1968 will be even further reduced and that aid for Vietnam will be a larger proportion of it. Percentages of national income devoted to foreign aid by developed countries in 1965 were calculated by the OECD as follows: United Kingdom, 0.6 per cent; West Germany, 0.5 per cent; Japan, 0.4 per cent; United States, 0.7 per cent; and France 1 per cent.*

The increasingly wealthy countries, therefore, could hardly claim that they were straining themselves to meet the imperative economic requirements of the other two-thirds of the world. It has often been pointed out that what they devoted annually to this end was a very small fraction, usually less than 5 per cent of their military budget, and was also less than their citizens expended annually for either cigarettes, liquor, cosmetics, or similar attributes of gracious living. Furthermore, while the underdeveloped countries were often unrealistic in their judgment of the amounts of foreign aid they could effectively use at any given time, experts estimated that they could in the aggregate easily and profitably use—indeed desperately needed—at least $3 billion more annually than they have been receiving in recent years.

It is only fair to say, however, that the West, like the East, has some reason to be disillusioned with the achievements of its aid effort so far, some reason to question whether the massive enlargement of that effort, to which it is always being exhorted, would be either effective or in its own vital interest. Critics of massive aid cite the following arguments, which are not of course all cited by the same critics or all consistent with each other.

First and foremost, it is alleged with considerable logic that as long as population in many underdeveloped countries is permitted to grow at the present fantastic rate, feasible development, even with greatly increased foreign aid, could barely keep pace with population increase. Hence aid does not improve living standards, meet rising expectations, permit modernization or enhance political stability, and is therefore merely pouring money down the drain. Second, in the same connection, it is pointed out

* These figures would be even lower if developed countries used percentages of gross national product, as the United Nations has now recommended, as their target for economic aid.

that fundamental progress is impossible in most underdeveloped countries without radical improvement in agricultural productivity and that many governments and most farmers have so far been unwilling to take the drastic measures required for such improvement. Third, it is argued that nationalism and chauvinism are so intense in many underdeveloped countries that, not only is foreign private investment discouraged by punitive discrimination, but also the governments extending aid are prevented from exercising such control over its use as alone would assure its efficacy. Implicit in this argument is the fourth, borne out by all too frequent experience, that the governments of new countries have often, through delusions of grandeur, faulty economics, inexperience or rampant venality, wasted or misappropriated a substantial part of foreign assistance, as well as domestic resources.

A fifth allegation is that privileged classes, military cliques, or traditional customs are so deeply entrenched that it is impossible to carry through the economic and political reforms which alone could permit development to proceed on a sound basis and foreign aid to be used in the interests of the mass of the people. Sixth, it is claimed with varying motivations that either because efforts are being made to effect these reforms or because they are not, because Communists or militarists or dictators or fanatics have taken over or are about to take over, political instability, civil war, anarchy, communism, fascism are so inevitable and so imminent that aid would be wholly lost or would even profit elements hostile to the donor country. Similarly, and seventh, it is pointed out that when recipients of massive aid, such as India, Pakistan, the United Arab Republic, Israel, and many others, indulge in equally massive military buildups, involving sophisticated equipment and leading to belligerent confrontations and even war, they divert great segments of both foreign and domestic resources which might otherwise have been used for development.

Western governments have for years practiced the benevolent chicanery of solemnly assuring their parliaments that foreign aid is primarily intended to "stop communism" or otherwise promote "hardnosed" national interests and, at the same time, professing

to recipient governments that the same aid is altruistic, unconditional and not politically motivated. This ambivalent posture
is becoming more and more difficult to maintain in both directions.

Electorates in Western countries—tired of annual subsidies for
which little gratitude is expressed and little political profit observed, increasingly skeptical of the annual invocation of the
Communist "wolf," swayed by the array of arguments, both sound
and specious, outlined above—are more and more resistant to
continuing even at lower levels a steady expenditure which seems
to bring no clear and reliable return. The question is increasingly asked whether in hard fact the power of the Third World
for good or ill is not so limited, its conceivable impact on the
strategic balance and on the security of the developed nations
so uncertain and remote, that it could not be safely left to stew
in its own juice.

On the other side, in the new countries, as political mobilization proceeds and sensibilities sharpen, it becomes more and more
difficult for their governments to accept aid on the conditions on
which donors more and more insist, or to tolerate a posture of
dependence in which foreigners conspicuously restrict the exercise of "sovereignty" and interfere in "domestic affairs."

The Somber Prospect

A possibility therefore exists of progressive breakdown in association and communication between the two worlds, of a widening gap not only in living standards and political practice but
in mutual comprehension and tolerance, of a prolonged separation not only in space and color but in time and style. One can
conceive that the pursuit of instant modernization, which both
opinion and survival so often seem to demand, might prove too
much for many of the underdeveloped states and that they might
go down in a welter of warring factions to chronic anarchy or
revolving dictatorship. One can easily imagine in Southern
Africa, for example, a race war, a blood bath of appalling proportions, in which the black majority would assert with a bru-
tality bred of long oppression its demand for equality of status
and power.

Under such circumstances there might emerge a state of the world comparable to that prevailing during the decline of the Roman Empire, an island of affluent but withering civilization surrounded by a sea of ravenous, multiplying and encroaching barbarians. The new "barbarians" might either be rigidly organized and inspired by some evangelistic doctrine, in accordance with the dream of Lin Piao, or might simply be split into a confusion of hostile tribes and petty tyrannies from which the contagions of brutalization and reinvigorated disease would inevitably seep back into the Atlantic redoubt, even if it were stoutly defended.

The peoples of that redoubt might, under these circumstances, react in a variety of ways. They might shut themselves off as best they could from the rest of the world, make themselves self-sufficient at a lower level of affluence, arm themselves to the teeth and use their arms ruthlessly, disown responsibility for the lives and deaths of the "barbarians," and even no doubt in time disavow a common humanity with them. They might, as Wells and Orwell imagined, compete for useless empire over devastated hemispheres. It is quite obvious that such a reaction would soon harden, brutalize and degrade the "civilized" to the level of the "barbarians," and in the realm of the spirit there would be little to choose between them.

Fortunately no such bleak fantasy, though conceivable, is probable. Neither is the native genius of the South likely to be so warped nor the awakened conscience of the North to grow so cold. There is every probability, it is true, that during a crisis of modernization extending over many years, many developing countries will undergo much worse political turmoil and much more human suffering than they have hitherto known. Things are almost sure to get worse before they get better. There is no inherent necessity, however, that they suffer more or struggle longer in this crisis than their forerunners in a Europe which survived the abominations of the industrial revolution and the horrors of two great civil wars.

It is true that the peoples of the underdeveloped world are starting from much farther back, without the accumulations of capital and cadres, without the sophisticated social and political structures, that many of their forerunners enjoyed before they had to face the crisis of modernization. It is also true, however, that the new nations have the advantage of coming to the crisis in a world where the capital and cadres, the social and political structures for meeting it, do in fact exist, even if the first are only insufficiently available and the latter incompletely adaptable. The duration, scope and consequences of the crisis will depend to an extraordinary degree on the role that the affluent states, from which the crisis involuntarily but inescapably flows, will be willing to play in meeting it. They can aggravate it by competitive intrusion, prolong it by pharasaical abstention, or reduce and abbreviate it by provident collaboration.

They will, in the circumstances, be wise to recall the warning of Pope Paul VI in his encyclical "On the Development of Peoples" of March 1967: "When so many people are hungry, when so many families suffer from destitution, when so many remain steeped in ignorance, when so many schools, hospitals and homes worthy of the name remain to be built, all public or private squandering of wealth, all expenditure prompted by motives of national or personal ostentation, every exhausting armaments race becomes an intolerable scandal."

The concluding part of this book will be concerned with how the three current and impending confrontations dealt with in this part, and the much more fundamental challenges described in the first part, may or may not be met in those decades just ahead which will decide the future of man.

Reflections and Conclusions

PART III

Reflections and Conclusions

CHAPTER 6

Where Do We Stand?

The time has come to pull together the threads, to assess the prospects for men and women within the bounds of their nature and their inventions, to draw conclusions about rational and necessary relations among nations, and to point out some partial remedies for our self-induced predicaments.

It is worth repeating again and again, because it has not yet been fully comprehended, not yet felt in our bones, that never before in human history has so much hung in the balance. Never before has it been physically possible for men to achieve at least a material utopia in a few decades; never before has it been both physically and psychologically possible for men in a matter of months or days to come so close to destroying life on this planet, at least to setting back civilization a thousand years.

Albert Camus wrote in *The Fall:* "I'm going to tell you a great secret, my friend. Don't wait for the last judgment. It's taking place every day." In each small daily act of statesmen and ordinary men and women in these critical times, the future is imperceptibly and cumulatively determined, judgment is pronounced on ourselves by ourselves.

Possible Catastrophe

As of today the judgment can hardly be hopeful. Sometimes it seems as though we of the wonderful twentieth century were

determined to act out Thomas Hood's parable of the early nineteenth:

> The vine unpruned and the neglected peach
> Drooped from the wall with which they used to grapple;
> And on the canker'd tree, in easy reach,
> Rotted the golden apple.

Not only does the golden apple rot, but the Damoclean sword
more than ever hangs by a thread. It is common knowledge,
repeated again and again by Presidents Kennedy and Johnson,
that a general nuclear war could cause as many as 100 million
casualties on each side within days or hours. That would be only
the beginning. Many would be stricken and maimed by fallout.
What is most difficult to realize is that, in the closely knit industrial societies of Europe and America, where far more than half
their populations are massed in cities and towns, wholly dependent for food, water, heat, light and medicine on intricate and
vulnerable systems of transport and communications, even the
areas only moderately damaged might be subject to almost total
breakdown under such conditions and incapable of helping those
more massively hit. If half the population were casualties and
more than half the cities destroyed or totally disorganized, it
would be likely that the nation as a whole would be unable to
cope with the situation in any effective or civilized fashion.

Law and order would break down wholly, those city-dwellers
who were alive and capable of movement would pour into the
countryside in desperate and ruthless search for food and water,
diseases of all kinds would break out, production and distribution on all but the smallest and most local scale would halt,
pillage and murder would become the normal way of life. In the
circumstances, which would constitute something much worse
than any historical Dark Age, even the course of human evolution would be distorted. Those fittest to survive would no longer
be the ones adapted to the civilized way of life—the scientists,
the industrial managers, the professionals, the skilled workmen,
the bureaucrats, the artists—but would be precisely those most
unfit for such a life, those that modern society is trying to reform
or root out—the delinquent, the bully, the psychopath, the hood-

lum, the congenital savage. These would be the ones most likely to survive, to be the rulers of what was left of the human race, the progenitors of whatever might come afterward.

Thinking the unthinkable, indeed. Such things are conceivable, you say, but hardly likely. Why not? Statesmen and soldiers are almost daily announcing that under certain circumstances they would be "obliged" to use their fantastic weapons. No doubt they make such statements with a view to maintaining a "credible deterrent." But if one says often enough that he will act or react in a certain way, he creates in his own mind and that of his followers a pattern of expectation which tends gradually to tighten like a vise around him and becomes inescapable. In the present anarchic state of relations among nations, in the present archaic state of human behavior, there can be no reliable barrier to resort in time of desperate crisis, when personal and collective prestige, "national honor," and entrenched habits of thought may be governing, to the full arsenal of arms that lies at hand. The opportunities, moreover, for genuine misunderstanding, miscalculation, misreading of a gesture intended to be only admonitory or of an accident not intended at all, are so enormous in the present complexity of international relations that, even if one assumes statesmen are never reckless, eventual catastrophe is all too conceivable.

Assume, however, that while it is conceivable, it is nevertheless avoided. There are still other catastrophes brewing which may prove less evitable. Suppose that the population explosion should proceed merely at its present rate for another ten or twenty years. According to extrapolations of this rate, in 1980 there would be 840 million people in China, 680 million in India, 150 million in Indonesia, 380 million in Latin America, to mention only the most striking increases. Would the governments of these and similarly affected countries, whether capitalist or Communist, whether or not aided to the full extent of foreign capabilities, be able to avert the starvation of millions of people, disorders and revolutions, the breakdown of organized society and morality which would follow famine on that scale? Even if famine is held to "acceptable" proportions, what about the effect on international as well as domestic order of the frustrated expectations of hundreds of millions of angry and armed proletariat, what chance of security for the rich and complacent leisure class in the North?

Another nightmare is that portrayed in varying but similar terms by H. G. Wells, Aldous Huxley, George Orwell and many others. The nightmare of a world in which miracles of genetic manipulation and psychological conditioning, devised by the biologists and the psychologists with the purest of intentions but exploited by the publicists, drug manufacturers and communications media, would be taken over by governments with an appetite for power and used to produce a race of docile robots, perfectly endowed with whatever servitude their test-tube manufactured elite might choose to apply. Pure fantasy, of course, but with just enough truth in it to be frightening.

More likely than any of these one-dimensional catastrophes would be a gradual universal degradation partaking of all of them. One might, in this sad spectrum, foresee a general failure of courage, trust and hope among both developed and underdeveloped peoples, a dissolution of such international organization and common purpose as have been evolved, an intensification of national and ideological passions and rivalries, a proliferation of nuclear weapons among two or three dozen major states and a multiplication of conventional arms among others, a world rigidly divided between callous "haves" and desperate "have-nots" more loosely divided among an ever-growing, ever-shifting host of artificial nationalisms, and a never-ending series of wars of conquest, wars of liberation, wars of containment, wars of hunger, wars of pillage, wars to make the world safe for this and that, and wars of Jenkins' ear.

How long this might go on it would be hard to say. In many respects the picture does not differ from much of human history and might therefore plausibly be given, like other Dark Ages, a life expectancy of several centuries. However, there are now at least three radically new factors: nuclear weapons, extreme rapidity of transport and communications, sheer weight of numbers. The presence of these factors would seem to make it probable that the phenomena foreseen in the preceding paragraph, if they were permitted to occur, would rather quickly involve most of the world in one or several apocalyptic episodes, which would carry the human race back to the Bronze Age or earlier.

Possible Utopia

Sixty years ago many men and women were confident of continuous human progress under the benevolent auspices of science. Today, in what has been called the age of anxiety, very few are. Too many advertised Utopias have turned out to be slave societies. We remember Eric Hoffer's warning: "When hopes and dreams are loose in the streets, it is well for the timid to lock doors, shutter windows and lie down until the wrath has passed."

Yet never before has it been anywhere nearly so feasible for men, if they will use their heads, discipline their passions, and stick to righteous means, to move into a state of society very close to Utopia. To ignore that golden option, in the name of "realism" or any other shibboleth, would be the height of stupidity. There is a Moroccan proverb which says, "If you want your furrow to be straight, attach your plow to a star." A contemporary American poet, Richard Wilbur, has written:

> What is our praise or pride
> But to imagine excellence and try to make it?
> What does it say over the door of Heaven
> But homo fecit?

There is no need to expatiate at length on the elements of the Utopia that lie at hand. A flood of books every year describe in detail attainable aspects of that fat and pleasant land. Much of it is growing up before our astonished eyes. Much of our indignation at all that is still lacking arises from our knowledge that it need not be, that the absence of excellence is more and more unnecessary.

We could have in the developed countries, after a relatively few years of intelligent and concentrated effort, an economy producing affluence and leisure for all our citizens. We could have even in the vast underdeveloped countries, through an equally vast cooperative venture in modernization, including of course population control in the South commensurate with that in the

North, a sufficiently rising standard of living also to give those peoples assurance of eventual affluence and longevity.

We could have gradually invigorated techniques of democracy in both government and other aspects of social organization, first inside those states with longest experience of this kind but eventually, as economic development permitted more education and freedom, even inside those where democracy has only marginally or never appeared. We could have progressively stronger international organizations, at first with peace-keeping powers sufficient to restrain not only small but great states and to relieve single nations of this dangerous responsibility, with nation-building powers sufficient to bring new states to viability without dependence on East or West, but eventually evolving into what is essential for general security—a single federal government. We could have, without sacrificing wide diversity of belief, custom and structure, a single universal faith in the obligations, brotherhood and destiny of mankind, in a world which can be made habitable by science but can be kept civilized only by man himself.

All these things could be, but they are not likely to be unless we work at them much more rationally, dispassionately and intensively than we now are. We may need a clearer picture of a plausible Utopia to inspire us, but what we need more are guidelines for urgent first steps in that direction. Politics, it is said, is the art of the possible. It is also the art of the indispensable, and any politician who does not have a feeling in his bones for what is necessary, not just this year but five or ten years hence is not likely to survive that long. First steps toward world order must be practical and acceptable, but they must not be so modest and slow that the catastrophes we have foreseen overtake us before the new measures have taken hold. The problem is to determine what has to be done soon and what people will accept soon, and to try to bring the two as close together as possible.

The remainder of this book will address itself to that problem. We shall first set down a few concluding reflections on the underlying forces which account for the insecurity of nations and which, unless consciously and quickly corrected, may soon destroy them. We shall then attempt to lay down, in the light of the whole survey, some simple and practical guidelines for the conduct of international relations in their general aspects, in the geographic areas discussed, and, finally, in the ultimately decisive sphere of international organization.

Reflections on the Sources of Insecurity

There is no reason to believe that the nature of men, any more than that of other animals, obliges them to slaughter their own kind. It is obvious, however, that over many generations habits of pugnacity, of violent and often exorbitant response to threats or supposed threats, have become deeply embedded. Such habits have, since nations existed, governed relations between them. Sometimes these habits are imprinted in neglected or mistreated children; sometimes they are impressed on misguided or abandoned young people; often they are magnified by the obstinacy of old men clinging too long to power in a world they no longer understand; always they are aggravated by persistently indoctrinated national myths and delusions.

The instruments of response through which such habits are expressed internationally—that is, nuclear and other modern weapons—have now become so lethal and so indiscriminate that they no longer, if they ever did, foster the survival of the fittest. On the contrary, these habits and their instruments now threaten the extinction of fit and unfit alike, or perhaps favor the marginal survival of those least adapted to civilization and most to barbarism.

Among animals aggression against their own kind is rarely carried to mortal lengths. Among men it more and more is. The character of modern weapons, which so often take effect out of sight of the user, renders inoperative the deep-seated inhibitions which normally preserve the species by circumscribing the combat. The aviator or missileman, when he impersonally releases a mechanism, has no impression, because he cannot *see* the consequences of his act, of exceeding the bounds not only of humanity but of common sense, of jeopardizing rather than preserving his race.

Salutary mutations in human behavior away from obsolete "warrior virtues" have been occurring for many centuries, and have found human society gradually more and more hospitable to them. If selection remains "natural," these mutations toward virtues more adapted to civilization will persist and dominate. But if the selection is unnatural, for example nuclear, such mutations will have no value or durability.

Faith of any kind has always been a tricky, two-edged affair, hard for men to live without, almost equally hard to live peacefully with. If a man believes something passionately, he can hardly resist preaching it to others; if they prove deaf to his preaching, he is often tempted to impose it by fire and sword. This is even more true of churches and nations.

The old faiths have in the last hundred years so far cooled that they have lost much of whatever effect on international relations they once had. This is fortunate insofar as it has caused the adherents of one religion to stop slaughtering or persecuting those of others. It is unfortunate insofar as compassionate and fraternal ideals of Christianity, Buddhism, Islam and Judaism are able to exercise so little restraint on the unscrupulousness and exorbitance of nations.

Little heed is paid these days to the solemn appeals of religious leaders for peace and brotherhood. Little credit is given such sentiments as that Saint Thomas Aquinas voiced long ago: "We must love equally those whose opinions we share and those whose opinions we reject. For both have made the effort to discover truth, and both, in so doing, have assisted us."

New faiths and ideologies have caused more trouble and shed more blood in the last fifty years than at any time since the seventeenth century. Nazism, an incredible witches' brew of atavism and savagery, proved intolerable and was soon destroyed. But some of the causes which produced it continue to operate, and there are few countries in the Western world where vestiges of it do not persist. They could grow.

The new faith of communism continues to circumscribe the rationality of about a third of the human race. The fact that it is miscalled a science compounds the confusion. Insofar as it is a form of economic organization, it has advantages and disadvantages, depending on the character of the society in which it appears. Insofar as it is a form of political organization, it is at first a revolutionary and later a counterrevolutionary expedient, effective in social mobilization, obstructive to the evolution of democratic government. Insofar as it is a crusading faith and a militant church, seeking to impose itself by force, it has kept the world in turmoil for twenty years and is a threat to everyone's security, including its own.

Fortunately, having mostly material goals, its zeal tends to be subdued as these are approached. In China, and elsewhere among the dispossessed, it continues to fascinate and to fanaticize. In its original habitat, however, Eastern Europe, it is already settling down into a conservative institution with some of the features of a church, some of a giant business corporation, and some of a parvenu aristocracy. Its revolutionary impact is not ended, but it has been blunted and weakened.

The most prevalent and persistent faith of our times, for which most men have most often been ready to die, is nationalism. This passionate attachment to an often accidental and artificial aggregation of men and women has produced great heroism, great cultural achievement, internal stability. In the belligerent xenophobic form it so easily assumes, it has also caused, as Toynbee said, the breakdown of several civilizations and many of the wars, including the two World Wars, which have plagued the world since 1789. It has come in the past fifty years, in relations among nations, to contribute more to the insecurity than to the security of their citizens.

How long the nation-state will exercise its fatal charisma, or how long the human race can stand it, no one can say. Science has already made it in some respects obsolete and may before too long cause it to be superseded. For several more decades, however, it is likely to continue to be, along with human nature and technology, one of the most conspicuous factors governing human affairs.

Science during the past century has substantially revolutionalized both the physical environment and human society. With scientific process still accelerating, the revolution in human affairs during the next thirty years may well be greater than during the past hundred. Human habits, attitudes and institutions have failed to keep up with this dizzy progress. The gap between the two realities, one physical and the other social, is already so great as to cause grievous trouble and danger. It could easily in the next few decades, in a variety of ways, cause disaster. This is particularly true of the relations among nations, which are conducted essentially as they were two thousand years ago and in almost total disregard of how far science has transformed the basic factors and postulates.

To be sure, even the scientists, for all their marvelous ingenuity, do not really understand much better than the laymen either the universe or the new environment they have created. Perhaps they cannot. As one of them, J. B. S. Haldane, has said: "The universe is not only queerer than we imagine—it is queerer than we can imagine."

Many scientists have in effect washed their hands of the world and withdrawn into some "pure" specialty, claiming that nothing else is of comparable importance or is not in any case their responsibility, even if it arises in part from what they have done. Others feel a great and terrible responsibility. "In some sort of crude sense," said Robert Oppenheimer, "which no vulgarity, no humor, no overstatement, can quite extinguish, the physicists have known sin; and this is a knowledge which they cannot lose."

There is some reason for claiming that the pursuit of science, with its requirement of openness and objectivity, is conducive to virtue in the broadest sense. Thus there is still a possibility that scientists may play an increasing part in maturing and civilizing their fellow men.

One of the most significant achievements of science is the solution of the problem of production. In principle, there is no longer any reason why there should not, within a relatively short space of time, be sufficient necessities and too many luxuries for everyone. It is true and ominous that, if population goes on increasing at its present rate, we may all starve or smother. It is also true, however, that if population can be decently controlled, we may all be as rich as Croesus and much happier. This remarkable achievement, once completed, would remove the major rational cause of most of the wars of history—the desire of poor peoples to seize or share the wealth of rich peoples. Of course until it is completed, until the presently widening gap between the impoverished two-thirds and affluent third of the world's population has been substantially narrowed, this cause of war will persist in high degree, however the means to make war may be divided.

At the same time, rivalries between modern economic systems, all of which use in varying ways the same scientific processes, appear more and more artificial and obsolete, less and less an intelligent reason for fear or conflict. Indeed, technological imperatives are causing the various systems more and more to converge and conform. Capitalism is tending to become more "collectivist," communism more "individualist," and the differences between them more political than structural. It is, however, true that both systems have become so caught up in the momentum of weapons-making, in "the military-industrial complex," that many of their managers share an unhealthy vested interest in the continuance of international confrontation and insecurity.

Political systems during the past half century have displayed neither the progressiveness nor the convergence of economic systems. The effect on them of technological imperatives is far less immediate and inescapable. Indeed, one consequence of progress in science and production has been to spawn a gaggle of revolutions which have set back democracy, generated new and fanatical political systems, put in power reckless and psychotic leaders, flung old and new systems at each others' throats.

These confrontations continue in almost every part of the world, though the incompatibility of differing political systems seems a little less total than it did twenty years ago. Even here some intimations of convergence, or at least of mutual toleration, are beginning to appear. Of course, as has happened before, they appear first and most strongly among the common people, rather than among leaders and custodians of dogma. As an historian of the medieval world, Friedrich Heer, has pointed out: "Ordinary people, in the day-to-day circumstances of ordinary life, were practicing co-existence with 'deadly enemies' long before, often centuries before, theologians and ideologists swallowed their scruples and their pride sufficiently to provide the intellectual basis for the religious toleration which the common people had already instinctively adopted."

The most pernicious curse of modern times is the archaic

habit of violence carried over into an era when it no longer serves an evolutionary or a social purpose. This habit is now expressed in weapons so outrageous, so disproportionate, so revolutionary, so fundamentally subversive of human institutions and civilization, that they have long ceased to be rational—have indeed become incompatible with human decency and human survival.

For this reason it is not only a waste but a flagrant abuse of human devotion and talent that so many gifted and vigorous men all over the world, soldiers and scientists, are required to spend their lives multiplying and elaborating arms and armies. These hosts of dedicated men on each side of international confrontations work and prosper solely by virtue of the corresponding diligence and achievement of their counterparts on the other side with whom they compete but on whom they depend. Their reciprocal action and reaction, their natural bias and vested interest, the prestige and sentiment attached to their professions, maintain a perpetual momentum and aggravation of armament which is contrary to the real interests of every nation concerned. This sterile competition has been going on throughout human history, insofar as we know it, but in the last half of the twentieth century, like the pollution of air and water, has become intolerable.

A substantial beginning must be made in the demobilization of soldiers and military scientists, as well as in the reduction and control of arms, if the prevalent insecurity of nations is to be even alleviated, let alone ended. Of course, just as the mobilization and escalation were reciprocal, so must be the demobilization and de-escalation, and that is the rub. The de-escalation, however, requires no more ingenuity than the escalation, and if the same energy, persistence and resources were devoted to the former as are still devoted to the latter, equivalent results could no doubt be obtained.

All these delinquencies, psychoses, crises, confrontations and catastrophes, indeed all the disintegrating forces of the times, were foreshadowed and reflected by the artists and writers of the twentieth century. These brilliant men, however, were far less successful, and too often less interested, in reflecting the extraordinary achievements and opportunities of the age, in foreshadowing the fantastic new order which a sufficient re-enforcement and diffusion of these achievements could bring. Too many of the artists and writers, in an obsession with their own alienation, failure of nerve, a fascination with the very brutalities and disharmonies that had shocked them most, sometimes in cynical exploitation of the public appetite for sensation, have in effect shortchanged their generation and the next.

When he was a very young man, Dylan Thomas wrote to Pamela Hansford Johnson: "On all sides of me, under my feet, above my head, the symbols moved, all waiting in vain to be translated." That of course is the obligation, as well as the rapture, of artists—to translate into fresh but comprehensible language the symbols of their times.

If they translate only the horrors and the abdications—unless that is really all there is—then they fail to nourish the young people who need them most. They "imprint" with folly and despair those who most want heartening and inspiration, they communicate a "death wish" to those just beginning to live, they constrict the choices of all their contemporaries. They leave "waiting in vain" in the shadows, unheeded and untranslated, the symbols men need in these desperate times to generate new faith, build new order, and create an enduringly habitable world.

CHAPTER 7

The Conduct and Misconduct of
International Relations

Systems of Security

The inherent insecurity of nations in the modern environment is such that there may be no safety for mankind except in a fundamental reform, an early supersession, of the nation-state system. The time may be approaching in the world when, as in France in the fifteenth century, in Germany and Italy in the nineteenth and the United States in 1787, only "a more perfect union" of traditionally separate but now interdependent parts will provide enough elbow-room for progress and survival.

It has always been considered utopian to suggest any fundamental change in the international system. More and more one wonders, however, whether there is anything so basically unrealistic as "realpolitik," as the traditional strategy of national egotism, national armaments, alliances, balance of power, deterrence, challenge and response. Certainly, going back in history no farther than the last fifty years, this system has brought no security to its strongest proponents, to Germany, to Russia, to France, to Britain, to Italy, to Japan, to China. It has brought temporary security to the United States only because this country has hitherto been protected by distance and allies, but even the United States is now subject to the loss of half its population in a few hours.

There is a rather awful sense of *déjà vu,* of recurrent night-mare, about all the military and academic plans and studies for achieving security by introducing some new weapons, by reshuffling the jigsaw of alliances in some other way, by fostering bipolarity or multipolarity, balance or imbalance, or by devising cunning new tactics of "crisis management." As if the other side, or other sides, could not and would not be equally ingenious and ruthless. As if science were not fast making all these games obsolete and childish.

The traditional international system has never provided security to nations any more than the feudal system provided security to baronies or principalities or towns. In the latter case, only the introduction of a new and more sophisticated system finally did so.

New political systems of the complexity and magnitude the world now needs will not, even in this age of vertiginous novelty, be built and accepted easily or rapidly. A new international system may first emerge in regional rather than ecumenical form, though there are important respects in which the ecumenical may prove more efficient than the regional. We shall take a careful look at both of them in the final chapter.

On the assumption, however, that, while both new forms exist in embryo and both should be fostered, neither will in the immediate future be decisive in international relations, we shall begin by suggesting some measures whereby the vices of the traditional system might be mitigated and its conduct made safer until it can be effectively replaced.

The first principle on which the foreign relations of states have, behind a screen of pious rhetoric, been conducted is national security and national interest. But what is the real content of these abstract and hallowed conceptions?

Do they really derive from and support the fundamental interests of the individual men, women and children who constitute a nation; their health, their bread and butter, their jobs and housing, their education and equality of opportunity, their civic rights, their freedom to worship and freedom from fear? So often national security and national interest are interpreted in rather mythological terms having to do with glory, honor, grandeur, prestige, or with the "freedom" of peoples who have never been free to do much more than barely subsist, the "way of life" of those who ask not to preserve but radically to change their customary ways. National security and national interest are ideas that need to be very rigorously cross-questioned. The issue is not "my country, right or wrong," but what does my country really need and what do its people really want.

For instance, does power, particularly military power, really enhance national security and national interest; and if so, up to what point? Certainly there are many cases in history in which a people was overwhelmed and subjected because it was defenseless or weak. As long as there is no superior force to protect nations, weak or strong, they must rely on themselves and their allies. But great power may be fully as hazardous as great weakness.

In 1914, and again in 1940, Germany had the most powerful army in the world; at neither time was it used in such a way as to promote the interests or preserve the security of the German people. In 1968, the United States and the Soviet Union have far and away the most powerful military establishments in the world. Are their peoples more or less secure than those of Switzerland or Uruguay? In the event of a "small" war, like that in Vietnam, the Great Powers could not be too badly hurt. The real danger lies in the escalation of a small war into a great one, where they would be the first to be struck and the most likely to be destroyed.

National power, even relatively disinterested power, inevitably provokes fear and eventually more-or-less matching counterforce. Uncontrolled national power, moreover, creates in those who possess it an almost irresistible temptation to use it; but its use, even for seemingly legitimate ends, provokes still more fear and still more counterforce. The law of disproportionate response, triggered by such fears, quickly takes over.

It is rarely clear to governments and peoples up to what point the accumulation and use of power in fact promote their interests and their security. The accumulation and use are never unilateral, are always, when they reach an undefinable point, competitive and provocative. When they reach and pass that point they create national insecurity and impair national interest.

The heart of the problem of the conduct of international relations is the rational and restrained exercise of power. That has always been most true about the exercise of military power. During the past two decades, for the first time in history, that proposition has become conclusively true, since the misuse of military power in its nuclear form could be fatal to the security and interests of all the peoples involved.

The Control of Arms

People are learning to live with modern weapons the way they live with volcanoes, forgetting that, unlike volcanoes, we make weapons and can do away with them whenever we honestly and collectively decide to do so. Of course, this will not be easy. No nation is willing to give up weapons on which it conceives, rightly or wrongly, that its security depends. No nation trusts others to keep agreements they may sign on such a life-and-death matter. No watertight system has been devised of locating nuclear weapons already in existence or preventing the fabrication of more. The same is even more true of chemical and biological weapons.

This is not the place to examine in detail the ways of controlling and eventually limiting these preposterous and seditious arms. What is first necessary is to convince people everywhere that they *are* preposterous and seditious, preposterous because they are so excessive as to cause, if used, what they are designed to cure; seditious because they would, if used, be destructive of all lawful authority, including that of the governments that used them. Once people are persuaded generally that these weapons are not a protection but a plague—a plague like malaria, cancer, pollution, overpopulation, and venereal disease—then the same ingenuity and resources that cured or are curing those plagues, indeed the same ingenuity and resources that created these weapons, can no doubt be as successfully employed to control, reduce, and eventually do away with them.

People and governments must be convinced, however, that the control of weapons of mass destruction must have first, absolutely and indisputably first, priority on the agenda both of international relations and of domestic politics. Such control is not more important than national security—it is *itself* the heart and core of national security. It *is*, however, infinitely more important than world revolution, imperialism, containment, liberation, development, Vietnam, Kashmir, the reunification of Germany, or any other of the great issues of the day which monopolize the time and energies of statesmen, soldiers and legislators.

What is first of all necessary is firm agreement to prevent the further proliferation of nuclear weapons. It is no doubt "unfair" that some nations should have these weapons and others not, that there should be "first- and second-class nations" in this respect, that both, but the latter more than the former, should be limited and controlled in their peaceful use of nuclear energy, that great nations and groups of nations should be denied future "options" on the subject. All this "unfairness," however, pales into insignificance beside the deadly peril to everyone, "first- and second-class nations" alike, if unlimited and uncontrolled proliferation occurs.

It is bad enough to have five fingers on the doomsday trigger; to have twenty or thirty would be intolerable. If there is to be cutoff in proliferation, and there must be, the place and time to act are here and now. All arguments against that overriding imperative, no matter how persuasive, are intrinsically and necessarily secondary. Any government that should take upon itself the responsibility for blocking international agreement on nonproliferation would earn the odium of all mankind, including first of all its own citizens. Not only would the substantive failure to stop further proliferation probably be fatal; the psychological effect of the failure would degrade and envenom the whole range of international relations.

In one essential respect, however, the nonnuclear states are perfectly right. They should not be required to forego these weapons altogether, while the nuclear powers continue compulsively and lavishly to accumulate even more of them, with freedom to use them whenever they choose. It would be hard to imagine, for example, anything so sterile and self-destructive as the deployment of vast antiballistic missile systems by the Soviet Union and the United States. Such systems would almost certainly not save the cities they were built to protect and might indeed multiply the fallout around them; they would almost certainly provoke a powerful demand for vast civilian shelter systems; they would revive the poisonous psychological climate of the Cold War at its worst; they would oblige both governments to expend huge sums at the cost of domestic progress; they would almost certainly in the end, taking account of all these factors, impair rather than sustain the security of each. All that would have been demonstrated would be what is already clear, that there is no such thing as a stable nuclear deterrent, or indeed a stable *national* deterrent of any kind.

What the non-nuclear states have a right to expect in exchange for their renunciation is a serious commencement by the nuclear states in the reduction and control of their arsenals. A non-proliferation treaty would contribute to that end since it should be obvious to the nuclear powers that the treaty could be maintained only if they also soon submitted to some comparable limitations.

What is now required of the nuclear states is agreement at least on the following measures: a cessation of all testing, including underground testing; a cut-off in all production of nuclear materials for weapons use and a rapid diminution of existing stockpiles; a prompt and steady reduction in the deployment of nuclear weapons and missiles wherever they are. What is required of *all* states is agreement on the limitation of conventional arms and armies, on a total prohibition of chemical and biological weapons, and on reasonably effective systems—we cannot expect and should not seek perfect systems—for inspecting and enforcing these agreements.

All these stipulations are contained in one form or another in both the American and Soviet draft treaties which have long been gathering dust in the dossiers of disarmament commissions. What is necessary is that all governments concerned, enjoined by an aroused public opinion, firmly decide that, no matter what the impediments and distractions, comprehensive treaties for all these purposes must be concluded and a substantial beginning made in their implementation within the next five years. Are such comprehensive agreements, limiting national sovereignty in such fundamental respects, realistically conceivable in this short span of time?

If through some hideous accident or miscalculation a hydrogen bomb should explode over a great metropolis somewhere in the world, wiping out a million or more people in a few minutes, a wave of horror and outrage would engulf the world. If the disaster did not automatically set off a nuclear war, there would be a sweeping demand to punish those responsible and to take the most drastic measures to ensure that it did not recur. Many of the same individuals who had previously denounced as impractical and subversive any limitation on national sovereignty or on the use of nuclear weapons would, particularly if their own kith and kin had been incinerated, scream the loudest for the abolition of such weapons or for an effective international authority to control them. What was wholly "unrealistic" one week would become an obvious necessity the next.

It seems a pity that the human race requires the conspicuous sacrifice of many lives before it will take—as in the case of air pollution, automobile accidents, cigarette smoking and nuclear war, for example—the necessary preventive measures. Nevertheless, it may well prove that only after some such catastrophe will nations be willing to entrust themselves collectively with responsibilities none of them can carry alone.

One other point should be made on the question of arms control. It is hard to escape the judgment that aerial bombing, except in close support of ground operations, is becoming a more and more dubious form of warfare on both practical and moral grounds. On the practical side, exhaustive surveys conducted after World War II showed that it had been far less effective in damaging industry and transport than its proponents claimed. Even in total war it has not been decisive without the aid of other arms and without an appalling and probably unnecessary toll of noncombatant lives. German industry was more productive in mid-1944, after being heavily bombed for four years, than in 1940 when the bombing began. Both in Korea and in Vietnam bombing proved incapable of bringing an adversary to his knees or even of interrupting relatively primitive lines of communication. Particularly in its use against people incapable of retaliating in kind, it has proved more of a political liability than a military asset.

As to the moral factor, when bombs from German Zeppelins first killed women and children in World War I, the Allied reaction was that such crimes could be committed only by "the unspeakable Hun." Since that time all of us in "civilized" countries have become accustomed with hardly a qualm to inflicting and sustaining hundreds, sometimes thousands, of noncombatant casualties in a single raid. For this callousness one should certainly not blame the aviators, who are brave and honorable men doing their duty at great risk to themselves, but rather the character of their weapons and the moral climate of their times—that is, the convictions and standards of all of us who dispatch them on their missions and rely on them for our protection.

National Use of Force

There is little need to argue that nations should not start wars. At least since World War I that has become accepted doctrine. Even when the responsibility is as clear as in the case of Hitler's attacks on Poland and the Soviet Union, or North Korea's on South Korea, the guilty government felt obliged to claim that it was acting in self-defense.

Often, of course, the responsibility has been so clouded by provocative action on both sides that it is impossible to determine which really started the hostilities. Experts have been trying in vain for the past fifty years to define aggression. As the United Nations has discovered, it is difficult even to identify a breach of the peace, particularly when a decision to this effect by the Security Council morally obliges its members to follow up with measures of enforcement, which are always embarrassing and often ineffective. The embarrassment is generally avoided by the useful expedient of calling for a cease-fire without assessing guilt. It is relatively easy to determine who refuses to accept, or who breaks, a cease-fire.

Given the experience of the past fifty years, there still is an extraordinary readiness on the part of states to resort to war, or to take action that is so provocative as to make war probable. Over and above the rivalries of superpowers and their allies, the states of the Near East, those of the Indian subcontinent, some African states having territorial disputes are perpetually baiting each other and perpetually on or over the brink of war. The Great Powers, moreover, rightly or wrongly, feel their interests are involved in most of these lesser confrontations and sometimes risk escalating them to great ones by their support of one party or the other.

Every shot fired across a frontier is therefore these days a shot heard round the world. Every clash between states, no matter how small or irresponsible, may contain the seed of World War III. There can be no sure reliance, as the behavior of both dictatorships and democracies bears witness, on the self-restraint of nations and governments. Ambition, fear, prestige, commitments to allies or ideologies are all too often more persuasive than self-imposed inhibitions on the exercise of national power.

This is of course why armaments and alliances exist, but armaments and alliances have not solved the problem. Indeed, as often as not, they have aggravated it: in the case of armaments, by inspiring fear and disproportionate counterarmament; in the case of alliances, by running powder trains from state to state. Alliances gave Austria in July 1914 the power to drag Germany and the whole of Europe into war. Alliances in the 1960s gave a few men in Hanoi the power to create on their remote peninsula a confrontation which involved, directly or indirectly, three of the world's strongest powers and set back for several years an accommodation between two of them which was almost universally desired. The least that should be demanded of alliances is that their members stand together as firmly in mutual restraint as in mutual support, that the strongest partners see to it that no one of the weaker in its own narrow interest drags all the rest into war or jeopardy.

We have earlier asserted that, unfortunate and probably transitory as is the division of three ancient nations, Germany, Korea, and Vietnam, the world cannot in its present inflammable state tolerate that force be used to reunite them or to violate the demarcation lines which divide them, any more than it can tolerate the use of force across frontiers, even when, as in the Near East, Kashmir, some parts of Africa, or along the Oder-Neisse, these frontiers have not been recognized as legitimate by all the parties they circumscribe.

We have also noted the deceptive nature and the grave hazards of "wars of national liberation." In these times of fundamental change in human society the preservation of a status quo that so many of those most concerned wish to modify is neither desirable nor possible. In some cases men have always felt, and no doubt always will, that the status quo is both so entrenched and so intolerable it has to be changed by force. The traditional "right of revolution," however, while it is sure to be frequently applied in internal affairs for many years to come, can no longer be applied in international relations without unacceptable consequences for national and individual security.

This is particularly the case when a so-called war of national liberation is in fact an attempt to impose a new political or social system by force on a nation which is already sovereign and free of foreign domination. This Communist ploy to appropriate the panoply of nationalism and apply it for their quite different ends in Vietnam has deluded a great many people. If the Soviet Union and China, or either of them, should apply, as the Chinese at least have indicated they intend, their technique throughout the vast areas they designate as "rural"—Asia, Africa, and Latin America—the world will remain in turmoil indefinitely and World War III will eventually result. If the Soviet Union genuinely desires, as it well may, a world from which the threat of such war is removed or at least greatly reduced, it must abandon as too dangerous this means of propagating its doctrine, and take steps to ensure that its disciples throughout the world do likewise.

On the other hand, if the perils and limitations of armed insurgency must be recognized by the Communists, the perils and limitations of armed counterinsurgency exercised by anyone other than the international community should, particularly after Vietnam, be recognized by everyone else. Counterinsurgency by the armed forces of states other than the one attacked, even at the request of the victim, even by a state as powerful and relatively as disinterested as the United States, is obviously very hazardous. It risks pitting soldiers of one race and culture against those of another, on ground where the militarily weaker combatant has many advantages, in a manner in which noncombatants are likely to suffer much more than combatants. Sir Robert Thompson, who played a major role in the defeat of insurgency in Malaya and observed it during four years in Vietnam, contends that its essence is political and that a primarily military response to it is bound to be indecisive and to create more problems than it solves. Military counterinsurgency risks arousing as much resentment against the foreign protector as against the domestic insurgent. It is altogether a very chancy business.

Indeed it is becoming rapidly clear that no single nation or group of nations can be safely entrusted with the responsibility either for bringing about peaceful, not to mention violent, change or for interpreting and maintaining international security. With the world as politically divided, physically close-knit and precariously balanced as it is, the exercise of force by a state or group of states either to impose change or to maintain the status quo almost always provokes military counteraction by a rival state or group of states. When Great Powers are involved, and they usually are, an escalation of the use of force on both sides is likely to occur and a great confrontation to take place or be risked.

Thus, the unilateral assumption by states of roles, which in past eras were more or less successfully performed by Rome and by Britain but which in the modern world can probably be carried only by the international community, is likely to jeopardize as much as to re-enforce international peace and security. It is quite true that so far the international community has been insufficiently empowered and equipped to play these roles. The reasonable answer would seem to be to empower and equip it sufficiently.

In the meantime, the only instruments we have, unreliable and inadequate as they are, are the nation-states. For the time being, the world must make do with them as best it can. How may they in the future more rationally conduct themselves in their relations with each other?

National Style and National Discipline

Disraeli once remarked: "A practical politician is one who practices the errors of his predecessors." Too often this is true. It is more popular to pursue accepted errors than to confront novel facts.

On the whole, however, it is advisable, when possible, to determine one's course of action by a judgment of long-range consequences rather than of immediate ends. This is especially the case in the conduct of international relations when impetuosity and miscalculation can have such horrendous results. George Kennan is quoted in Arthur Schlesinger's *A Thousand Days* as saying: "We both know how tenuous a relation there is between a man's intentions and the consequences of his acts. There is no presumption more terrifying than that of those who would blow up the world on the basis of their personal judgment of a transient situation. I do not propose to let the future of mankind be settled, or ended, by a group of men operating on the basis of limited perspectives and short-run calculations."

Among the weaknesses of statesmen and chanceries have been their failure to look ahead, to scrutinize the end of what they are beginning, the degree to which they allow policies of the gravest import, questions of life and death for their citizens, to be determined by the flood of emotional appraisals and pressures which sweep over them at a moment of crisis. Under these circumstances, decisions are all too likely to be set by the character or lack of character of the statesmen and soldiers involved, by their temperamental bias and style, by a sense of personal or political insecurity, which may in the heat of the moment weigh more heavily in the balance than a cool judgment of the welfare of their people.

Even when planning councils exist in foreign offices, they often succumb to the fascination of the day-to-day diplomatic game and neglect the responsibilities for which they were created in favor of heady participation in it. This has been a shortcoming of planners in the U.S. State Department and accounts in part for the American failure sufficiently to foresee new trends in world affairs. It is all too rare everywhere, in past and present, that the costs of alternative courses are weighed soberly and objectively in due time, that policy is wedded to honorable principles which give it dignity and consistency and is operated flexibly but coherently within the framework of those principles.

A significant case in point is cited in a recent essay by a British

Member of Parliament, Evan Luard, wherein he contrasts the effectiveness of the posture of conciliation or appeasement as practiced by Britain and France toward Hitler in the thirties, with the posture of deterrence practiced by the West toward the Communist states since World War II. He remarks first about both of them: "Which type of policy is in fact conducted seems normally to be determined not so much by careful analysis of the circumstances and likely effects as by the mood of the moment and general assumptions inherited from the past." In other words, a posture is likely to be adopted because its opposite is presumed to have failed on an earlier occasion, even though the circumstances may have been and usually were quite different.

Luard goes on to say: "The record demonstrates that neither a policy of conciliation nor one of deterrence can ever be successful if conducted in isolation from the other." Conciliation alone, he argues, will be ineffective or even provocative if the adversary is in fact ambitious and reckless, whereas deterrence alone settles nothing and leaves unresolved explosive issues lying all over the map. Alluding to our present situation, he concludes: "A policy of pure deterrence may be as ill-conceived in this case as a policy of pure conciliation was between the wars. In certain circumstances deterrence, by preventing the transition from open hostility to mutual toleration, and so increasing the believed *necessity* for deterrence, may represent a form of self-fulfilling prophecy, condemning both parties to a permanently congealed attitude of mutual threat."

Luard's comment recalls our earlier conclusion that the security of a nation can be preserved only if that of its potential adversary is equally protected; for if the latter feels insecure, it will amplify armament or political warfare or both and thus jeopardize the security of the former. The two are as mutually dependent as two men on a life raft at sea or two falling with a single parachute. Only policies designed to re-enforce the security of both will in fact re-enforce the security of either. Only accommodation and coexistence, at the very least, will prove to be in the real national interests of the two of them.

The validity of these judgments is unaffected by whether or not the states in question share the same ideology or the same political or economic system. The decisive fact is that they share the same planet, the same weapons, and the same mortality. They have therefore the same fundamental interests, however contradictory their ephemeral aims may appear. This truth is supported by the ease with which nations shift alliances; the deadly enemies of yesterday are the bosom friends of today.

Nietzsche said: "Convictions are more dangerous foes of truth than lies." He might also have said—"more dangerous foes of peace." Nothing was more sterile and inconclusive than the millennial war between Christians and Moslems, the hundred years' war between Catholics and Protestants. It would be a stupid mistake, an appalling tragedy, to repeat them with a war between Communists and anti-Communists.

The American Secretary of State, Elihu Root, wrote more than forty years ago: "When foreign affairs were ruled by autocracies and oligarchies the danger of war was in sinister purpose. When foreign affairs are ruled by democracies the danger of war will be in mistaken beliefs." The danger arises even more from crusading communism than from crusading democracy. Both must henceforth enforce upon themselves the strictest sort of national discipline in the conduct of foreign affairs. They do not have to accommodate conflicting beliefs, but they do have to confine the application of these beliefs to willing objects and peaceful means.

A form of "mistaken beliefs" other than that intended by Secretary Root, but equally incendiary, is the belief born of fear that an adversary is stronger or more aggressive than he actually is. Military establishments, despite repeated lessons, seem congenitally unable to resist the temptation to overestimate the armament of their opponents. This is partly "playing safe" but partly also wishful thinking, used to justify arms increases on their own side. The consequence of the increases is eventually to produce on the other side the very escalation which was mistakenly alleged in the first place. The pyramiding of misinformation, miscalculation, and misspent resources has been characteristic of every arms race in history. Most recently it has been exemplified by the purported "bomber gap," "missile gap" and "antimissile missile gap" between the Soviet Union and the United States, each of which was the excuse on both sides to arm far more heavily than was necessary and to aggravate considerably the very fears which caused the armament.

Similarly, even when adversary arms and armies are estimated more or less correctly, there is a curious tendency, never applied of course to one's own side, to equate intentions with capabilities: to assume, for example, that if Soviet armies at one time had the capability to march to the English Channel, they were going to do so, or that if American offensive missiles had the capability of wiping out Soviet cities, they would be used in this way unless deterred by Soviet defensive missiles. In other cases it is presumed on the Western side that if the Communists advance in Korea, they are also going to advance in Europe; or on the Communist side that if the Americans move into Southeast Asia, they are also bound to move into China or the Near East.

In each case, as we have repeatedly seen, the fatal law of disproportionate response, nourished by all the vested interests that have grown up around it, inflated by the venal sensationalism of press, television and radio, sanctioned by the panic of politicians, generals and the public, takes hold and sweeps all before it. Yet in the end only if this "law" is resisted and checked, will rational and peaceful conduct among nations be possible.

There seems to be, as a matter of fact, a long-standing consensus among masters of diplomacy that coolness and deliberation are the prime essentials both to a successful foreign policy and to the preservation of peace. Talleyrand, who vainly advised Napoleon when to stop and who subsequently acted on the belief that France's true interests lay with Europe rather than with the Empire, is known for his dictum: *"Surtout point de zèle."* Napoleon brought about his own destruction, but Talleyrand's coolness and foresight spared France the worst of its consequences.

Lord Salisbury, twice Prime Minister of Great Britain, remarked that the victories of diplomacy are won by "a series of microscopic advantages; a judicious suggestion here, an opportune civility there, a wise concession at one moment and a farsighted persistence at another; of sleepless tact, immovable calmness and patience that no folly, no provocation, no blunder can shake."

Rather remarkably, a statesman more notable for indomitability than conciliation, Winston Churchill, advocated the same approach. "Those who are prone by temperament and character," he wrote in his memoirs of World War II, "to seek sharp and clear-cut solutions of difficult and obscure problems, who are ready to fight whenever some challenge comes from a foreign power, have not always been right. On the other hand, those whose inclination is to bow their heads, to seek patiently and faithfully for peaceful compromise, are not always wrong. On the contrary, in the majority of instances, they may be right, not only morally but from a practical standpoint. . . . How many wars have been precipitated by fire-brands! How many misunderstandings which led to war could have been removed by temporizing! How often have countries fought cruel wars and then after a few years of peace found themselves not only friends but allies."

In a review of B. H. Liddell Hart's *Deterrent or Defense* in 1960, John F. Kennedy praised the author's credo: "Keep strong, if possible. In any case, keep cool. Have unlimited patience. Never corner an opponent, and always assist him to save his face. Put yourself in his shoes—so as to see things through his eyes. Avoid self-righteousness like the devil—nothing is so self-blinding."

Kennedy followed this counsel faithfully in the missile crisis of 1962, a classic example of a successful mixture of firmness, adroitness, and conciliation. That episode also illustrates the fact that the essence of "crisis management" is not the perfection of *intra-alliance* arrangements for deterrence or defense, but the establishment of *inter-alliance* connections for avoiding or deflating the impending or the instant danger.

It is also worth remembering that neither side in future crises, no matter how perfect its tactics, can expect to produce on the part of the other the substantial capitulation achieved by one side in the Cuban crisis. That capitulation was possible, indeed necessary, only because the other side had in 1962 recklessly moved into an untenable position, from which its only exits were either general war or withdrawal. In a more normal international crisis, capitulation by either side is not to be expected, indeed should neither be desired nor sought. Experience in the years before World War I and on many other occasions in history demonstrates that a series of diplomatic defeats, inflicted on one or both adversaries, is likely to create in a subsequent crisis such an accumulation of domestic and inter-alliance pressures on those that have capitulated in the past that they can neither yield nor compromise again, and an unwanted and unnecessary war occurs. The object of the style just described, therefore, should normally be not to bring about diplomatic triumphs but mutually tolerable, even if mutually unpalatable, accommodations.

Finally, among the obstacles to cool and deliberate "crisis management" by statesmen are some of those adolescent aspects of human behavior to which we alluded at the outset. We do not refer to anything so universally deplored as bullying, sabre-rattling, blackmail, or even to pugnacity, arrogance and self-righteousness. We mean rather the simple, pathetic human fear of appearing to be a coward or a fool, of giving the impression to friends and foes alike, but most of all to the leaders's own public opinion, that he is easily frightened or deluded.

Nothing has more often magnified trivial incidents into great confrontations than this fear on both sides. Yet these are essentially the reactions of little minds. As Jacqueline Kennedy wrote to Nikita Khrushchev a week after her husband was assassinated: "The danger which troubled my husband was that war might be started not so much by the big men as by the little ones. While big men know the needs for self-control and restraint—little men are sometimes moved more by fear and pride. If only in the future the big men can continue to make the little ones sit down and talk, before they start to fight."

While we may hope that the prescriptions set down in this chapter—about the real meaning of national security, the control and reduction of arms, the inherent drawbacks to national use of force, the conduct of foreign relations with becoming discipline and style—may be at least partially observed by all governments, we must be prepared for the conviction on the part of each that no such prescriptions are being or will be observed by its adversaries. The enormous deposit of mistrust accumulated during twenty years of confrontation in Europe, in Asia, and elsewhere will not soon be dissipated. Confrontations will, at the very least, continue for a number of years along much the same lines and with much the same instruments as in the past.

Even here, however, foresight and self-restraint, coolness and objectivity, discipline and style can be applied in ways that may make the difference between crescendo and diminuendo, between escalation and accommodation, between war and peace in each of the confrontations over the next decade. It is to these specifics for curbing particular confrontations that we now briefly turn.

CHAPTER 8

Curbing Confrontations

Europe

The history of Europe during the past hundred years is a tale of such folly and tragedy that it would be incredible if it had not happened. This enormously gifted people on their small continent had by their talents, energies and inventions achieved a position of unprecedented and uncontested leadership of the world. In the short space of three decades, in a savage spasm of self-destruction, they threw it all away.

Toward the end of the nineteenth century Europe slipped into a state of international anarchy in which two fortuitous alliances unnecessarily and meaninglessly confronted each other, arrogated to themselves the right and power to determine when the whole world should go to war, and finally did go to war without wanting to or knowing why. When they had done so, they were unable to stop until they had slaughtered the flower of Europe's youth, undermined many of its basic institutions, further fragmented its patchwork structure, rewarded the victors with indigestible loot, saddled the vanquished with a psychosis of revenge, loosed a cascade of revolutions and a mafia of dictators, and made another war in very short order almost certain.

After the second war, things went somewhat differently. By its folly Europe had for at least two decades forfeited the capacity to decide its own destiny, even the capacity to make decisive mistakes. The two superpowers moved in over its prostrate body to protect, often wrongheadedly, their own security and interests. The Soviet Union seized and held Eastern Europe; the United States and Western Europe successfully rallied to prevent further Soviet expansion. Europe was once more divided into two hostile alliances; Germany was partitioned into two incompatible states; an enormous panoply of murderous armament was massed and frozen along the arbitrary line that divided both.

After twenty years it began to be obvious that, however necessary it might originally have been, this armed and obsolete confrontation was now contributing more to the insecurity than to the security of all concerned. No one, however, seemed to know how to end it.

In the meantime the irrepressible peoples of Europe were rapidly reviving in strength and confidence. In Western Europe they had recovered physically but not psychologically; that is, they were economically contemporaneous with the United States and the Soviet Union, but were still spiritually disoriented. One might say that the older generation had recovered by attaching itself to old symbols and to economic affluence, but that the younger generation was still adrift because it believed in neither. Both ideals and ideologies had failed and were repudiated. In Eastern Europe the same trends were discernible, except that economic recovery and modernization had not proceeded so far, whereas stronger political motivation was provided by the arduous process of detachment from Communist orthodoxy. Both Germanies were particularly disoriented because of their defeat, their division, and their vulnerability.

All the Europeans, moreover, were becoming more and more resentful of their dependence on the superpowers, of the servitudes imposed by confrontation and of the artificial separation between East and West. "Polycentrism" began to appear in Eastern Europe as early as 1956 and ever since has moved by fits and starts but inexorably in the same direction. De Gaulle made himself the spokesman of an analogous trend in the West. Concern with NATO slackened notably, and long latent frictions between the United States and its allies worked up to the surface. At the same time both Europes, even occasionally both Germanies, displayed a mounting interest in mutual contact, even in some cases mild fraternization. These insubordinate tendencies on the part of their allies evoked an ambivalent response from the superpowers but for the most part, perhaps willy-nilly, were tolerated.

There was, in short, a marked and healthy, though still far from conclusive, movement toward détente in Europe. At the same time, however, an ancient and far less healthy phenomenon emerged from the shadows. The Europe of the Fatherlands, which so often had spilled so much of its own blood and that of others, began to reconstitute itself. De Gaulle majestically insisted on French nationalism, which obliged all the rest to think more of theirs, including of course the Germans whose nationalism had the most reason to feel frustrated. With the diminution of the threat from the East and the solace of growing affluence, the West Europeans seemed to be losing interest, as they encountered difficulty, in the once captivating movement toward unity. Although the Economic Community is being consolidated, it is also being strictly circumscribed both in size and in political content. Yet a mere end of the confrontation and a return to the Balkanized Europe of 1914 or 1932 would be a prescription neither for peace nor for lasting revival.

The challenge to Europe is to create itself. The old nations, even if restored as fully as France has been by De Gaulle, do not have a role to play in the modern world commensurate with their past glories, their present capabilities, or the spiritual requirements of their young people. If they persist in trying to turn back the clock, they might be punished by success. As Santayana said, those who have learned nothing from history are condemned to repeat it.

With its tragic and traumatic history still so close, with a diminishing but unresolved confrontation in its midst, with outstanding economic revival but continuing political fragmentation, with a mood of mounting confidence but persistent sensitivity and frustration, especially among the young, what course should Europe follow? And what example in Europe should the United States and the Soviet Union set?

One conclusion is very clear. Both Western and Eastern Europe are now strong enough to stand steady exposure to each other without fear of revolution or loss of identity. This holds particularly true for the two Germanies. It is high time that in their own interests they stop trying to out-maneuver each other and begin the long painful process of mutual adjustment which must proceed any form of reunification. The time is approaching to take down the walls. However, the reunification of Germany now, if it meant only the revival of an old autonomous power in the center of Europe, would be at best an anachronism and at worst a major element of disequilibrium and danger. The reunification of Germany, it should be clear, will only become possible, may indeed only be desirable, within the framework of a reconciled and progressively uniting Europe.

For this, as de Gaulle has so wisely recognized, the end of the Cold War and a growing accommodation with the Soviet Union and its allies are necessary. The differences between Western European society and Communist, not to mention Soviet, society will long be too great to permit real union. It would be impossible to effect, and dangerous to attempt, a detachment of East European states from Russia and their closer integration with the West. On the other hand, a united Europe "from the Atlantic to the Urals" is hardly possible, or even expedient, since it would presumably exclude Britain and divide the Soviet Union.

What are immediately possible and expedient are détente, accommodation, cooperation in a wide variety of fields. These are indeed both essential to European security and the contribution which Europe, after disquieting the world for a hundred years, should make to its peace.

The most constructive policy to which the United States could address itself in Europe during the next five years would be precisely to make *its* indispensable contribution to détente with the Soviet Union and its allies. Such a policy would certainly not mean dismantling NATO until East-West reconciliation has proceeded much further and has become much firmer than it shows as yet any sign of being. It would certainly not mean giving the West Germans legitimate cause to feel that they were being abandoned or their interests forgotten, but would have to take full account of the legitimate concerns of all friends of the United States in and out of Europe.

This policy would, however, be based on a few hard indisputable facts: that the peace of Europe and of the world cannot be assured or even significantly re-enforced as long as the two superpowers are in hostile and precarious confrontation; that Europe is the area where their confrontation has habitually been most direct, most acute and most persistent; that whatever reduces the temperature of that confrontation is conducive to the security of Europe as much as to that of the two powers themselves; and that the overriding interests of Europe are therefore served by measures significantly contributing to détente between the United States and the Soviet Union, such as arms control and reduction, even when these may seem to conflict with narrower European security preoccupations.

Most directly relevant to all these considerations, and most operative in the real interests of European security, would be a prompt, progressive and substantial reduction in the deployment of armies and nuclear weapons across the fragile epicenter of Europe. There are many formulas through which this can be accomplished, but the means are secondary. The essential thing is that the end be reached, and reached soon. The ultimate objective, beyond the rollback of armaments and the dismantling of walls, is the establishment across the center of Europe of a gradually tightening nexus of East-West, intra-German, and intra-European relationships, conducive to the security of all concerned and inhibiting either to renewal of European civil war or to the abuse of Europe as an arena of alien conflict.

As far as Western Europe is concerned, the Americans have for almost twenty years wisely promoted union among as many of its states as possible. They have, however, usually overestimated their ability to bring about such union, indeed have perhaps occasionally impaired its prospects by excess of zeal. The Europeans must and will decide for themselves if, how, when, and to what extent they will cooperate, federate or unite. It is to their interest to recognize that economic modernization and equality with the superpowers are possible only through a much fuller union than is now contemplated. It is their responsibility to determine how much and what kind of a union in the Western part of Europe is compatible with symbiosis and reconciliation with the East.

Much has also been thought and said in Europe and North America about the "Atlantic Community." This is at the same time a grand and a nebulous conception. For it to become a supranational reality, both the United States and its European and American partners would have to sacrifice to it far more important elements of sovereignty than they seem likely to relinquish in the foreseeable future. Being necessarily so limited, the "Atlantic Community" should not be misused as a competitor or obstacle to some West European union which could much sooner be much closer and more real. In the sense, however, of a strong nexus of common culture, common interests and common political and economic institutions, the "Atlantic Community" does exist. The nations it embraces can very profitably and intimately cooperate, not only to the degree required in NATO but, even more important, in otherwise dealing with, mitigating, and eventually dissolving both East-West and North-South confrontations.

We reiterate, however, that the principal duty and privilege of this generation of Europeans is to create Europe. This is the only objective that is now commensurate with their history, their capacities, their needs and their pride. If they aim for less, they will not achieve even that but will sink back into a welter of anachronisms and trivialities, and will soon lose their children to new nihilists, witch-doctors and demagogues. The Europe of tomorrow need not and will not be all-embracing, need not and will not be highly centralized, need not and will not assume exactly the form that any of its members want; but it must be a living process, clear, coherent, and convincing enough to win belief and allegiance and to constitute a noble cause. Given that, it can be a common market, a confederation or a federation; it can reach from Iceland to Poland, from Norway to Greece, or more, or less, but it must feel itself essentially one.

The use it makes of its unity is of course another question. Would it be just another superpower, just the sum of its ancient parts, another vast, ambitious, vainglorious nation-state seeking prestige, power, resources, markets, conquests, in the tradition of Louis XIV, Clive and Bismarck? Or would it use its enormous talents and experience to join in modernizing Asia, Africa and

Latin America, in disciplining and mastering the bomb, the machine and the test-tube, in preparing for the Renaissance of the twenty-first century?

East Asia

It would be unprofitable while the "Great Proletarian Cultural Revolution" in China and the war in Vietnam are in full swing and shifting daily, to make predictions about their outcome or to suggest policies for dealing with them. Certain fundamentals in East Asia, however, persist.

China, with its 700 million industrious people, its sophisticated traditions and its vigorous elite, is almost certain, eventually if not immediately, to play a primary role in the area and a major role in the world. It would fail to do so only if it should fall back into the fragmentation and anarchy which overcame it during the hundred years before 1949—which is conceivable but improbable.

The only internal force strong enough to destroy the Communist regime is that regime itself. From time to time it has seemed possible that it might do so. The interests of the Communist elite, however, despite the diversity in their interpretations of Marx, Lenin and Mao, would seem to be so overwhelmingly bound to their maintaining sufficient unity to hold their grip on the country that there is a high probability they will do so. Which man or clique will come out on top, whether the primary instrument of the victors will be the army or the party bureaucracy or the "revolutionary mass organizations" or a combination of all three, is of secondary importance. This year or the next or the year after, just as after the disastrous experiment of the "Great Leap Forward," sufficient equilibrium and control will probably be re-established to permit modernization, development and the buildup of military power to resume.

A return to more settled conditions would not mean that the "Great Proletarian Cultural Revolution" would vanish without a trace. There can be little doubt that this miscalculated convulsion has quickened and unleashed latent animosities among many elements of the Chinese population—peasants, workers, tradesmen, bureaucrats, technocrats, soldiers, intellectuals, students; those of "bourgeois" and those of "proletarian" origin; the older and the younger generations; partisans of Mao, of Peng, of Liu, of Chou; et cetera, et cetera. All these antagonisms and vendettas can neither be satisfied nor erased overnight. Moreover, the disorganization and evisceration of education, the purge and intimidation of teachers, the infatuation and licensed lawlessness of so much of the youth, will for a long time degrade standards of knowledge and behavior and retard progress in science, modernization and civilization.

Even if and when the effervescence subsides, order is re-established, economic and military development resumed, the problems confronting the regime—population, food, transport, industrialization, foreign exchange—will be so enormous, and their solution so impeded by the vagaries of Maoist ideology, that the regime is unlikely to have substantial capacity for external aggression, as distinct from external trouble-making, for a good many years. It is even possible that China will once again for some time be displaced by Japan as the leading indigenous power in East Asia.

We noted in Chapter 4 that a sober recognition of these inhibitions has for the most part governed China's foreign policy since 1953. Necessarily, though no doubt grudgingly, its policy has been so governed during the past three years when its domestic convulsion coincided with the augmented war in Vietnam. Whether its policy will continue to be so governed, however, even in the presence of its vast internal problems, will no doubt depend in part on a number of external factors.

It will depend on whether the regime feels itself so threatened by external military pressure or so humiliated by hostile military activity close at hand that, against its better judgment, it feels obliged to make a military response. It will depend, on the other hand, on whether or not some of the small countries along China's borders are so vulnerable and unprotected that their seizure by subversion or guerrilla war would seem irresistibly cheap and easy. It will depend, finally, on whether or not the rest of the world, during the next few years while China is still weak, not only creates the instruments of containment but, more important, uses the breathing spell to re-establish significant contact and communication with the Chinese leaders and people.

These factors, which will tend to determine the future foreign policy of the Chinese Communist government, equally delineate the policies which the rest of the world, and particularly those states most concerned with the region, would be well advised to follow. Partial escalation of the Vietnamese war into the North was carried out with impunity, as escalation of the Korean war was not, because China was incapacitated by internal strife. When that incapacity has been to some degree relieved, it will be provocative, dangerous, and in the broad view counterproductive for other major powers to carry out military operations immediately adjacent to China's frontiers, unless the Chinese themselves have first moved out across these frontiers.

On the other hand, it would also be dangerous and provocative to leave the small states on China's periphery exposed and unsupported in the shadow of a great power which has, at least in principle, assumed a mission of universal revolution. Until the United Nations is able to defend them, states inside and outside the region must be prepared to help to do so. Outsiders, however, can provide only military force and economic aid. These will be highly important but they will be only palliatives. Vietnam, Laos, Thailand, the Philippines, Burma and Indonesia will remain critically vulnerable until their governments provide themselves with a much more solid popular base through social reform and economic modernization. Most of them have hardly begun to do so. Unless and until they do so, all help from outside will prove ephemeral and ultimately in vain.

In the long run, primary roles in both the containment and the assimilation into the world community of China should be played by her great neighbors, the Soviet Union, Japan, and India. They should be encouraged and helped to do so, for the sake of general security as well as their own. This is a further reason why the Soviet Union may wish and, if so, should be accorded greater relaxation in Europe and vis-à-vis the United States elsewhere. This is a further reason why Japan should be encouraged to take the lead both in building regional organizations and in reviving relations with China. This is a further rea-

son why India should be assisted in every way possible to meet
the enormous problems she confronts.

The United States has already made clear in Korea, in Taiwan,
in Laos and in Vietnam that it is prepared to contribute to the
containment of China and its ambitious allies in Pyongyang and
Hanoi whatever force and whatever funds for development are
required. It may have to commit more of the former; it will certainly have to provide much more of the latter. There are, however, clearly discernible limits to what the United States or any
single state can or should do alone. President Kennedy's warning
applies here: "The United States is neither omnipotent or om-
niscient . . . we cannot impose our will . . . we cannot right every
wrong or reverse each adversity . . . there cannot be an American
solution to every world problem."

The war in Vietnam has already cost the United States outside
East Asia some of the stature of world leadership it had so painfully and justly won; it has dangerously divided American opinion and delayed the repair of serious flaws in American society; it
has postponed the application of urgent measures of international
security and international reconciliation. This is not to say that
the war should not have been fought, once the North Vietnamese
had provoked it, but rather that it should not have been allowed
to pre-empt such a disproportionate amount of the resources and
passion of a great power with multitudinous responsibilities at
home and abroad. There was an inapt extrapolation to East
Asia, where the adversary power had limited capabilities and was
pursuing a cautious policy, of the dissimilar experience in Europe
with two dictators, Hitler and Stalin, whose ambitions and
capabilities both were vast.

A wiser policy for the United States to have followed in Vietnam would have been: to check and contain in the South the
attempt of Hanoi to take it over by force; to have limited bombing in the North to infiltration routes close to the boundary
with the South and with Laos; to have exercised much more
sternly its leverage with the Saigon government to obtain more
genuine political reform and more effective participation in the
war; and to have persistently sought negotiations which would
have included the chief adversary in the South, the Viet Cong;

to have pursued the military and economic effort at a level commensurate with the size and power of the adversary; and, finally, to have been prepared, if necessary, to maintain this effort at this level over a period of years.

Walt Rostow in early 1967 said: "If we have the common will to hold together and get on with the job, the struggle in Vietnam might be the last great confrontation of the postwar era." We can devoutly hope he is right. There is serious doubt, however, whether Vietnam can properly be called a "great confrontation," since it was a war between the world's strongest state and a very small one, even though the latter was supplied with arms and other necessities by its friends. What it was of course was a revolutionary war in a small country, abetted from outside, and certainly not the last of its kind. Indeed, there are likely to be a great many wars of this type in the next few decades. It would not seem, moreover, that they can be most successfully, safely or economically dealt with by the intervention of a single Great Power. We will come back to this point below.

A concluding and paramount counsel about East Asia is in fact the one with which we began: namely, on the assumption that the job of containment will be adequately done one way or another while China is weak, what is essential is that the present opportunity be seized to establish practical and healthy relations with her before she is strong. Even if there were no other reason, it would be necessary to do so in order to proceed with what we have called the first item on the agenda of mankind—the control and reduction of nuclear armaments. If China will not participate, there are grave limits to how far other nations can go. Yet China cannot reasonably be expected to take part in this international enterprise if she is excluded from all others. She should be invited without delay, and without regard for her current disorders, into the United Nations and into all other appropriate international organizations. Initially, she will no doubt refuse; she will prove, when she does come in, a most prickly and disruptive partner. A nation does not recover overnight either from a century's humiliation or a twenty-year intoxication. The stakes in this case, however, are too high to permit or excuse boggling by the rest of the world. Those nations which have suffered the least should show the most understanding and patience. Both China's sobriety and its friendship are essential to world order.

The Third World

The peoples of what are euphemistically called the "less developed countries," those distributed around the world in the great arc from East Asia through the Middle East and Africa to South America, are confronting a prodigious complex of problems for which there is no exact precedent. The closest analogy in Western experience might be Europe in the fifteenth century.

Their problems fall into three categories: those involved in keeping alive and in developing their resources; those involved in creating a convincing political identity and a viable political structure; those involved in establishing stable relationships with their neighbors, with the Great Powers, and with international organizations. Each of these sets of problems is inextricably meshed with the other two; substantial progress in meeting any one of them is improbable if there is conspicuous failure in meeting either of the others. To speak only of one of them is necessarily misleading, because the three constitute an unbroken circle.

The leaders and elites of the Third World have staggering obligations to meet in coping with these problems. They are, however not the only ones who have such obligations. The traumatic racial gap, the persistent psychological gap, the widening economic gap between most developed and underdeveloped countries cannot be ignored by the leaders and peoples of either. If the gaps widen and deepen, if unrelieved population growth, widespread famine, frustrated expectations, internal turmoil, and internecine conflict occur in the Third World, neither the developed countries of the West nor those of the East will profit or escape the consequences. Both will be involved, contaminated, brutalized and, in the end, stricken together. On the peoples of the North, therefore, there also rest obligations, which are at the same time humanitarian and self-serving, to meet the problems they inescapably share with the South.

The first category of obligations, those relating to food and development, include the following: in almost all countries the population explosion must be checked. In countries where it is extreme and where available resources are limited, it must be checked drastically and quickly; the leaders of these countries have no more important duty than to ensure by every feasible means that this is done; religious leaders have the duty to lift their archaic bans on its being done; foreign governments and international institutions supplying aid to such countries have the duty to assist with the means and the right to insist that they be widely used. The same reciprocal and imperative obligations on recipients and donors apply to the provision of food to the hungry, the maximization of agricultural production in the recipient countries, and the adoption there of technical, administrative and political measures essential to that end.

In this category there also falls the obligation, which is of course a political necessity as well, to meet, not extravagently but at least to a modest degree, the rising expectations of the peoples of the Third World. This involves, in the first instance, energetic and persistent self-help on the part of the governments and citizens of these countries. It also involves substantial and steady foreign assistance in the form of technical aid, bilateral and multilateral loans in sufficient volume and on easy terms, and the stipulation by donors, wherever it is feasible, of regional economic cooperation among recipients. Finally, this obligation involves, on the part of developed countries, the prompt revision of their commercial practices to permit limited preferential treatment for the exports of less-developed countries in order to reduce the need for external aid.

Obligations in the second category, those concerned with political identity and political structure, fall of course almost entirely on the leaders and elite of the less-developed countries. These are intimate cultural needs, involving painful divorce from ancient custom, which can be met only in ways and by means reflecting the indigenous spirit. An attempt to impose foreign systems and structure will be resented and will usually fail.

The second obligation is often described as "nation-building." The term assumes, no doubt rightly, that the nation is the characteristic and indispensable form of political association in the

twentieth century, and that peoples newly emerged from colonialism or hibernation will and should insist on full national status,
if they have not had it before. Nationhood is relatively easy for
those, such as the Latin Americans, who have long enjoyed it,
though even here a strong sense of nationality has often failed
to penetrate the whole society. Nationhood is far from easy, however, for those who have been deprived of it for a century or more
or have never enjoyed it.

Having in mind the perils of fragmentation in small units,
which have made the Balkans a byword and which Europe as a
whole is still striving to overcome, one is tempted to wish that
smaller new countries, just as they are leaping from the oxcart
to the airplane, might skip the stage of the small state and, profit-
ing by the very absence of a strong sense of nationhood, move
swiftly into the era one can already see emerging, that of the great
regional or continental federation. Unhappily most recent experience has been in the contrary sense of the breakup of much more
modest federations in East and West Africa, Malaysia and Nigeria; the barely contained centrifugal forces in larger countries
such as India, Indonesia and the Congo.

The fact is that the problems of almost all less-developed states
are so monumental that their leaders are only precariously able
to maintain themselves in power in the existing structure and fear
to complicate their venture by amalgamating with other structures and other elites. They have an understandable preference
for holding the maximum number of prestigious places and emol-
uments which the existing structure provides rather than risking
the loss of some through merger with other elites. They have not
yet perceived what the experience of larger states and of large
private corporations demonstrates, that merger not only reduces
friction, facilitates development and usually serves the general
welfare, but also multiplies jobs for the governing elite and mag-
nifies the power of the ablest among them. It would not seem
wholly unreasonable to expect that these simple facts would
become more apparent as time goes on, as they are belatedly
becoming apparent in Europe. Certainly if the fragmentation of
the Third World continues at its present level, neither its peoples nor its leaders will achieve the stature and progress they

seek; indeed under these circumstances the risk of total frustration and collapse will always be close at hand.

Obligations in the third category, stable relationships with neighbors, with the Great Powers, and with international organizations, fall once again on the leaders of both South and North. The former have the obligation to their own people and to all others in the same plight not to exacerbate it by trying to subvert, dominate or overthrow their neighbors, or by wasting the precious patrimony of their nation on armaments and military adventure.

Equally the Great Powers have obligations in this category to the Third World. They owe it an early end to racialism, certainly inside their own countries but also elsewhere where it is still brutally dominant, as in southern Africa. Most of all, they have the obligation to spare the Third World, which suffers enough from its own creeds and conflicts, the extra burden of theirs. In particularly troubled regions like the Near East and Southeast Asia, they owe its peoples not competitive intervention, not incitement and arms to already intoxicated sects and nationalisms, but impartial, effective and multilateral peace-keeping and peaceful settlement.

The Soviet Union and eventually China will have to learn that it is not really in their interest to promote wars which have a way of spreading and involving their authors, not even perhaps in their interest to promote revolutions which may either veer into unmanageable "deviations" or end in savage counter-revolution. Possibly even the Russians may lose their enthusiasm for "wars of national liberation" when they awake to the fact that there remain only two substantial areas of the world, Southern Africa and the Soviet Union, where very large ethnic groups remain dependent and "unliberated."

As to the West, within the next few years it will have soberly to review its posture and policies toward the Third World. The West needs to check to the best of its ability its abuse of these countries as arenas of East-West conflict and intervention, to develop other more neutral instruments of peace-keeping there, to revive its own flagging compassion and sense of common destiny with these disconcerting millions, to reaffirm its commitment to devote to their development each year no less than 1 per cent of its prodigious income. The West will find, no doubt, that the leaders of the Third World will prove "reasonable" and "responsible" in Western terms to the degree the problems they confront do not seem insoluble. Where they do seem insoluble, the leaders will be "revolutionary" in whatever direction and to whatever degree appears necessary.

Any observer of this troubled scene would be foolish if he did not anticipate for two-thirds of the world a prolonged time of troubles, famine, and confusion. On the other hand, he would be callous and irresponsible if he thought the remaining third should or could ignore such tribulation and pass by on the other side. The world is now so close-knit that it will live or die together; a disease or wound in one member will soon infect the whole body; a nation which in the future minds only its own business will not be minding that.

Perhaps the only practical means of bringing this time of troubles to an end will prove to be gradually evolving East-West cooperation, expressing itself primarily through strengthened international organization with a wide variety of competence and scope. It is to this requirement that the final chapter will be addressed.

CHAPTER 9

Organizing International Security

In one of his great speeches shortly before he died, Adlai Stevenson said: "The central question, as I see it, is whether the wonderfully diverse and gifted assemblage of human beings on this earth really knows how to run a civilization. Survival is still an open question, not because of environmental hazards but because of the workings of the human mind. And day by day the problem grows more complex. It was recognized clearly and with compassion by Pope John; to him, the human race was not a cold abstraction. Underlying his messages and encyclicals was this simple thought: that the human race is a family, that men are brothers, all wars are civil wars, and all killing is fratricidal."

At the outset of this book the proposition was put forward that the insecurity of nations cannot be explained merely by a study of foreign policies or by the conventional weighing of power, arms, doctrines, alliances and resources. The grounds for insecurity, it was argued, are far deeper, and only a comprehensive and dispassionate understanding of real causes offers hope of real solution. Such an understanding is what we have tried to achieve. Is there any comprehensive conclusion that we can finally draw?

Human nature and habits, scientific progress, traditional nationalism, nuclear weapons, new political faiths and systems, economic change and expectations, all play their part in the insecurity of nations, but none of them alone, not even all of them together, would seem to be necessarily uncontrollable or fatal.

Indeed scientific and economic progress offer almost miraculous opportunities for reducing both individual and national insecurity. Even new faiths and regressive political systems, corrupting and destructive as they have been during the past half century, are clearly neither irresistible nor unalterable. They are being contained and are beginning to evolve in directions dictated by the same forces that govern the rest of the world.

However, the primary cause of the insecurity of nations persists, the very attribute on which nations pride themselves most —their sovereign independence, their "sacred egoism," their insubordination to any interest broader or higher than their own. The tragic character of their condition lies, moreover, in their habitual failure to understand what their own interests really are, to recognize that the interests of all are in the modern world so bound together that those of one nation cannot be served over the long run without all being served, that those of one nation cannot be imperiled without all being imperiled.

If mankind is to continue to prosper, perhaps even to survive to the end of this century, there is going to have to be a rather rapid assimilation of nation-states into a more coherent and functional international system. Balances of power among nations have never long maintained a balance tolerable to all, nor have stable deterrents long proved stable. This is true whether the balances and deterrents are set up by two superpowers or by half a dozen, by two or more coalitions or by a host of small states; it will also be true if and when the world is organized into four or five great confederations, if those confederations insist on acting with the same license and lawlessness as nations do now.

There will never be security for nations and peoples until there exists some impartial and effective international authority, expressing man's best instincts and common interests, designed and empowered to keep the peace, restrain aggressive governments, control national armaments, negotiate and enforce peaceful settlements, facilitate peaceful change, and assist new states to develop and modernize. When single states or coalitions take it upon themselves to perform these tasks in their own way, they inevitably raise up rival states or coalitions which insist on performing them otherwise. The nature of the modern world is such that it will not tolerate a pax Romana, pax Britannica, pax Sovietica or pax Americana. Peace-keeping, if it is not in practice to become war-making, is a task that henceforth has to be performed collectively.

This said, it must be frankly admitted that the present United Nations family of international organizations is still extremely weak, particularly in the most essential fields of peace-keeping and peaceful settlements. To mention only its most conspicuous shortcomings, the United Nations has no standing armed force and is obliged to rely entirely on national contingents mustered in time of crisis and subject to withdrawal at any moment. It has no decisive power to control national armaments, limit national conflict, or enforce peaceful settlements. Its principal organ for the maintenance of peace, the Security Council, is often immobilized by Great Power antagonisms and the veto, is prevented from dealing with East Asia by the exclusion of the largest Asian power, is obliged to rely for enforcement of its decisions either on the voluntary compliance of governments or on economic sanctions of doubtful force.

The organ in which all members sit, the General Assembly, suffers from the fact that it cannot order but only recommend, that the "sovereign equality" of its members and the influx of "ministates" progressively dims its reflection of real power and hence the impact of its recommendations, and that the preoccupation of its more numerous and least powerful members with vestigial problems of "colonialism" distracts it wastefully from the major problems of today and tomorrow. The International Court of Justice is impotent to enforce international law or to settle international disputes because most of them are never brought before it and, when they are, no machinery exists to enforce its decisions.

Despite the efforts of three great Secretaries-General—Trygve Lie, Dag Hammarskjöld, and U Thant—the authority of this "chief administrative officer of the Organization" to negotiate peaceful settlements, even to carry out Security Council decisions, is still contested by Great Powers and hence sharply curtailed. The numerous "specialized agencies" associated with the United Nations perform increasingly useful international functions and help knit tighter the fabric of international interest, but each has its separate powers and burgeoning bureaucracy, which it is impossible for the Secretary-General or anyone else to coordinate or control.

Perhaps most serious of all, action by the United Nations is tightly circumscribed by the niggardliness of its members, particularly the wealthiest, who protest the cost of collective peace-keeping in the Congo, about $400 million over four years, and then, for example, spend $25 billion over three years for unilateral peace-keeping in Vietnam. This same selective parsimony reduces, though not quite to the same degree, the capacity of the United Nations and its related agencies to perform, in the development and modernization of new states, the paramount role which their impartial character particularly equips them to do.

Nor are regional organizations any more generously endowed with power by their members. The Organization of American States has a relatively long tradition, but neither the United States nor the other twenty republics are willing to confide to the Organization the right to intervene or to forbid intervention, the right to determine levels of economic assistance or standards of social and political performance. The Organization of African Unity is hardly out of swaddling clothes, as are narrower and less formal regional associations in East Asia. Europe is engaged in a great debate as to whether the unity of only Six, which in any case is only economic, shall become a unity of Seven. Except in those great federations which are nation-states, the United States, the Soviet Union, India and perhaps China, even the organization of regions and continents is still primitive and half-hearted.

Yet if the United Nations is weak it is only because governments and peoples, through whose aspirations and commitments it alone can exist, have denied it the necessary power. If, as and when governments, representing a more enlightened public opinion, come to the conclusion that the inborn insecurity of nations can be remedied only by the same means through which the insecurity of feudal baronies and city-states was remedied, that is, by entrusting greater responsibility and power to a central authority, then the constitutional and administrative process for doing so will prove relatively simple. The Charter of the United

Nations was not too badly drawn; its main shortcomings are obvious; it can be amended whenever there is sufficient consensus to do so; new life can be breathed into it whenever nations wish.

The catalogue of its weaknesses can equally well serve as a prescription for its reform and its adaptation to a larger purpose. Briefly, what it most requires are: authority conferred on it by its members, first of all by the Great Powers, to determine and apply effective measures to forestall or stop armed conflict between nations great or small; reform of Security Council procedures to facilitate and validate such determination; establishment of a small standing U.N. police force, to be supplemented immediately in case of need by national contingents previously earmarked, organized and trained for the purpose; authority conferred on a reformed Security Council, assisted by an invigorated International Court, to arbitrate and, if necessary, enforce peaceful settlements of disputes judged to constitute imminent threats to the peace; authority conferred on a reformed Council or Assembly, with appropriate subsidiary bodies, to negotiate agreements for the control and reduction of national armaments and to enforce implementation of these agreements; authority conferred on the Secretary-General to supervise the execution of most of these measures and to coordinate all U.N. organs and "specialized agencies"; either firm agreements by member governments to finance all these activities adequately or grant of authority to the General Assembly to levy appropriate and limited taxes; a much more extensive use of U.N. agencies as instruments for the development and modernization of less-developed countries; such strengthening of regional organizations as is compatible with authority conferred on the United Nations itself.

The basic proposition on which the United Nations was established, as the Russians never cease to remind their fellow members, was "the unanimity of the Great Powers." That unanimity evaporated within a year or two after the Charter was signed, and the organization suffered accordingly. During its first decade and a half, however, the vast majority of its membership was sufficiently homogeneous to enable it to carry out effective peacekeeping, sometimes through the General Assembly, without the unanimity of the Great Powers. That recourse still exists and on rare occasions may be usable. The present crisis of the United

Nations, however, arises primarily from the fact that over the last few years the majority of its enlarged membership has come to be much more heterogenous, consistently united only in "anti-imperialism" and rising expectations, for the most part "non-aligned" and unwilling to override a Great Power on a vital issue. Under these circumstances effective peace-keeping action over the strong objection of a Great Power is almost as unlikely to be taken in the Assembly as in the Security Council.

Over the long run, therefore, the revival and re-enforcement of U.N. peace-keeping must depend upon either a renewal of Great Power unanimity or a revulsion of the new Assembly majority against Great Power obstruction. Superficially, the latter might seem the more probable, but it would be very difficult, in view of the majority's limited military and financial resources, for that revulsion to express itself in effective peace-keeping unless the action were supported by one or more of the Great Powers. Such support by either a Western or an Eastern Great Power, but not by both, would mean, however, that many of the nonaligned would have to align themselves; and that is what, except on rare occasions, they will be unwilling to do.

It is probable, therefore, that the assimilation of nation-states into a more coherent and functional international system, which our whole argument has tended to conclude offers the only reliable escape from the insecurity of nations, indeed from eventual disaster, depends on the restoration of a significant measure of Great Power cooperation. At present that means primarily United States-Soviet cooperation, though at a later date the participation of a more united Europe and a stronger China, Japan or India may be equally essential.

Given the profound ideological and political disparities between East and West, it is quite obvious that one cannot expect between them in the foreseeable future anything approaching the confidence and accord which exists, for example, among most Western states. Fortunately, that is not necessary. What *is* necessary, what stands out with sharpest clarity from experience in Southeast Asia and the Near East, is that both the Soviet Union and the United States, with their principal allies, should conclude (1) that the absence of more effective means of peace-keeping is creating unacceptable risks to their national interests, (2) that unilateral and competitive peace-keeping seems likely to magnify rather than reduce those risks, and (3) that a gradual re-enforcement of multilateral peace-keeping through the United Nations offers a mutually acceptable and mutually manageable means of limiting those risks.

Until the two superpowers reach a conclusion along those lines, it is unlikely that the United Nations can be substantially strengthened, that it can be substituted for the posture and paraphernalia of Great Power confrontation all over the world, and that the inherent insecurity of nations, most of all that of the Great Powers themselves, can be relieved. This is why, as many Afro-Asians and a few Europeans constantly remind us, at least a limited accommodation between the United States and the Soviet Union is the essential prerequisite to any solid stabilization of world affairs and should have clear priority over all other national stratagems and gambits. Such a course is still distasteful to the custodians of dogma and confrontation in both countries, but in the end no other can create for their peoples and the world the security that these custodians, for all their fanfare, have utterly failed to provide.

The revival and re-enforcement of the United Nations no doubt seems, and at the moment may be, Utopian. The point to be made again and again, to be hammered unmercifully into our proud, hard, silly heads, is that the attempt to achieve the security of nations by national means under modern circumstances is still more Utopian. Even assuming uncommon sense or, more likely, some tragic demonstrations of calamity, the invigoration of the United Nations will take a number of years. The passing of powers from old to new, from parochial to ecumenical, from states separating peoples to institutions uniting them, will not be accomplished quickly or easily. Still, it seems high time to begin.

When he was over eighty and had retired to a farm in Lorraine, Marshal Lyautey instructed his gardener to set out some fruit trees. But they will not bear for twenty years, protested the gardener. Then we must lose no time, said the Marshal, but plant them tomorrow.

Bibliographic Notes

PART I: THE DISORGANIZATION OF TWENTIETH-CENTURY SOCIETY

Chapter 2: Underlying Causes of National Insecurity

THE RELEVANCE OF HUMAN NATURE

CARRIGHAR, SALLY. *Wild Heritage.* Boston: Houghton Mifflin, 1965.

DURBIN, E. F. M., and BOWLBY, JOHN. *Personal Aggressiveness and War.* New York: Columbia University Press, 1939.

FROST, ROBERT. "Two Witches," in *Complete Poems of Robert Frost.* New York: Holt, Rinehart & Winston, 1949.

LORENZ, KONRAD. *On Aggression.* Translated by Marjorie Kerr Wilson. New York: Harcourt, Brace and World, 1966.

MEERLOO, JOOST A. M. *That Difficult Peace.* Manhasset, N.Y.: Channel Press, 1961.

ROSTAND, JEAN. *Life, the Great Adventure.* Translated by Alan Houghton Brodrick. New York: Charles Scribner's Sons, 1956.

SCOTT, HERBERT. "Crow Box." Copyright © 1966 by *Harper's* Magazine Inc. Reprinted from the August 1966 issue of *Harper's* Magazine by permission of the author.

TILLICH, PAUL. *The Eternal Now.* New York: Charles Scribner's Sons, 1963.

OLD AND NEW FAITHS

KIPLING, RUDYARD. "We and They" from *Debits and Credits.* Copyright 1926 by Rudyard Kipling. Reprinted by permission of Doubleday and Co., Inc., the Macmillan Co. of Canada, and Mrs. George Bambridge.

RUSSELL, BERTRAND. *Portraits from Memory and other Essays.* New York: Simon and Schuster, 1956.

TOYNBEE, ARNOLD. *A Study of History*. London and New York: Oxford University Press, 1949.

WOOTON, BARBARA. "Winners and Losers in the Rat-race," in CALDER, NIGEL (ed.), *The World in 1984*. Vol. 2. Baltimore, Md.: Penguin Books, 1965.

THE RELEVANCE OF SCIENCE

BETHE, HANS A. "Science," An Interview by Donald McDonald. Santa Barbara, Calif.: Center for the Study of Democratic Institutions, 1962.

BORN, MAX. "Reflections," *Bulletin of the Atomic Scientists,* November, 1965.

BOURLIÈRE, FRANÇOIS. "A New Balance Between Man and Nature," in CALDER (ed.), *The World in 1984*. Vol. 1.

BRIDGMAN, PERCY W. *The Way Things Are*. Cambridge, Mass.: Harvard University Press, 1959.

BRONOWSKI, JACOB. *Science and Human Values*. Rev. ed. New York: Harper & Row, 1965.

BROOKS, HARVEY. "Scientific Concepts and Cultural Change," *Daedalus,* Winter, 1965.

HEISENBERG, WERNER. "From Plato to Max Planck," *Atlantic Monthly,* November, 1959.

POPPER, KARL. *The Logic of Scientific Discovery*. Translated by the author with the assistance of Julius Freed and Jan Freed. New York: Basic Books, 1959.

SCHRÖDINGER, ERWIN. *Science Theory and Man*. Translated by James Murphy and W. H. Johnston. New York: Dover Publications, 1957.

SEN, B. R. "The Race Will Not Yet Be Won," in CALDER (ed.), *The World in 1984*. Vol. 1.

WEINER, NORBERT. "Dynamical Systems in Physics and Biology," in CALDER (ed.), *The World in 1984*. Vol. 1.

EVIDENCE OF THE ARTS

BALDWIN, JAMES. "As Much Truth as One Can Bear," *The New York Times Book Review,* January 14, 1962.

BOTSFORD, KEITH. "Report from a Surrealist Capital," *The New York Times Magazine,* September 11, 1966.

FITZGIBBON, CONSTANTINE. *The Life of Dylan Thomas*. Boston: Little, Brown, 1965. Quoting letters of Dylan Thomas to Bert Treich.

GILOT, FRANÇOISE, and LAKE, CARLTON. *Life with Picasso*. New York: McGraw-Hill, 1964.

KAFKA, FRANZ. *The Diaries of Franz Kafka*. Edited by Max Brod. 2 vols. New York: Schocken Books, 1948–49.

WILLIAMS, TENNESSEE. Interview in *The New York Times*, Section II, March 28, 1965.

THE IMPACT OF ECONOMICS

BERLE, ADOLF A., JR. *Power Without Property: A New Development in American Political Economy.* New York: Harcourt, Brace, 1959.

KEYNES, JOHN MAYNARD. "The End of Laissez-Faire" (1926). Reprinted in *Essays in Persuasion.* New York: Harcourt, Brace, 1932.

THE DILEMMAS OF GOVERNMENT

ACHEBE, CHINUA. *A Man of the People.* New York: John Day Company, 1966.

GROUSSET, RENÉ. *Figures de Proue.* Paris: Librairie Plon, 1949.

KISSINGER, HENRY. "Domestic Structure and Foreign Policy," *Daedalus,* Spring, 1966.

MENDEL, ARTHUR P. "The Rise and Fall of 'Scientific Socialism,'" *Foreign Affairs,* October, 1966.

MORSTEIN MARX, FRITZ. *The Administrative State: An Introduction to Bureaucracy.* Chicago: University of Chicago Press, 1957.

NAMIER, LEWIS. *England in the Age of the American Revolution.* 2nd ed. New York: St Martin's Press, 1962.

THE ESCALATION OF ARMS AND VIOLENCE

JOHNSON, LYNDON B., speech at the National Legislative Conference of the Building and Construction Trades Department of the AFL-CIO, quoted in *The New York Times,* March 25, 1964.

LOVELL, BERNARD. "Search for Voices from Other Worlds," *The New York Times Magazine,* December 24, 1961.

McCLOY, JOHN J. "Balance Sheet on Disarmament," *Foreign Affairs,* April, 1962.

WIESNER, JEROME B., and YORK, HERBERT E. "National Security and the Nuclear-Test Ban," *Scientific American,* October, 1964.

WOLFE, THOMAS W. *Some Factors Bearing on Soviet Attitudes Toward Disarmament.* The RAND Corporation, P-2766, July, 1963.

PART II: CONFRONTATIONS, 1945–67

Chapter 3: Challenge and Response in Europe

CHURCHILL, WINSTON. *Triumph and Tragedy. The Second World War,* Vol. 6. Boston: Houghton Mifflin, 1953.

DAWSON, RAYMOND, and ROSECRANCE, RICHARD. "Theory and Reality in the Anglo-American Alliance," *World Politics,* October, 1966.

DULLES, JOHN FOSTER. Address by the Secretary of State, New York, January 12, 1954, in CURL, PETER V. (ed.), *Documents on American Foreign Relations, 1954.* New York: Harper & Row, 1955.

FEIS, HERBERT. *Between War and Peace: The Potsdam Conference.* Princeton, N.J.: Princeton University Press, 1960.

———. *The China Tangle: The American Effort in China from Pearl Harbor to the Marshall Mission.* Princeton, N.J.: Princeton University Press, 1953.

McNEILL, WILLIAM H. *America, Britain and Russia: Their Cooperation and Conflict 1941–1946 (Survey of International Affairs, 1939–1946,* Royal Institute of International Affairs, vol. 3.) New York: Johnson Reprint; London: Oxford University Press, 1953.

McNEILL, WILLIAM H. *The Rise of the West: A History of the Human Community.* Chicago: University of Chicago Press, 1963.

MOSELY, PHILIP E. *The Kremlin and World Politics: Studies in Soviet Policy and Action.* New York: Vintage Books, 1960.

MURPHY, ROBERT. *Diplomat Among Warriors.* Garden City, N.Y.: Doubleday, 1964.

SCHLESINGER, ARTHUR, JR. *A Thousand Days: John F. Kennedy in the White House.* Boston: Houghton Mifflin, 1965. Quoting John F. Kennedy on the Cuban missile crisis.

SORENSON, THEODORE. *Kennedy.* New York: Harper & Row, 1965. Quoting John F. Kennedy on nuclear strategy.

TOYNBEE, ARNOLD and VERONICA M. (eds.). *The Realignment of Europe. (Survey of International Affairs, 1939–1946,* Royal Institute of International Affairs, vol. 6.) London: Oxford University Press, 1955.

TRUMAN, HARRY S. *Years of Decision. Memoirs,* Vol. 1. Garden City, N.Y.: Doubleday, 1958.

XYDIS, STEPHEN G. *Greece and the Great Powers 1944–47, Prelude to the "Truman Doctrine."* Thessaloniki, Greece: Institute for Balkan Studies, 1963, and Chicago: Argonaut, n.d.

Chapter 4: Challenge and Response in East Asia

ECKSTEIN, ALEXANDER. *Communist China's Economic Growth and Foreign Trade: Implications for U.S. Policy.* New York: McGraw-Hill, 1966.

FEIS, HERBERT. *The Atomic Bomb and the End of World War II.* Rev. ed. Princeton, N.J.: Princeton University Press, 1966.

FEIS, HERBERT. *The China Tangle: The American Effort in China from Pearl Harbor to the Marshall Mission.*

LACOUTURE, JEAN. *Vietnam: Between Two Truces.* Translated by Konrad Kellen and Joel Carmichael. New York: Random House, 1966.

MAO TSE-TUNG. "In Memory of Norman Bethune," "Serve the People," and "The Foolish Old Man Who Removed the Mountains," quoted in *The New York Times,* December 10, 1966.

REES, DAVID. *Korea: The Limited War.* New York: St Martin's Press, 1964.

RIDGWAY, MATTHEW B., and MARTIN, H. H. *Soldier: The Memoirs of Matthew B. Ridgway.* New York: Harper & Row, 1956.

SCHLESINGER, ARTHUR, JR. *A Thousand Days.* Quoting Harold Mac-Millan.

"The Southeast Asia Collective Defense Treaty," in CURL, PETER V., (ed.). *Documents on American Foreign Relations, 1954.*

TANG, TSOU. *America's Failure in China, 1941 to 1950.* Chicago: University of Chicago Press, 1963.

U.S. DEPARTMENT OF STATE. *United States Relations with China, with Special Reference to the Period 1944-49, Based on the Files of the Department of State.* Washington, D.C.: U.S. Government Printing Office, 1949.

WHITING, ALLEN S. *China Crosses the Yalu: The Decision to Enter the Korean War.* New York: Macmillan, 1960.

Chapter 5: The Crisis of Modernization and the North-South Confrontation

GIDE, ANDRÉ. *The Immoralist.* New York: Alfred A. Knopf, 1948.

HEILBRONER, ROBERT L. *The Future as History: The Historic Currents of our Time and the Direction in which They are Taking America.* New York: Harper & Row, 1960.

PART III: REFLECTIONS AND CONCLUSIONS

Chapter 6: Where Do We Stand?

FITZGIBBON, CONSTANTINE. *The Life of Dylan Thomas.*

HOFFER, ERIC. *The True Believer: Thoughts on the Nature of Mass Movements.* New York: Harper & Row, 1951.

OPPENHEIMER, ROBERT. Quoted in *The New York Times,* February 20, 1967.

WILBUR, RICHARD. "For the New Railway Station in Rome," in *Things of This World.* New York: Harcourt, Brace, 1956.

Chapter 7: The Conduct and Misconduct of International Relations

CHURCHILL, WINSTON. *The Gathering Storm. The Second World War,* Vol. 1. Boston: Houghton Mifflin, 1948.

LUARD, EVAN. "Conciliation and Deterrence," *World Politics,* January, 1967.

MANCHESTER, WILLIAM. *Death of a President, November 20-November 25, 1963.* New York: Harper & Row, 1967. Quoting Mrs. Kennedy's letter to Premier Khrushchev.

SCHLESINGER, ARTHUR, JR. *A Thousand Days.* Quoting B. H. Liddell Hart.

THOMPSON, SIR ROBERT. *Defeating Communist Insurgency: The Lessons of Malaya and Vietnam*. New York: Frederick A. Praeger, 1966.

TUCHMAN, BARBARA. *The Proud Tower*. New York: Macmillan, 1965. Quoting Lord Salisbury.

Chapter 8: Curbing Confrontations

ROSTOW, WALT W. Quoted in *The New York Times*, February 24, 1967.

SCHLESINGER, ARTHUR, JR. *A Thousand Days*. Quoting John F. Kennedy on the United States in a pluralist world.

Chapter 9: Organizing International Security

STEVENSON, ADLAI. *International Convocation on the Requirements of Peace*. Santa Barbara, Calif.: Center for the Study of Democratic Institutions, 1965.

Index

COUNCIL ON FOREIGN RELATIONS

PUBLICATIONS

FOREIGN AFFAIRS (quarterly), edited by Hamilton Fish Armstrong.

THE UNITED STATES IN WORLD AFFAIRS (annual). Volumes for 1931, 1932 and 1933, by Walter Lippmann and William O. Scroggs; for 1934-1935, 1936, 1937, 1938, 1939 and 1940, by Whitney H. Shepardson and William O. Scroggs; for 1945-1947, 1947-1948 and 1948-1949, by John C. Campbell; for 1949, 1950, 1951, 1952, 1953 and 1954, by Richard P. Stebbins; for 1955, by Hollis W. Barber; for 1956, 1957, 1958, 1959, 1960, 1961, 1962 and 1963, by Richard P. Stebbins; for 1964, by Jules Davids; for 1965, by Richard P. Stebbins; for 1966, by Richard P. Stebbins.

DOCUMENTS ON AMERICAN FOREIGN RELATIONS (annual). Volume for 1952 edited by Clarence W. Baier and Richard P. Stebbins; for 1953 and 1954, edited by Peter V. Curl; for 1955, 1956, 1957, 1958 and 1959, edited by Paul E. Zinner; for 1960, 1961, 1962 and 1963, edited by Richard P. Stebbins; for 1964, edited by Jules Davids; for 1965 and 1966, edited by Richard P. Stebbins.

POLITICAL HANDBOOK AND ATLAS OF THE WORLD (annual), edited by Walter H. Mallory.

HOW NATIONS BEHAVE: Law and Foreign Policy, by Louis Henkin (1968).

THE INSECURITY OF NATIONS, by Charles Yost (1968).

PROSPECTS FOR SOVIET SOCIETY, edited by Allen Kassof (1968).

U.S. POLICY AND THE SECURITY OF ASIA, by Fred Greene (1968).

NEGOTIATING WITH THE CHINESE COMMUNISTS: The U.S. Experience, by Kenneth T. Young (1967).

FROM ATLANTIC TO PACIFIC: A New Interocean Canal, by Immanuel J. Klette (1967).

AMERICAN AGENCIES INTERESTED IN INTERNATIONAL AFFAIRS (Fifth Edition), compiled by Donald Wasson (1964).

JAPAN AND THE UNITED STATES IN WORLD AFFAIRS, by Warren S. Hunsberger (1964).

FOREIGN AFFAIRS BIBLIOGRAPHY, 1952-1962, by Henry L. Roberts (1964).

THE DOLLAR IN WORLD AFFAIRS: An Essay in International Financial Policy, by Henry G. Aubrey (1964).

ON DEALING WITH THE COMMUNIST WORLD, by George F. Kennan (1964).

FOREIGN AID AND FOREIGN POLICY, by Edward S. Mason (1964).

THE SCIENTIFIC REVOLUTION AND WORLD POLITICS, by Caryl P. Haskins (1964).

AFRICA: A Foreign Affairs Reader, edited by Philip W. Quigg (1964).

THE PHILIPPINES AND THE UNITED STATES: Problems of Partnership, by George E. Taylor (1964).

SOUTHEAST ASIA IN UNITED STATES POLICY, by Russell H. Fifield (1963).

UNESCO: Assessment and Promise, by George N. Shuster (1963).

THE PEACEFUL ATOM IN FOREIGN POLICY, by Arnold Kramish (1963).

THE ARABS AND THE WORLD: Nasser's Arab Nationalist Policy, by Charles D. Cremeans (1963).

TOWARD AN ATLANTIC COMMUNITY, by Christian A. Herter (1963).

THE SOVIET UNION, 1922-1962: A Foreign Affairs Reader, edited by Philip E. Mosely (1963).

THE POLITICS OF FOREIGN AID: American Experience in Southeast Asia, by John D. Montgomery (1962).

SPEARHEADS OF DEMOCRACY: Labor in the Developing Countries, by George C. Lodge (1962).

LATIN AMERICA: Diplomacy and Reality, by Adolf A. Berle (1962).

THE ORGANIZATION OF AMERICAN STATES AND THE HEMISPHERE CRISIS, by John C. Dreier (1962).

THE UNITED NATIONS: Structure for Peace, by Ernest A. Gross (1962).

THE LONG POLAR WATCH: Canada and the Defense of North America, by Melvin Conant (1962).

ARMS AND POLITICS IN LATIN AMERICA (Revised Edition), by Edwin Lieuwen (1961).

THE FUTURE OF UNDERDEVELOPED COUNTRIES: Political Implications of Economic Development (Revised Edition), by Eugene Staley (1961).

SPAIN AND DEFENSE OF THE WEST: Ally and Liability, by Arthur P. Whitaker (1961).

SOCIAL CHANGE IN LATIN AMERICA TODAY: Its Implications for United States Policy, by Richard N. Adams, John P. Gillin, Allan R. Holmberg, Oscar Lewis, Richard W. Patch, and Charles W. Wagley (1961).

FOREIGN POLICY: THE NEXT PHASE: The 1960s (Revised Edition), by Thomas K. Finletter (1960).

DEFENSE OF THE MIDDLE EAST: Problems of American Policy (Revised Edition), by John C. Campbell (1960).

COMMUNIST CHINA AND ASIA: Challenge to American Policy, by A. Doak Barnett (1960).

FRANCE, TROUBLED ALLY: De Gaulle's Heritage and Prospects, by Edgar S. Furniss, Jr. (1960).

THE SCHUMAN PLAN: A Study in Economic Cooperation, 1950-1959, by William Diebold, Jr. (1959).

SOVIET ECONOMIC AID: The New Aid and Trade Policy in Underdeveloped Countries, by Joseph S. Berliner (1958).

NATO AND THE FUTURE OF EUROPE, by Ben T. Moore (1958).

INDIA AND AMERICA: A Study of Their Relations, by Phillips Talbot and S. L. Poplai (1958).

NUCLEAR WEAPONS AND FOREIGN POLICY, by Henry A. Kissinger (1957).

MOSCOW-PEKING AXIS: Strength and Strains, by Howard L. Boorman, Alexander Eckstein, Philip E. Mosely, and Benjamin Schwartz (1957).

RUSSIA AND AMERICA: Dangers and Prospects, by Henry L. Roberts (1956).